18 95

Broken Greek

a language to belong

D1616148

Adrianne Kalfopoulou

Plain View Press
P. O. 42255
Austin, TX 78704

plainviewpress.net
sbright1@austin.rr.com
512-440-7139

Cover Art:

Thanks to Voula Liaka and Maria Kostaki for the final image, and to
Alexei Kyrilloff, Marili Papadopoulou and Jordan Karatzas for working
through the first idea with me.

"My only experience of telling stories in my life is from periods when I had to make things up to have people believe me; in plain words, lies."

Mihali Papagyropoulos, student in *Introduction to Literature*

"If I have tried to define something, it is […] simply the common existence of history and of man, everyday life with the most possible light thrown upon it, the dogged struggle against one's own degradation and that of others."

Albert Camus, *"The Artist and His Time"*

To my parents, Kitty and George
And for Dyanne

Acknowledgments

My thanks are deep and to many. The 2001 Salzburg Seminar crowd on "The Continuing Challenge of America's Ethnic Pluralism" got me going as wondrous listeners to my half-joking anecdotes about Athens traffic. Dr. Beverlee Bruce's casual discussions of cultural anthropology influenced me more than she knows. Jose Itzigsohn encouraged me through much doubt. John Psaropoulos' journalism remains a model of how to tell "the whole story" whole. Dyanne DiSalvo and Stephen Butler sustained me with love and a room of my own. And without Emily and George's *philoxenia* through the fall of 2003, I could not have imagined my way to a conclusion. I thank Linda Manney, Helen Maravegias, Margot McPherson, Anne Nebel, Alicia Stallings, Elina Stratigakis and Olga Taxidou, for conversations that made a difference, Aliki Barnstone and Maria Kostaki for *politimo* help, Alexandra Nikiforidou and Sotiris Lappas for being *koumbari*, Theodora Tsimpouki for her support, Stratis Haviaras for his example, Kosta Doukas for his discussions of Kapodistria, and Vali Lambridi for always opening her door. The people I encountered over the years related here were integral to how I saw or experienced the events described; this narrative was born because of them. Finally, I thank Susan Bright for her careful attention to this manuscript, and Jordan *yia tin triferi tou stirixi*. My deepest gratitude, παντα, goes to my daughter Korina, σ'αγαπω νουνου μου.

Sections from "Traffic Politics," "Academic Phallicisms," and "Saints and Anarchists" first appeared in the *Athens News* in a column titled "The Furies."

Author's Note

Like much of modern Greece this book was shaped by fragments of memory, history and myth. It begins when one of the determining influences on the contemporary world of Greece, the Pan-Hellenic Socialist Party (*PASOK*), founded and headed by Andreas Papandreou, was first elected in 1981 under the party slogan of *Alagi* (Change) directed at the common population or *mi pronomiouhi* (the under privileged), in the hopes of providing access to power, knowledge and decision-making that was traditionally in the hands of the few. It ends over twenty years later with the election of *Nea Democratia* (New Democracy), the party of the right, who came into power on a platform of 'anti-corruption' and re-establishing rules thought to have been abused by the socialist government. While the narratives are not directly political, they foreground the lives of people living under and within the terms of current government and its policies. In another sense, how Greece and Greeks have negotiated historically oppressive and less than acceptable contexts of authoritative bodies, informs profound issues of culture and character; these stories are an attempt to address the richness and contrariness as well as the elegies of what, finally, is a narrative of coming of age in a country similarly catching up with itself.

Contents

A Confusion of Titles
by way of preface

Prayer is not something I do, at least not consciously, so it was curious when the word presented itself in my first idea for a title. *In Prayer and Broken Song*, the working title of my manuscript for the three years I was writing it, expressed the overwhelmed sense I experienced when I started this narrative. The religious aspect of prayer seemed appropriate too, but more in regard to a metaphysics of faith than any specific religion. The reflexive 'Oh God' or the Greek *thé mou* articulates the acute helplessness and vulnerability felt when there seems no visible, immanent salvation in the face of desperate circumstance.

In a real way the act of writing this narrative is, for me, a form of prayer to an unknown God. As a result of ancestry and a childhood love of the country, I found myself returning to Greece in young adulthood in a quest for self-reference. I wasn't prepared to settle into a first after-college-job in a New York publishing firm, and I thought, vaguely, that returning to Greece to live with my paternal grandparents who were then alive, would give me a clearer idea of what I wanted to do with my life. I could never have fathomed the current of events that spun and raveled like Arachne's webs, or that they would provoke the cunning and vengeance of the gods and goddesses, Athena in particular. Greece, or my journeying of Greece, is that web of complexities, it is the story I have wanted to write and been reluctant to, afraid the urgency to record my experiences threatened to distort what I wanted to say; and so I felt I prayed.

But when I mentioned the title to the writer and translator Willis Barnstone at a Greek taverna the night he gave me a copy of his translation of *The Apocalypse*, he shook his head. "Bad title," he said, "but one will come to me in a minute." By the end of our meal, at a table with a lot of noisy conversation, he said, "How about *Trial by Greek and Passion*" or was it *By Passionate Trial and Greek*? I don't remember the order, but I remember 'Trial' 'Greek' 'Passion'. I also remember his enthusiasm for the fact that the words represented something of earnest effort. "'Trial' and 'Greek' are positive," he went on, and I remember thinking quietly, "Is this positive?" My story was not about 'Greekness' as a supplement to an outsider's lack of cultural mythology as was often the case with books by foreigners who put a Goddess or God's name in the title after a brief sojourn in the country; this narrative is about my failure to belong as much as it is about moments of affirmation. "It's about trial," Willis pointed out, "and Greek gets in the language that you're speaking through." I realized then that it was my broken Greek that has long been the language of my relationship to this world. And its trials, or my trials, have been a result of that brokenness, of being set afloat, broken off and fragmented by my less than fluent command of the language that barred access to parts of the culture as much as it allowed for entrance into the rifts of those worlds. Prayer was also part of the story, but more essentially it was a way of describing the story as broken. We pray when faced with merciless events, or their possibility, circumstances which challenge our faith, and if we have none, then our existence.

Greece. My father's country. My paternal grandparents' home. A place of childhood and myth, of childhood narratives and mythic history. The place my mother, an Italian-American, always remained wary of. The word 'Greek' resonates with its originating meaning: *Greki* or *Graikos*, a word with Latin roots, one Greek elementary school texts state the Ottoman Turks used pejoratively to mean slave or servant. "We will no longer refer to ourselves as Greeks," Costas Mitsotakis, a former Prime Minister of Greece declared publicly on TV. "We are Hellenes," and went on, always, to refer to Greece as 'Hellas.' But for me it is Greece, the places and spaces I've journeyed, and continue to live; it is the landscape and mindscape of a people whose history still reverberates with what it meant to be *Grekoi*, so I will write the journey as I lived it.

As much as possible I have chosen to speak through the spoken discourses of the people I met whose exchanges fed, educated and challenged me. I've also tried to remain true to the unabashed grittiness in those dialogues and discussions. For one, the direct expression of what it means to be living the moment, unadorned of any romanticism implied by the phrase, has more to do with being caught or trapped in a life and culture that gives little choice or ability for transcending day-to-day survival. For another, as is the case of oral traditions, there is an involvement in language at the level of the spoken which is impoverished by the more self-conscious choices, and omissions, available to someone writing. I realize the irony as I write the spoken, trying not to write/right it beyond the context within which I have experienced it. In this I am indebted to the invaluable contributions of African-American writers, (Zora Neale Hurston, Toni Morrison, Gayle Jones) and the literature of Native American writers (Louise Erdrich, Sherman Alexie, Leslie Marmo Silko) for empowering what was firstly only an intuitive sense of the importance of spoken language and the cultural treasure house it preserves.

In an essay titled "Choosing the Margin" bell hooks, the feminist African-American cultural critic, writes of an all-night conversation she had with a friend "talking about the struggle of oppressed people to come to voice." She judges her friend Eddie George's comment as 'very down' when he says, "ours is a broken voice." Hooks is remarkable in her cultural assessment of brokenness and her wariness of its dismissal by those who either cannot account for it or are threatened by it: "My response was simply that when you hear the broken voice you also hear the pain contained within that brokenness – a speech of suffering: often it's that sound nobody wants to hear" (hooks 146).

I've borrowed hook's phrase because it foregrounds the difficulty of speaking in contexts of pain. The written word gives a more enduring shape to what might otherwise be dismissed as the diatribe of the moment it attempts, in good faith, to provide a context for. But it can also be deliberately misread to maintain the dominant contexts responsible for those expressions of rage and grief. Such cultural whitewashing is paradigmatic in the now classic last paragraph of Chinua Achebe's *Things Fall Apart* when the white missionary police, after witnessing Okonkwo's hanging, suggests he will devote "not a whole chapter but a reasonable paragraph" to his book "*The Pacification of the Primitive Tribes of the Lower Niger.*" Ultimately, as hooks articulates it, "language is a place of struggle"; she repeats the refrain several times when she speaks of how we, inevitably and problematically, speak "to those who dominate" as we voice (or rage) our oppression.

Greek, for me, was always the language of an incensed rhythm. As my grandparents spoke, as my father spoke to them, I witnessed, a child, something I always misunderstood as argument. Greek was the language of impassioned opinion, of intimacy. I remember a first image from my early twenties when I came to Greece to work at an English language magazine. An older woman was crossing the street, yelling in a full stream of words. I was transfixed by the absolute focus of her rage. A driver had not stopped for her when she had the right of way; she was fascinating in her relentlessness. She was also an omen. I remember thinking would I ever come to that? The oppressor's presence "changes the nature and direction of our words," hooks says, and I think of Greece, of that woman hurtling her voice like something solid at the driver who almost ran her over. I think of the country's long history under Ottoman oppression, of what are, after centuries, the visible consequences and maybe more importantly the invisible ones, of those three to four centuries of cultural domination. *Ti na kanoume* is the expression of resignation. One often hears *Ti na kanoume* (What can we do?) muttered with a shrug, a vague backwards nod, and then answered rhetorically with *dhe variese* (never mind).

In my first encounters with Greece I had no story to attach to the sounds and gestures I listened to and watched. It all looked like grand theatre, but also like something oddly impossible to fit into the language of the American world I had been educated in. The more I understood of Greek, the more feeble English seemed in its ability to reflect the layered depths of a world that had no analogous word for privacy but four to describe variations of love: *eros* (physical desire or love), *agape* (spiritual or platonic love), *latria* (devotional love) and *philia* (the love of friends). Language is culture and culture remains embedded in language. As I journeyed more deeply into the culture of my ancestry, I started to feel obstructed by the English I was born into, and took for granted. Efficiency, a word that connotes a satisfactory, measurable outcome for an analogous amount of energy or product investment, does not exist in Greek. *Apotelesmatikotita* (the measure of results) is used to refer to systems rather than individuals; a priority and privilege of first world cultures, the analogous absence in Greek for 'efficiency' suggests a western understanding of the word is not relevant or applicable to a Greek context. *Paragogikotita* (productivity) and *ikanotita* (capability) come close to paraphrasing the notion, but the words foreground individual abilities as opposed to a systematized investment controlled by measurable outcomes. An individual could put in tremendous effort to produce what, by western standards, might be considered a disproportional result, but one nevertheless viewed as worthwhile in a non-western context.

A comment on a story I wrote for a writing workshop in college said, "Too involved," for asking language "to hold up to too much." What is it that written language tries to reach for, what drama beyond language does it try to replicate? I didn't know then that I would write so much about a country whose language I only knew through the lilt and lull of words I listened to without always understanding. Perhaps this is why the country drew me; it became the landscape of absolute feeling where language could 'hold up to,' or break under, what, conventionally, it was not meant to do.

The Sound

Don't you want to come home, take the old ship
with its rusted body, its faded curtains,
find the island you've dreamed of
so far from where you lived, discover the patience
to sit sleepless in the hard, uncomfortable chairs,
listen to the voices of stubborn vacationers
drunk on cheap wine, let the view of the sea lull you
while you stare through salt-streaked windows?
Try to eat the heavy kitchen food ladled out by
exhausted cooks, pay for stale bread, let yourself
hope to arrive, finally, where you never believed
you could be. Listen to the ship's reluctant groan,
wait for the clanking anchor chains, watch the thick
ropes tossed into night, hear village voices
calling to shipmates, see them grab the frayed hemp,
tie the ship to land: the sea's swell and breath, the slap of
waves against the battered hull, an ancient song.

"God gave man a mind, a heart, hands…he has to make with them what he can," the taxi driver says to me. When I tell him I'm from America he states the fact that it is a very large, very rich country. "And democratic," he adds emphatically.

"Not always," I tell him. "It has problems, some worse than the problems in Greece." He laughs out loud, entertained. This is early 1981, before the Gulf War, months before PASOK (the Pan-Hellenic Socialist Party) would come into power for over two decades, before my grandparents died, before 9/11, before the younger Bush administration's avid aggressions. "Ah!" he exclaims, "You should never expect life to be satisfying." He tries to glimpse my expression in his rear view mirror, but doesn't see me smile. "You're a young girl," he says, "probably without a husband or children. You don't know the struggle yet…"

157 Syngrou

My grandparents' house is on Syngrou Avenue, then a tree lined thoroughfare of villas that led to the sea, not the thoroughfare of large multinational
companies and car dealers that it is today or the stopping point for trans-
vestites and prostitutes that it now turns into by night. My grandfather is
waving to me, his dark beret over his bald head; he's watering the date tree
in his flannel blue robe. "Work is health," he says, as the thick scents of
autumn fill the air.

I tell him he shouldn't tire himself; he's always up and down the marble
steps he built to the apartment where he and my grandmother Ismini live,
then down more steps to the garden and his work place, a small shed where
he keeps his tools, the old machine that makes the fabric spools he sells to
clothing factories. "When God banished Adam from the Garden of Eden
he told him from now on it was from the sweat of his brow that he would
have to earn his bread." He winds the long hose, says he's going to prune the
bougainvillea once the weather gets cooler.

The lights are still not on when we go upstairs. Electricity is expensive.
My grandfather jokes that money doesn't come easily to elderly hands. I smell
meat cooking; my grandmother's in the kitchen. She leans her head against
the doorframe, lets her cane slip. "He's waiting for me to die! He says I don't
do anything…" I pick up the cane, look at the dark circles under her eyes,
her perfectly wound hair pinned into a bun. My grandfather comes into the
kitchen; her face is haloed in steam as she stirs the meal wordlessly.

"Don't cook if you feel badly," I say.

She shakes her head, her hair loosening in the steam. "I have to or I'll
die."

Every night my grandfather sits and listens to opera in the darkened living
room. Around midnight my grandmother negotiates the distance from the
kitchen; balancing on her cane, she brings him his nightly brew of chamomile
and *telio*, the herb that brings on sleep.

Those first months of my visit are plagued with dreams of war. The house
bred them; my grandfather's stories inspired them. In the downstairs apartment where I stay, the furniture is sheeted like ghosts, except for in the two
rooms I use. I hear sounds every night, not of a chair being moved upstairs,
or the drag of my grandmother's cane across the wood floor, clear sounds, but
the sounds of my dreams: shuffling boots. Gunfire. Gravel. Stones scattering
like pellets. I wake sweating. I face a canon, smell pitch and metal. I see the
tips of leather soles beneath the door, hear voices, never see faces.

"They were treated like traitors," my grandfather says as we walk toward
Omonia square. The place is dense with market vendors. Everyone is hawking something: large plastic bags in pinks, blues and yellows, rows and rows

of cassettes. Music blares from the stalls. Men crouch or sit, begging, shining shoes. My grandfather points to a plaque, almost invisible in a wall black from pollution. The plaque is high up, but I can see the curved shape of an olive branch with its leaves. "This was the building," he says, "the resistance fighters blew up during the German Occupation. Those men should have been made heroes, but instead they were treated like traitors when the war was over and the Allies came in." He is more sad than angry and changes the subject.

The past takes up space, presses in, I feel a need to outrun it, sense the impossibility. My grandfather takes the bus from Syngrou to the center of Athens and walks to Omonia, then makes his way back to Syngrou again. Movement gives him purpose. One morning I don't see him come down to get his paper. I go upstairs, he's in bed, not well. The tea my grandmother made for him sits untouched, steaming next to a hardboiled egg. He asks me to sit next to him and begins a story of a politician sent to Smyrna to meet an English diplomat. Apparently he wasn't qualified for the meeting, but he had known Karamalis, the prime minister then, and was friendly with everyone in government. A man stood behind him during the whole interview, repeating: "I have no comment. I have no comment," to all the questions the English diplomat asked him. Ismini sits in a chair, her hands clasped in her lap; she looks at my grandfather like he's her child. She wants him to eat; she thinks food will stop the gnawing in him; he raises himself on the pillow and gestures to me: "*This* is Greece!" he almost yells. "The Greeks could be first in everything, but in taking responsibility they're last! They're always thinking 'how can I use this person for my own interests?'" I breathe out audibly, cornered by his passion. He falls back heavily against his pillow.

"We must make room for others now," he says with a sudden smile. He describes the blood he saw in his urine. "The body finally collapses under the burden of years. We're useless, taking up space that should be filled by younger bodies." When he goes on about death Ismini leaves the bedroom; the kitchen smells of spinach; she's making *spanakopita*.

"Life is sweet," she says to me. "As long as you live life is sweet." She begins to weep. "I don't listen to the things he says."

"But you do," I move the strands of hair from her eyes.

"I think he's crazy sometimes," she says, "like his mother and sister…I don't know what goes on in his mind."

"He's just tired, like you." I want her to lie down but she won't.

"He'll want to eat soon," she says, going back to the cooking. I go into the bedroom and find my grandfather dosing; he opens his eyes without moving. "You know, Adrianna, when your father was born your grandmother's hips were too narrow and your father's head was too big. The doctors had to cut her and your father came out without breathing. She suffered…The doctor put him head first into cold *ice* water…he *gasped* for air!" He sits up against the pillow smiling. "The shock *made him* gasp!"

That night I sleep upstairs and the sound of my grandmother crying wakes me. My grandfather roars with pain; his prostrate gland has closed up. It's Sunday, almost dawn when I walk to the clinic across the street; there's a night nurse who doesn't understand me when I tell her I want someone to come to the house. I finally find a young doctor who comes and checks my grandfather, says he must have an operation soon; he must carry a urine bag until then.

〰

"*Kyrie Eleisson…*" my grandfather waves the sack of urine like church incense, and laughs. He's downstairs in the garden watering the plants. "You know Adrianna, the Turks have a saying; 'old men become ridiculous.'" We laugh together but his eyes are sad.

"When I was only ten years younger I was taking frozen showers in the middle of winter." I take his hand; his fingers fold over mine. The sky's dark with thunder clouds, shadows fall across the garden. As we walk back up the stairs he talks of how people have betrayed him, he talks obsessively. "Relatives," he says, "come and go. They say 'Good Morning,' then they're gone. A French proverb says, 'Once I was an angel then someone took my place. Once I drank then someone came to drink'…our time has passed." He sighs.

I squeeze his hand without thinking.

We climb the wide marble steps. I think I cannot imagine the house without him. I want to call my father, tell him about the prostrate operation. "No," he's reproachful. "They have their own problems."

〰

Christmas day my grandfather has a stroke. I'm in a village outside the city. When I come back at twilight, the garden whispers in a thin breeze. I think, simply, he cannot die. Church music is on the radio. My grandfather's in bed, his hands stretched against the radiator; he barely turns when I kneel next to him taking his hands into mine, kissing them. "For five days I looked at the hospital ceiling," he speaks with difficulty. "I can't do any work now, nothing. Everything is finished, Adrianna." I start to cry.

In the kitchen my grandmother leans against the stove, the circles under her eyes like charcoal smudges. "It doesn't matter how I feel as long as he gets better," she murmurs, telling me she's been up all night: he had to go to the bathroom; she cleaned the sheets herself, then he fell. She called the young

16

doctor who diagnosed the prostrate; he called an ambulance. My grandfather yelled and complained so much the nurses wanted him out; they couldn't do the operation until he was better. My grandmother takes my hand, puts it against her heart so I can feel its hurried beat. My grandfather is suddenly in the doorway, making halting steps. Ismini murmurs something and spits. The words are Turkish.

"Why are you spitting?"

"For hope," she says.

∿

The day nurse hired to help is Armenian, but Ismini refuses to let her do anything; no one can cook or clean or take care of her husband as she can. The Armenian woman looks at me suspiciously. She says older people never change their ways, she tells me she's been in Greece for fourteen years and only has one friend from all those years. "You must be careful with people," she says, "for every step you take, take five backwards." I avoid her gaze that says bread, even if you split it, is never enough.

My grandmother lies over her made bed, my grandfather's in his. Despite the volume of the radio there's a quiet to the room. My grandfather looks at me blankly, gestures toward my grandmother, her lips pale, her cheeks sunken. I sit down next to her, absently adjusting the combs in her falling hair.

"*Yiayia* is going to go to a dance now," my grandfather says from his bed.

"Yes, *Yiayia* is going to go dance tonight," she says with some color in her cheeks.

"*Ach*…Adrianna, I was at the threshold of death and not allowed to enter." He looks at me, changing the subject, "You must have a plan. You're young, beginning your life." I look past the mirror's reflection, past the ceiling high closets. "Us," he goes on, "we're going to be garbage soon." He sees my face crumble. My grandmother goes out and comes back with tea precariously balanced on a tray.

"Only *Yiayia* will go to the garbage," she says.

"*Yiayia*!" I grab the tray from her.

"In fifteen days I'll be going to Athens again," he says as Ismini sits on the edge of the bed.

"You're still weak," I say.

He laughs, mocking. "In one month, two months…God knows where I'll be going."

∿

"*Look* Adrianna…" My grandfather lifts his trembling fingers and tries to press them together to make the cross. Five days have passed since the stroke. My grandmother stoops, exhaustion straining her movements. His right arm moves clumsily across his chest as he slowly completes the sign of the cross. "I knocked on the door of Paradise, but Saint Peter was busy so I have to call another time."

"You see *Papou*, you're a man with energy," he nods, indulging me.

"I've lost track of time. I don't know how life has passed so quickly, a whole lifetime gone," my grandmother murmurs. I talk of how I remember the jams she made from the quince trees. "It's a good thing if you have good memories, but we have difficult ones." At night in the shallow light my grandfather reads by, my grandmother sees her brothers and sisters, tells me her father was a good man. "A very good man," she repeats.

〰

The taxi driver lights a cigarette. "Why bother," he exhales, leaning into his seat while we're stuck, unmoving, in traffic. "They tell us everything is okay. Everything will be all right." A huge sigh escapes him. He talks about the news on the radio, something about cutbacks. I take a liking to him. Someone honks, leans on his horn like he's fallen asleep over it. "You light a cigarette," he says, ignoring the blaring. "What can you do but light a cigarette?" He laughs. "If you get upset you'll go mad. Smoke a cigarette and relax, at least we Greeks know how to relax." I laugh now and he smiles as we inch forward. "What can anyone do," he repeats, changing gear. "It's all bigger than us."

I'm in Piraeus, walking in a street full of fish taverns. I think of the taxi driver, my grandmother's stubborn exhaustion, what we call depression in the States seems not to apply here; everything is too immediate, too extreme. Fried onion and charcoal scents lace the evening.

I go upstairs in the morning; tea's on the table, but the radio is quiet.

My grandfather refuses to kiss me. "We're both sick," he says, "and you left us alone. Your wash has been hanging downstairs for two days. Don't you feel shame?" I ask them where the Armenian nurse is. "We had her here to help us, not for us to serve her. She drank coffee and was on the phone all the time. She should have been the one to pay us!"

My grandmother pulls the bed sheet tight, folds it. I lift the mattress. She looks at me, "Go drink your tea before it gets cold." I notice a sore scratched open on her neck. She tells me she lay awake bothered by her itching skin. She says she never says anything while my grandfather moans through the night, but can't sleep. I follow her into the kitchen where she leans against the marble counter to squeeze oranges for me to drink.

18

"Adrianna," she asks almost reluctantly. "Go downstairs and get the wash that's hanging. It's not nice for the neighbors to see it hanging on the line for so many days."

≈

Sun soaks the bedroom curtains. My grandfather is playing a record of Attik's music. "Attik!" Ismini smiles when I ask her who he is, a rare lightness in her voice. My grandfather hums. "Attik died of starvation in the war." She is calmer than I've seen her in awhile. "He's singing, *don't forget…the grandmother says to the granddaughter…don't forget.*"

All week there are political gatherings in the streets. Banners fly, placards are carried through the main thoroughfares: bold wavering letters spell lack and need. The Greeks rally their dissent. I sit in an open-air café with Caroline, a journalist from Australia who came to cover the *PASOK* elections some months ago. Caroline tells me the Greeks still haven't realized the reality of their own limitations.

"They want to blame it all on the Junta…or if it's not the Junta, it's the Ottomans."

"They haven't had a chance to grow at a pace that wasn't interrupted by something," I suggest.

Caroline shrugs. She says she's tired of politics, wants to go back to Australia and have a baby before she gets too old. A group passes with the KKE Communist banner protesting low retirement benefits. "I used to like the Communists," Caroline adds "a beautiful ideal, isn't it? But it doesn't work," she says matter-of-factly. "We're just naturally selfish."

"It's too easy to put yourself first." I think of my grandparents in their apartment. Ismini's passions, her need to see me eat, to see my grandfather well, someone who doesn't know how to put herself first. Then I remember the rubber cleaning gloves I bought for the Armenian nurse stashed in Ismini's closet. When I asked her why she didn't give them to her, she was short. "She doesn't need them. Why did you spend money on her?"

≈

"I'm dying and all he can say is I didn't help him put on his socks!" Tears stream down her face. A hard rain pelts the windows and wild cat screams rise from the garden. Ismini lies across her bed, her shoes mud spattered, her stockings rolled up above her knees. I stroke her back and forehead.

"I went down in the rain to get him the newspaper. That's why I wasn't here. Now he holds it against me. He wanted to get up, put on his shoes. I do what I can." The tears don't stop; she turns her face away from me so I won't see.

"He understands. If you tell him he'll understand," I say.

"No…" she swallows stiffly.

"He doesn't mean what he says," I pull strands of her hair back into the hair combs. We play a game. I tell her the same things to console her and she repeats the same complaints. Our pact says she will do everything as she always has and I will soon see them stronger.

"They're my helpers." She points to three Russian icons on the wall. I rub camphor ointment into her skin, spread it through her shoulder blades, listen to her breathing grow steady.

〰〰

My great aunt Corinna arrives one day from Patras where she lives, her appearance like a sudden rain; she moves wordlessly through the house tidying up, and startles me when she finally speaks. "The cats are from the same mother," she says in mid-sentence.

"The cats?"

Corinna never looks at me as she speaks: "There are twenty-five of them with the same coloring," she says, taking the dishtowel from its hook to dry a plate.

When I tell my grandfather Corinna has counted twenty-five cats with the same coloring, he answers as if he didn't hear what I said. "She never obeyed me. She's so stubborn!" Then he laughs, "Like you." I look at him surprised. "Like me?" He nods with a glint in his eye. "She told a man who wanted to marry her that she liked waking up and going to sleep whenever she felt like it." I laugh out loud and start to pay more attention to Corinna. She comes downstairs one afternoon to bring me tea and toast on a tin platter.

"No wonder you have a cold. All your blankets are on the floor." She picks up the fallen corners to readjust them over the bed. I watch her through my fever: a large woman with a head of grey cropped hair clumsily pinned away from her eyes. She glances around the room noticing the closed shutters. "You can't see a thing here," she exclaims, letting in a cold gust of air with the light.

Corinna, my grandfather's sister and my great aunt, was considered mad by the family. The fact that Corinna never married was, for Ismini, the damning fact of her life. My grandmother endured her like bad weather. What I viewed as independence Ismini judged as self-indulgent, what I understood as free will, Ismini considered selfish, but in her heart I think Ismini was more curious than she allowed herself to admit. Her favorite story was the one she told of the seal skin coats she had made for herself and Corinna. The skins had been given to her as a gift; she asked a seamstress to make two coats, one for each of them. "What a beautiful piece of seal that was," she would start. "A gift from one of your grandfather's clients in Persia. I had Pitza cut it so it would be enough for two knee-length coats; I had a very fashionable design for them." She would then pause before starting with what happened next. "When the coat was made I sent it to Corinna for Christmas; I had a dress of hers so I knew her measurements." At this point in the story Ismini's thin lips would disappear; she pursed them tight and shook her head. "I never saw the coat. Corinna never called to thank us. When she came to see us in the summer I asked her if she received it." Now Ismini swallowed as if gathering the strength to say what she had to say next, "'*Oh that!*' Corinna said, 'I have it in Patras. I cut it. I couldn't walk with that material flapping around my knees.'" The first time I heard the story I tried not to laugh, but my grandmother saw the smile.

"You think it's *funny!*" she demanded. I shrugged, saying I thought Corinna probably didn't understand the value of the material. Ismini always finished the story by describing the incident as a perfect example of her sister-in-law's barbarism.

When I go back upstairs I find my grandmother gauging her steps down the hallway, a teapot in one hand and her cane in the other. "Go sit," she snaps as I take the pot from her. She gives a resigned sigh, "I'm broken inside," she mutters. I take the tea into the bedroom where Corinna is darning a sock by the window light. Her eyes lift from her work to watch me pour tea for my grandfather who has the day's paper over his lap.

"I'll have a second stroke," my grandfather says, folding the paper. "I pray Adrianna that He will rest my soul; it's past time. We've lived our life."

"You look better," I tell him. He shrugs. Corinna dips crackers and sweet biscuits into her tea. My grandmother watches her from the bed. For no reason my grandfather bursts into laughter. "They used to bring ice from the mountains!" He slaps his knee with glee, "Ice from the mountains! Wrapped in jute leaves. Primitive methods. We didn't have such things as freezers." He claps his hands and Corinna starts to smile.

〰

Whenever I ask my grandmother how she is she answers, "Fine." She looks tired again this evening, spreading alcohol over her arms and legs. She tells me it eases her muscle pains. "From the morning he doesn't stop talking. He talks and talks and talks. I can't take it." She's breathless. "He's crazy like his sister," she whispers almost inaudibly. My grandfather manages to make his way down to the garden to pick mandarins. I find him next to the row of lime trees he tells me his father planted.

"I can't lie in bed all the time," he says, dropping the ripe fruit into a plastic shopping bag. The evening is overcast with humidity. He takes the garbage pail stuffed with leaves to the gate. "You never know with the garbage collectors. One day they're on strike, one day they're not. That's why this country will never get ahead. People are either on strike or on vacation." We stand at the gates, bird cries filter through the trees. Television antennae crowd the rooftops of apartment buildings, more and more of them are cropping up, taking over the houses with their small plots of garden. I watch my grandfather wrapped in his garden coat, the old flannel bathrobe with its torn pockets and frayed buttonholes, his profile more Roman than Greek because of his beaked nose broken from a fall; he likes to tell how during the war a car of German officers ran him off the sidewalk so he fell and his broken bone never healed straight.

As we're standing a group of adolescent kids pass; one of the girls is smoking. She pauses at the gates to adjust her shoe. The next minute my grandfather is by her side. "Cigarettes are poison!" he tells her. One of the boys edges close, so close I think he's going to touch him, and slurs, "Leave the girl alone old man." I move with a feeling of heat through my body but my grandfather turns away, his palms dangling by his torn coat pockets. "Young people," he murmurs, before I say anything.

"It's hard for them to listen," I mutter; he shrugs, making his way back upstairs.

〰〰

I hear quick footsteps across the upstairs floorboards, faster than either of my grandparents can move. I go upstairs in my bathrobe.

"He was yelling and crying. I didn't know what to do! What was I going to do! An old woman?" My grandmother is weeping into her hands. The doctor had just left.

"You could have phoned me," I say, sitting next to her.

"The gate was locked," my grandfather says from his bed. He's pale, his lips drawn and chapped. "Yes, I locked it last night," I say. I had gone out and come back and locked the gate.

"The doctor jumped the fence," he says, matter-of-factly, and smiles. "That's youth. Youth and health."

"You've been healthy too," I say, "for eighty-six years." He's pleased. My grandmother disappears into the kitchen to prepare the day's lunch. The smell of cooking wine and green peppers starts to fill the apartment. She tells me the doctor said if my grandfather didn't have the prostrate gland operation the pain would soon kill him.

"I don't believe in the Greek *tha*," he says when I say we have to make a decision about the operation. The doctor left painkillers. My grandfather points to the bottle. "The eternal future," he says. "Can we presume to turn back the clock? It's finished now, nature always wins." His skin is flushed, his voice almost ecstatic. "Only pray for my soul, Adrianna."

My grandmother stoops over the steaming peppers. She tells me her pain the night before was everlasting; she tells me she's worried, a streak of anger flashes across her features. "He could have done this sooner! Why did he wait until he couldn't urinate?" She forks up a chunk of lamb boiling with the peppers to look at it closely, tells me as an afterthought that my father called the night before to say her sister in Seattle died. I'm surprised.

"Was she old?" I wonder why Ismini is being so matter-of-fact.

She ladles the wine broth and sips through tufts of steam. "What can you do?" she says swallowing the broth. "Life passes."

〰

I come down from their apartment, back into the present, lock the front gate. Parked cars crowd the pavement and side road. A gambling casino has gone up behind the house. Syngrou Avenue, where my grandparents have lived for over half a century, once a strip of flying dust, is now a main road that connects the center, Hadrian's Gate, with the sea. My grandfather tells and retells the story of how he was chided for buying land so far from the city's center, a place covered by olive and pine trees where carts pulled by donkeys went by regularly. "Who would have ever thought Syngrou would become the road to the airport," he would exclaim, "to Sounion, to Piraeus…You can go anywhere from here!"

〰

My grandmother looks up at me from her bed. "God!" she hisses, "what pain!" The deep circles around her eyes have swallowed them. She turns with difficulty on her side as I lift her sweater to rub more camphor across her back. She inhales sharply. "You *mustn't* do anything today," I say firmly, rubbing the ointment into her skin with pressing upward movements. She says she can't stay in this position; her muscles begin to feel paralyzed. She gazes toward the wall. I see the flakes of dry skin around her hairline. "They're going to operate tomorrow," she mumbles. "I hope the operation will help him."

〰

The doctors put my grandfather through tests: they test his urine, blood, heart. The operation is postponed for the next day. He seems content when I visit him. "Patchwork," he says to me when I enter the plain room with three metallic beds. "All these operations are a nuisance to try and extend life." He waves the air, points to a tiny shelf where a Bible sits covered in dust. "The Holy book," he states, following my eyes. I've brought him a bar of soap, a green sponge, a shoehorn, a bottle of cologne. My grandmother prepared an overnight bag.

"I have two now," he says, delighted, picking up the cologne bottle. The one I bring him is unopened. My grandmother insisted I put it in the bag. "Take it back with you," he says, "so the young girls here don't feel tempted." He laughs and takes the opened bottle, twists off the cap so it goes flying across the floor. I pick it up; he splashes cologne over his neck and arms, rubs his hands vigorously and lifts the urine bag. "This will be gone tomorrow!"

∿

The tubing sways, my grandfather's white skin is a sickly shine under the light. I yell for a nurse. It's late, night. He grabs for me, almost slips from the bed; I pull him back, arms, hands, flaying. The hanging drip crashes to the floor. I am screaming. "You *can't* take your life!" His head falls against the pillow, tossing; his breath comes out in irregular jags. With all his strength he pulls himself up.

"The operation," he wheezes, "it was no good." Blood flows from his mouth, a brown liquid over my hands, down his neck. I am crying, wiping the stream of blood with the sheet. The nurse is still nowhere. His eyes are vacant.

"*Nurse!*" I'm yelling in the hallway. A young woman taking her time walks out of a room. She says my grandfather is one patient in a clinic with fifty-four of them. "He's spitting blood!" I scream. She's surprised by my tone, looks at me more closely. "Young one," she says, guessing I'm younger than my twenty-three years, "relax." I suddenly hate her and my expression says so.

I stay until very early the next morning, until my grandfather is calmer and urges me to go home. "Go sleep, Adrianna."

I tell him I'm afraid. "I think you're going to harm yourself."

He lays back heavily into his pillow and sighs. "Leave *Papou* alone," he says. "Leave him be."

I fold down the damp, blood stained sheet, looking at him; the tubes in his arm and nose. His eyes are still his sky-blue eyes, alive. "Promise me you won't take your life," I say, surprised at how calmly I am saying this. He doesn't move or answer. I kiss him and leave.

∿

My grandmother's footsteps cross and re-cross the floorboards through the nights. In the mornings she says, "I can't sleep with him away." We sit together for tea. She tells me stories of Russia, once her father bought a cow and she threw her milk out on the sly because she hated the taste. Her voice softens with nostalgia.

"In Turkey," she says, "My sisters and I wore veils so the men wouldn't rape us." Rain pours down outside, the luminous leaves look painted. Today my grandfather will come home. She is happy, talkative, her white hair up in a perfect roll around her head.

"You know all your peace of mind will be gone again," I chide. She nods, solemn. "Better that he takes it out on me than anyone else." The phone is dead; workmen have been installing a neighbor's line. The gas for heating has also run out and the house is cold. "*Papou* did it all," she says, reading my thoughts.

"I'll get someone to bring the petrol."

She shakes her head. "This is Greece. They won't listen to you when they hear your voice."

I look at her irritated. "They'll have to listen to me."

She moves toward the kitchen, starts to scour her steel pots, muttering: "You don't know what it is to want to do things and not have the strength."

〰〰

My grandfather returns to the house, pale and sunken. He is also angry. The man who was supposed to bring the gas for heat still hasn't arrived and the phone still doesn't work. I tell him not to worry though I'm upset. "They'll be coming," I tell him. "Right now, rest."

"*Who's* going to take care of this house?" His blue eyes flash. My grandmother motions me not to answer; he needs his strength. She sits on the edge of her bed, opposite his, unfolds the piece of cloth that holds her knitting. He points to her bad leg, the one broken on an iced sidewalk; doctors had not cared for it properly so it healed shrunken. Since then her right shoe sole is thicker than her left one. "Look at her mess," my grandfather murmurs. Over the rims of her glasses, her eyes tell me not to react. "We're patched," he says, and looks at me a long time. "May you enjoy progress." I take his hand tenderly; it's cold. "And may God protect you from the wickedness of men, from the suffering I endured at the hands of people." I kiss him goodnight, overwhelmed by my love for them. I also kiss Ismini but she keeps knitting.

〰〰

On March 3, 1982, my grandfather dies in his sleep. A yellow rose from the garden blooms a full blossom next to his bed. I can't touch my grandmother without tears welling up in her eyes; her face is flushed and bloated.

My grandfather lies in his bed, cold, the piercing blue eyes forever closed, his mouth a stern line I never saw in life. I cannot leave his side.

That morning the man for the heating gas arrives; my grandmother absently tells him to go away. The house is freezing, but no one cares. The garden is full of scattered mandarins and lemons, the roses are wide, palm-sized blooms. A smell of tar lingers in the basement from the machine that he worked. The pail filled with dead leaves sits against the steps. I take it to the front gate the way he did, where it will be picked up by the garbage collector.

All evening I notice small things, and keep hearing my grandfather. I see him with his arm outstretched, pointing to the ceiling dampness, saying he can't stand to see it, saying he can longer climb a ladder to tend to the house repairs. His blue eyes are angry, cobalt and relentless. My grandmother calls out his name all night. I touch her hands, her shoulder; she is stiff with grief.

〜〜〜
〜〜

The funeral is in Nea Smyrni, the neighborhood cemetery. Everyone is in black. A dark kerchief tied under my grandmother's chin twists her flesh, but she doesn't loosen the knot; I try to adjust it. She shakes her head, walks very, very slowly toward the casket at the back of the church. We gather inside, she is motionless in the chair nearest the casket. My grandfather's face is sallow, his lips so straight they look painted; he's in his best suit, his tie perfectly knotted. My grandmother clutches the sides of the casket, kneeling next to him. At the gravesite she is supposed to throw clumps of dirt. I am holding her and she is shaking, crying "*Aimilie..Aimilie…*" and throws the first clod against his clean suit; I see it spatter his motionless face, his ironed suit. Slowly he is lowered into his dug space, the casket is closed, slowly the spades shovel over more dirt. We all stand, crying, except for Ismini who is on her knees calling, "*Aimilie…don't leave me!*"

At home Ismini can barely move her feet. We sit on the edge of her bed as I unlace her shoes, the stockings slip loosely to her ankles.

"Watch the stockings," are the first words she murmurs after the funeral. "They belong to Efygenia…don't rip them." I lift her feet out of them. "There's nothing to do now, without him there's nothing for me to do."

I lace my fingers through the knots in her hair, twist strands into the combs. She shakes her head when she sees the combs. "They're grey," she says. "I only want black ones." She doesn't want to watch television or sleep. "Bring me my cane." She makes her way into the kitchen where she folds paper napkins into perfect triangles.

26

"People were different at one time," she says without looking up from her folding. "We all had gardens in Nea Smyrni, we would talk to each other from our balconies. Maniati had the best pistachios. Our trees never had such good pistachios, but our lemons were the best." She starts to speak, at eighty-three, of a life I have never heard of, a neighborhood where everyone bought from the same butcher, how during the war the mothers in Nea Smyrni gathered in someone's house to share news of their sons fighting in the mountains. "When Kalavrita was burned..." she begins another time. "We didn't know who was in those mountains. Efthymia's Petros was with the EAM fighters in that area. We didn't know anything for days, only that the Germans killed all the men and burned the village completely." She pauses, "They got people to come out of their houses by ringing the church bells. Everyone ran into the square. The Germans had circled the village..." she rarely finishes the story without beginning another. And they always ended with, "We're the only two houses left on Syngrou that have gardens. Maniatis and us."

〰

After the funeral Corinna disappeared, as quietly as she had appeared, and then as mysteriously, she reappeared. I found her in the kitchen with a chair pulled up to the window sunlight, pulling stitches out of a piece of cloth in her lap.

"Where's *Yiayia?*"

She motions to the living room.

The living room furniture was covered in white sheets to keep the dust off. Ismini sat in black on the edge of the couch, her hands folded over her cane.

"You look thin, and you have dark circles under your eyes," she says to me. I tell her I read at night. She tells me I'm like my grandfather. Sometimes I think she doesn't see me at all. After the funeral she gives me *Papou's* bathrobe to wear and his huge leather slippers.

Mrs. Pantazis, a neighbor, comes with a box of biscuits, her hair hidden under a black kerchief. My grandmother balances herself on her cane to get herself up from the couch. As soon as Mrs. Pantazis hugs her, she starts to cry. Mrs. Pantazis' eyes fill with tears.

"It's difficult Ismini. *Couragio.*" They talk in the living room through the evening. I hear fragments, "all my life..." Then Mrs. Pantazi's repeats, "I know, I know." I help Corinna spread a white tablecloth in the kitchen, the cotton folds heated by sun. We pile oranges in a basket, take out two bottles of ouzo, a leg of lamb from the oven. Eventually Mrs. Pantazi comes into the kitchen with my grandmother leaning against her arm. My grandmother takes a knife to slice the lamb, looks at me, lifts it to her neck, and shakes her head because I don't say anything.

When there are guests in the house Corinna hardly says a word, but once they're gone she doesn't stop speaking; she begins discussing the radio shows she listens to in Patras, the histories of the monasteries she's visited. My grandmother hardly answers, her mute expression says, *I'm being patient. I need her.* Once Corinna goes to bed Ismini sits in front of the television, her face washed in the white glare. I kneel by her and tell her how much I love her.

"I just want to go to a mountain," she murmurs, her eyes dim. "Somewhere far where I can think about Aimilios."

≈

"So you've seen the gowns of the Kings of Spain?" my grandmother chides. Corinna continues, "They have very long capes with burgundy fringes and blue silk linings." Exasperated, my grandmother tells Corinna to stop talking. I laugh at her abruptness. Corinna goes to see how the crumbs she's laid over a newspaper on the balcony are doing. She's waiting for the birds.

"They'll come now," she says when I follow her. "Aren't you too close?" She points to a shadow, the wing of a shadow. "There!" We wait but I never see any birds.

During Holy Week my grandmother and Corinna fast. Ismini says she will cook meat for me, but she and Corinna are eating fruit and bread and, in Corinna's case, sweets. All day I hear the liturgies from the radio. For the first time since my grandfather died, my grandmother hums, her psalm book open to the Easter psalms she sings aloud. By evening muted colors stretch over the floorboards, I watch the shadows lengthen until the dark envelops us. We keep the lights off to save electricity, sit for hours in complete darkness unless Corinna decides to light candles. Tonight she has a pair of *lambatha* candles from last year's *Anastasi*. When she lights them our shadows stretch up the wall across the ceiling. From the window I can see the almond trees in Maniati's garden next door; their limbs are long but the lower branches droop like weary arms over the uncut grass, wet in moonlight. Years ago when Nazi officers occupied the house, their tall stalks spun white in the glare of search-lights. Maybe the air smelled of lemon blossoms and wild roses, maybe no one had any idea what was to come, maybe Maniati in his house next door heard muffled cries through the shuttered windows as rain glistened the branches and the soaked scents mingled in air he thought acrid with blood.

Naxos

For the Easter weekend I go to the island of Naxos with a friend. My grandmother urges me to go when I tell her of the invitation.

"You're young, and Corinna's here."

Corinna smiles her toothless grin. "What are you going to do with two old women?" My grandmother flashes her angry look.

The village of Epiranthos sits high on the ragged tops of the island's mountains; the people from the village are, they say, originally from Crete. They speak a dialect that vaguely sounds like the Greek spoken on Crete. It is the only village on the island where (in 1983) there are no accommodations for foreigners. Unless someone has relatives or friends, there is no place to stay. A few years ago an effort was made to build a public toilet in the square for tourists and visitors. Two days before the toilets were finished, the men in the village went with pickaxes and demolished it. No one said a word. Epiranthos is the home of the famous Manolis Glezos, the man (then a boy) who risked his life climbing up the flagpole at the Acropolis that flew the Nazi flag during the German Occupation. He managed to tear down the flag, and became a national hero overnight.

As the bus climbs higher up the narrow mountain roads, the colors get darker, harsher, more vivid blues and greens contrast against rust colored hills.

"What grows here?" I ask.

"What can grow here?" Someone answers.

Isolated in the mountains, the villagers survive the winters with drink and talk, a melancholy life that leaves its marks in eccentric, sometimes savage, habits. There are lots of stories of fights, stories of killings called acts of love. The villagers shirk judgment by outsiders. Our bus stops in front of a row of eucalyptus trees. Children playing in the street suddenly call out, "Tourists! Tourists!" My friend has relatives in the village, his mother was from here and his sister married here. In the early 80s, most of the men are still shepherds. Most of the women I see are wearing black. My friend tells me there are a lot of accidents with lost shepherds found fallen off cliff edges. The women I see look widowed. He tells me, traditionally, a village woman will wear black if *any* of her relatives dies.

I look into the faces of the people we pass; the women usually look away or down. It's the men who meet my gaze. I notice a strange wariness in the look, defiant and proud, but caged. We ask for the house we're looking for; a man urges us up a mud path of stones to the whitewashed house where Tiporini lives. She's draped, from head to foot, in black. Tiporini is comfortable. Black cloth covers her hair and head down to her eyebrows. She must be Ismini's age, but her manner is relaxed, happier. She smiles and pulls up several short stools next to the fire when her son swaggers into the room. His obvious pride in himself is unattractive.

"He stole her," Tiporini whispers into my ear. "That's why there's no room in the house to put you up tonight." The whitewashed house is two rooms that include a fireplace in a corner that is also a kitchen. In the other room there is a bed and icons on the wall. I learn 'stole' (*eklepse*) is the word for 'elope.' The girl is eighteen; she laughs, her eyes are coy as she pinches her new husband. She seems amazingly confident for her age, a match for Tiporini's son who is much older than her. She slaps him on the arm, across his back, grimacing in exaggerated expressions of impatience. He laughs, encouraging her. I instinctively look away when I realize their performance is partly for our benefit, that they are enjoying it. The girl must have given his arm a hard pinch because he suddenly whirls her around so she falls. She is up off the ground in a second, dusting off her skirt; she smiles at me as if to say there is nothing to worry about, and walks over to check the fire.

Toward dusk Tiporini brings out the cooked lamb and two bottles of sweet wine. "No one's fasting?" I ask, surprised. It is Good Friday.

"*Fast!*" her son slurs the word. Tiporini cuts the meat quietly. Occasionally she gives him what looks to me like a brutal look. While we eat he teases her, pulling at her skirt or kerchief. She pushes his hands away roughly. When we gather around the fire she sits on the lowest stool. Her son pushes her with his foot; she ignores him so he pushes until the stool tips over.

"Stop it!" she hisses, but her voice stays muffled. He seems to gloat. I knew that for all his crudity if anyone were to criticize his mother he would be the first to physically defend her. But as his mother, there on her low stool, as he chewed on his leg of lamb, he possessed her utterly and unconditionally: more than any woman his mother would be his. What I understood as abuse were crude gestures at distancing himself from a woman who had given him the terrible freedom to do with her as he wished.

After the meal we take a walk through the village and run into Louizos, a man who asks us immediately who we know in the village. When Louizos hears Tiporini's name his face widens into a smile; he offers to buy us a drink in the coffee house.

"My father was from Epiranthos," he starts, eager to tell his story. "When he and my mother met they had two children. One day there was a fire and he lost half his arm and disappeared into the mountains for days. My mother thought he was dead and went with a friend to Constantinople. My father returned to the village to find her gone. He worked to save money to go to Constantinople where a cousin said he knew where he could find her." His smile becomes a broad grin that shows his missing teeth; he takes a drink of his *tsipouro* and tells us to do the same.

"His name was 'John the Marble Maker' because he lost his arm in the marble quarry when the fire broke out." He pours more *tsipouro* for us. "In

Constantinople he worked fifteen days in a bakery and sold over a thousand, maybe two thousand, cookies." He laughs, the *tsipouro* had gone to our heads and made us warm. "The baker tried to persuade Yanni…that's my father…to stay in Constantinople because he could become a rich man the way he was working, but my father said, 'No, I love my village,' so they returned to Epiranthos." Louizos laughs with sudden color in his cheeks. "My mother was pregnant with me!" He drinks the last of the *tsipouro* and toasts us. "So I was conceived in Constantinople though I was born in Epiranthos!" We laugh with him. The mountains are now a charcoaled uneven stretch through the windows.

"Have you ever heard of the cave of Zeus?" my friend asks. I hadn't. He tells me the story of a place the entire village of Epiranthos fled to during the Turkish Occupation. When the Turks arrived on the island they burned all the villages, but Epiranthos was empty, a ghost town. Someone told them about the cave. So when the Turks found it they rolled a boulder in front of it and burned the entire village alive.

A moon-paled darkness shrouds the road we walk to the next village. Distant headlights skim a far mountain curve; the lights are infrequent and the sound of cars very far away. In the village where we are staying the night, 'FOR RENT' signs and café tables in the main square give the village a friendlier mood. No one takes any notice of us.

Ismini

My grandmother's cheekbones are severe above her sunken cheeks. I watch her clasp the heating pipes to make her way slowly around the kitchen. The water's been cut off. We didn't remember to pay the bill; the envelope from the water company is on my grandfather's desk, unopened. The date reads March 2. I take two pails from the balcony and go to fill them across the street at a gas station. One of the gas station attendants eyes me as I fill the pail.

"What's wrong?" He asks, smiling.

"They've cut off the water from our house," I say. He takes the pail from my hand and finishes filling it, then carries it to the house with me. At the gate he pauses awkwardly. "This large house…do you live in it alone?"

I shake my head, "Of course not! There's my whole family, and my husband upstairs." He nods. "Well then, goodbye."

"I knew what I wanted," Ismini tells me, her hands clasped together over the tabletop. "I wanted to become a good seamstress." Her cheeks are flushed from brandy. "My brother wouldn't let me," she says simply. "He said I would learn bad habits." Her hand-embroidered cloths cover the tables, couch arms, the backs of the chairs.

"Then I met your grandfather."

"How?"

She tells me he lived in a house close to theirs, in Constantinople, and each day that he passed her house, they talked. One day he asked her if she would like to marry him. Her words are simple.

"Did you want to marry him?"

She looks at me, wipes loose strands from her eyes. "I saw he was a good man."

The next day a man with a thin mustache and plaid green jacket is at the door. He tells me he is from Constantinople and knew my grandfather. He looks suspicious, glancing vaguely behind me, toward the steps. I keep my hand on the door handle while he talks. He wants to trim the leaves from the date tree and sell them. He says for the past twenty years he has been trimming the tree, with my grandfather's permission.

"I sell them for charity," he says quickly, "for the Greeks in Constantinople." I look incredulous. He goes on rapidly telling me about his years in Constantinople, of the Greeks there. "The best Greeks," he reiterates, and for some minutes I am imaging it as he describes it.

"Is your mother home? Your father?" he asks finally, looking past me again.

"My husband," I lie. He offers me a cigarette. I shake my head and let him cut the leaves, thinking the date tree will look less neglected if it's pruned. I start feeling sorry that I am suspicious, and go upstairs to brew him some coffee. My grandfather used to say, "Paid help is too much work. You have to offer them lunch and coffee, and treat them like your guests." Yet for all his complaints, he never begrudged anyone a cup of coffee and insisted they eat some of whatever lunch my grandmother had made that day.

When the stranger took his coffee break, he told me he would like to bring me a flower, something special, "I have a gardenia all the way from Constantinople," he says. "Or would you prefer a rose?"

"A gardenia," I say, pleased. I watch him go back to the tree suddenly wondering if I should pay him for the service. I awkwardly ask; he looks suddenly insulted, then ironic. I know I've said something wrong. Perhaps he senses I live here alone.

He looks up at the balcony a second and asks, "Does the old woman still live there?"

"My grandmother, you mean? She's out shopping. She'll be back in a few minutes." He nods his head and goes back to his pruning.

When he leaves after several hours, cut leaves cover the pavement. He has done a clumsy job. Broken sheaves hang from the top of the tree; a dead limb hasn't been entirely cut away. The man never came back. He never brought the gardenia either. When I tell the story to Ismini she gets upset, tells me to lock the gate and keep it locked, and adds that I am old enough to know people are bad.

〰

A loud, blunt thud on the floor upstairs wakes me at night. I run upstairs. My grandmother is on the floor, calling out to the cat in a soft, despairing voice. "*Yiayia!*" I scream.

She looks at me. "I was trying to reach the cat's bowl to clean it." I pick her up, surprised by her weightlessness. She lets herself fall against me. "I made a whole chicken," she murmurs. "I was cooking it, waiting for you."

We go into the bedroom where I untie her shoes, lift her legs onto her bed. She suppresses a yell. "Scream!" I say, frantic.

She looks at me blankly. "I can't," and lays her head back.

The chicken in the kitchen pot is still warm. I spoon out broth for her, but she won't take it when I go to feed her.

"I don't want anything from anyone."

"Is there anything I can bring?"

She shakes her head, "Nothing." I stand, looking at her white hair against the pillow. She gazes towards the three icons on the walls next to her bed.

33

The next day Corinna reappears. I move through a daze of Corinna's cooking, radio liturgies, and Ismini's strained comments about Corinna's idiosyncrasies. For no apparent reason I start to cry one afternoon, relentlessly. Corinna looks up from the sewing she is doing at the window. She doesn't say a word. I stand in the kitchen leaning against the marble counter unable to stop crying. She fills a pan with water from the faucet and starts to heat it; she has brought tea with her from Patras, mountain tea she picked herself. She always brings things with her from Patras: olives, tea, *trahana*. When it is ready she pulls up a chair for me by the window next to her and gives me the tea to drink; I drink it slowly, letting it scald my throat.

Corinna goes into the bedroom where she grabs the cat, one of the strays my grandmother adopted. "I'll kill you!" The cat scratches her down the arm and bolts.

"She's not human..." My grandmother moans from her bed, and means Corinna. "She's been up since five this morning and the radio hasn't stopped."

"Why don't you tell her to lower it?" I say. Her mouth puckers with sudden hardness. "I can't. I need her to stay."

"I'm going to call a doctor."

"No!"

"Why not?" She looks desperate as she raises herself from the pillow and the combs fall from her hair. I pick them up absently.

"I saw the Black Angel..." she whispers, terrified. The curtains float out from the windowpanes. The trellis in the garden below is covered with climbing roses, peach and pink-colored. I look down on them from the bedroom window; they look up from the green vines like pinwheels.

"I think we need to call a doctor. Maybe your diabetes is taking your strength away."

"It never ends," she mutters, "never ends."

Newspaper pages cover the floor in the kitchen and tea leaves sit in a dark pile next to the stove. Corinna mops spilled milk. She has chased the cat out onto the balcony. I take a glass of water back into the bedroom.

"A doctor will give you a prescription for something that will make you feel better." I try to reassure her and myself. "*Papou* would have brought a doctor."

She looks at me sharply. "He doesn't hear anything now. Nothing at all," she says with bold satisfaction.

"Don't you believe in his spirit?"

She sighs, looking at me. "Do you?"

"Yes," I say.

"Why?"

"I don't know. I do, that's all."

Her eyes have a long, bottomless gaze; she looks at my sweater as if just noticing it, and fingers the neckline. "This needs more room here. Let me open it up for you." For a minute she seems to see me clearly, and then closes her eyes, turning against the pillow.

In the early evenings Mrs. Pantazis comes for her occasional visits, but this time she knows Isimini isn't well. She brings newspapers and jam into the bedroom, and sits at the bottom of her bed to talk. I go to boil water for tea and hear them discussing something in the paper.

"Did you see that picture?"

"The girl?"

"Yes."

"Her husband killed her yesterday and she was only twenty-three. It says her husband was seventy-five. Is that possible?" My grandmother is reading the article.

"No, no…" Mrs. Pantazi puts on her glasses to take another look at the article. I bring in the tea and spoon out her jam. My grandmother wants some too. I think of her diabetes, but she tells me she knows what sweets to eat and how much. So I get another plate.

"It just says he was a policeman."

"It's the light," my grandmother says, "I can't read well in the evening. She probably looked at another man and her husband killed her." Mrs. Pantazis nods. The doorbell rings. Corinna runs down to open the door forgetting there's a buzzer upstairs; it's the grocer who's brought vegetables and fruit. My grandmother rummages for money in a purse she keeps under her pillow; she also keeps her newspaper there.

After the grocer is paid, Mrs. Pantazi says it's time for her to get back to her house. Corinna is frying fish. My grandmother hears the oil spit and crackle. "She ruins the food!" she moans, pulling herself up from under the blanket. "I know she's going to burn the fish, I know it."

"She knows what to do; it's not the first time she's cooked fish," I say, starting to help her out of bed but she sinks back against the pillow, exhausted.

"I can't," she barely whispers. "Wait…I'll be better in a few days."

"People are trying to help you," I say, more harshly than I realize. She looks at me. "We have to take you to the hospital *Yiayia*." Her face sets and breaks, tears well up in her eyes slipping silently down her cheeks. She nods, and I sit by her, absently combing her hair with my fingers. She bends forward and I tease apart the knots at her nape.

〜〜

In the morning I call for an ambulance to take my grandmother to the clinic across the street, the same one my grandfather was operated in. Corinna and I prepare tea, toast. I tell *Yiayia* the ambulance will be coming in an hour. She asks for the hair spray on her dresser; she wants me to comb and roll her hair around her head in a braid. We do it together. I comb, she twists the silver strands, pinning them firmly into place. The spray stiffens the wayward tufts; she is pleased when she looks at herself in the mirror.

Two men from the ambulance come up the stairs with a stretcher then fold it into a wheelchair. They lift her from the bed in her sheet; she winces, some pins fall out of her hair, she fingers one of them in her lap as they adjust the straps around her waist. Balancing the chair down the steps they try to amuse her, making light jokes, but instead of smiling she cries. I reach for her hand, think she is thinking of all the people, all the times she has climbed these steps, up and down, a lifetime in them, my grandfather's slow climb after his evening watering of the garden, the careful balancing of his coffin down the same steps, and now her fragile body carried by efficient strangers. As we move out the gates her face lifts to the sun; she closes her eyes and the tears move fast down her lips and neck. She hasn't seen the garden in weeks. The grass is overgrown. A stray cat bolts through the geraniums. She gazes up to the balcony where my grandfather spent his mornings reading the paper; the leaf tips of the poorly pruned date tree skim the railings.

"Why are you crying?" one of the ambulance men chides her lightly. "You'll be back in a couple of days." She nods, without moving her gaze from the date tree, the balcony railing.

In the hospital lobby a doctor who took care of my grandfather comes to her side; he jokes with her, tells her everything will be fine. His presence soothes her. He talks of my grandfather to her and she feels him close, smiles.

She tells me, "The doctor says it's just my legs."

"That's right," the nurse reassures her, helping her out of the wheelchair and onto a stretcher that brings her into her hospital room. "All will be well, as happens always," the nurse goes on, irritating me. The words ring hollow. A doctor comes in chewing a toothpick; I notice he quickly pinches the nurse who grins. I want to hit him, but my grandmother immediately grabs his arm, pulling him down to her face.

"My husband loved you," she says almost desperately. "My husband said you were a good man." The doctor pats her hand. I ask him when they're going to do the tests. Something in my voice makes him look at me with some surprise.

"Tomorrow," he says as the nurse leaves. He then leaves too. My grandmother wants me to bring her hand lotion and knitting from the house; she forgot to pack them into the small bag we put together.

I go down to the small lobby to pay for her room with money my grandmother folded into an envelope. My grandfather always kept money in his desk drawer and in a safe in his bedroom. I had no idea how money got into the safe or who would be making the bank withdrawals now that he was dead. The clerk at the window wants my grandmother's I.D. I don't know where it was, so she asks me to bring it to her the next day and give her the necessary information:

> Name: Ismini Kalfopoulou
> Place of Birth: Constantinople
> Husband: Aimilios Yiorgos Kalfopoulos

One of the men in the office looks up from his desk, "Are you the daughter of Kalfopoulos?" he asks.

"No, his granddaughter."

He keeps looking at me. "I remember your father went to South East Asia…was it Singapore?" I'm surprised he's talking about my father and not my grandfather. I think of my father's absence, his quick visit after the funeral without my mother or brothers, of how he ordered a large television for my grandmother that arrived after he left, how it sent her into a fit of crying.

"Your father was involved with EAM, the resistance movement in the war wasn't he?" I nod again. "Isn't his name George?"

"Yes, George," I say.

Pages lay scattered in the garden weeds, caught in the branches of the lemon trees. Corinna threw food down from the balcony to the strays. She stayed on in the house, waiting for my grandmother to come home from the hospital.

When I visit the hospital in the evening the room is muted with the day's last light. There is a woman in the extra bed which was empty in the morning. The even hum of two women breathing is the only sound. Roses stand in a glass vase. My grandmother's hand is cold when I touch it. "I'm not well Adrianna," she says, opening her eyes. I kiss her forehead, the skin is flaking again. "An old woman died today."

"Who?"

"Someone on this floor." She pauses, looks through the curtainless window. Across the main street is the house. She tells me she can see the tips of the date trees' leaves. "Maybe it is best that I go to that other place now," she breathes, holding my hand. The sky is orange, a black strand of birds moves east. "Goodnight Adrianna," she lets go of my hand. "I'm not well right now." I kiss her goodnight, but stay until I am asked to leave by the night nurse. The woman in the next bed never woke up from her sleep.

As I climb the steps to the upstairs apartment I notice my grandfather's wooden ladder against the back balcony. I am not thinking when I call to

Corinna. She meets me half-way up the stairs as I'm running up to find her. "Did you use the ladder today?" I ask, leading her to the garden.

"What ladder?" I show her.

"*Thieves!*" she yells, picking up the corners of her shift to run faster up the stairs. "*Thieves!* Hurry! Close the door! We have to call the police." We shut the door at the top of the stairs, and I shut the windows too, terrified. Once we call the police we both go out to the front balcony to wait. They take over half an hour to arrive. Upstairs Corinna turns all the lights on. We hear the sirens before the police car pulls up to the gate. I think whoever was downstairs is long gone by now. We let in two policemen through the garden gate and show them the ladder against the back balcony. I suggest we go in the front door; they put their hands on their holstered guns as I unlock, then hesitate, so I go in first. The apartment is a mess, chairs and the kitchen table are turned over; drawers are pulled out. Clothing is draped haphazardly everywhere. There are burnt match sticks scattered over the floor.

It looks like they had known what they were doing. In the back, where the glass pane is broken to open the door from the inside, they had thrown water over the shards to clean off fingerprints. They had forced their way in with a broomstick. Loose papers lay everywhere. On the dresser top, in a crumpled envelope, I had cash; the money for the hospital payment. I had forgotten to take it upstairs to put back into my grandfather's desk. The thieves had missed it. Over sixty thousand drachmas; it occurs to me that if I had hidden the money they would probably have found it.

The police don't do much of anything besides look around. Once they leave, Corinna and I close up and go back upstairs. We leave all the lights on downstairs. Corinna tells me she's convinced the thieves knew the house, knew I had been away. I tell her it was pure chance that I went upstairs to her after the hospital; I wouldn't' have noticed the ladder if I had gone straight into my apartment. She crosses herself in front of the icons and lies down on the couch where she usually sleeps. I go to sleep inside, in my grandfather's bed, the second time since his death.

First thing in the morning, before breakfast, before tea, Corinna and I take the ladder away from the balcony. It's heavy as lead.

"You see how well your grandfather built this?" she says, tapping the sides with her knuckles, showing me the wooden slats, how solid they are. "He broke up doors and nailed the pieces together. That's why it's so strong." The wood *is* heavy; we barely manage the weight between us, dragging it into the basement where he kept his tools. Corinna makes me promise to keep the burglary a secret from my grandmother.

But when I go to visit the hospital after breakfast the first thing Ismini asks me is, "Why were there so many lights on in the house last night?"

"How could you see lights?" I ask her. She points out the window. From her bed she can see the corner of the gates.

"Tell me?"

"Some people tried to break in," I say.

She tries to sit herself up. "The things! There are precious things in the apartment!"

"Nothing was taken," I promise her, but she frowns. A light breeze enters the room. It's almost summer; time has evaporated.

"What's going to happen now?" she murmurs. "What's going to happen to me?" I feel a sudden, irrational anger at my helplessness and hers. My parents live in their distant world, convinced the monthly bank installments will take care of whatever there is to take care of. I rarely call anymore. Even when I do their reaction is the same. "Hire some help." When the hired help quits it is because my grandmother 'is difficult.' I put the flowers I brought from the garden in a cup by her bed.

She tells me to take them away. "I don't want them. I don't want anything," she says, sensing my withdrawal.

"I'm going to Tripoli," I say, "for the weekend. The doctors said you'll stay here till Monday."

"Tripoli?" she says, and suddenly sees orange groves and women in fields cutting fruit from the trees. She travels, her words soften. Before I leave she takes hold of my wrist and whispers, "Take some cologne. Splash some on your hands."

〜〜〜

In the morning I go upstairs to find all the windows and shutters open. Corinna is breaking eggs in the kitchen, letting their yellow centers swim into a soup dish. "Look," she says as I walk in, pale yellow ovals float in egg whites gradually bleeding apart. "These eggs from the grocer's are weak!" She throws the shells into an open newspaper and takes two more from the refrigerator, breaks them to show me their bright orange centers, thick as fresh paint. Next to the window, she balances the dish on her knees and whips them with a fork. It is for the *avgolemono* she says, the soup she is cooking. She wants me to take a Tupper full to my grandmother in the clinic. "They don't have good food in hospitals. It would be better not to eat at all in there." I ask her how I'm going to give it to her. "With this," she says, and lifts the dish. "Just take the dish with you, and a spoon. You can pour it in for her." She tells me she bought the season's first cherries from the market this morning. The fruit sit like gems on the countertop, perfect marbles in a ripped paper bag. Next to them are several long-stemmed carnations. "Those are for your grandfather," she says, noticing my gaze. "I'm going to take them to the cemetery."

~~~

When I get back from Tripoli my grandmother tells me my parents are coming to Greece; they're going to move her from the Syngrou house to an apartment. She won't say more. I try to coax her, but her mouth is a sealed line that swallows her lips.

"Are you sad," I finally ask, late in the day, "to leave the house?" She shakes her head. "Nothing makes me sad anymore, nothing at all."

My parents arrive and leave within five days; entering the house like focused packers, they move firmly through the rooms determined not to think beyond the task at hand. My father is especially steely. This is the house he was raised in, the one he left at sixteen to join the Greek resistance movement, to fight in the mountains during the German Occupation. He has never stopped fighting; now it is a battle no one sees. My mother follows, unquestioning, a woman from an immigrant Italian family in McKeesport, Pennsylvania.

"You're not the same person!" my grandmother blurts to my father one morning. He doesn't answer her, drinking his coffee. I keep thinking he has merciless demons. When my grandfather died, when my mother and brothers wanted to come to the funeral, he said, "What's the point. He's dead."

From the new apartment you can see the sea. Wild oleander grows along the boardwalk. At night lighted fishing boats bob through the darkness. In these nights, as the weather gets warm, the sweet blooming scent of night flowers drifts into the apartment, a pungent, sexual smell, thickening the darkness.

For months things stay in boxes in the Syngrou house. Corinna prefers to sleep on a cot in the basement where my grandfather kept his tools and had his afternoon naps; she would come by bus to the apartment until the Syngrou house was sold. One afternoon I go to find her; she is in the garden spreading newspaper scraps of food for the cats. I see *Yiayia's* black spotted kitten in the garden, but she runs when I go to pick her up.

"Let her be…" Corinna laughs. "She'll come back when she wants to."

"What if she doesn't?" I say, annoyed she let her out of the house.

"She will. She knows where she's fed." Inside Corinna holds up a large linen sheet to the light, studying it for holes. "I brought this for you," she tells me matter-of-factly. I look at the intricate ostriches and elfin children woven through winding branches and foliage. "I made it one winter next to an oil lamp," she explains, folding it.

"Why are you giving this to me?"

"Old people must give what they have to the young," she says, putting the folded sheet in my hands.

40

On Friday I take the bus with Corinna to Patras, the port town where she lives. It is the house her father built; the one her mother and father died in, the one where she spent over fifty years of her life. We pass hamlets along the Peloponnesian coast, lonely boats moored over a placid sea. The bus makes a coffee stop and we get out. A truck comes down the dust road throwing rocks and dirt into the air under its screeching tires. The man is selling watermelons. "Ready to be knifed!" he yells from his microphone. A boy who might be his son jumps out and cuts open a large melon balanced firmly against his stomach; its fuchsia insides gape open, dripping red juice. Several people from the bus buy the watermelons.

I don't like Patras, its air of abandonment, its old houses, its large plastered cornices around crumbling doorways lining the streets. Just outside the town the landscape is surprisingly green, Arcadia, one of the most fertile parts of the country full of orange and lemon groves. My great grandmother Kalliope lived here, her first home after she left the island of Andros to marry my great grandfather Yiorgos who lived most of his life in the city and died during the Second World War. Men stare off into the sea, sitting at tables lining the waterfront, swinging worry beads in their hands. Corinna will stay in Patras, but I'll go back to Athens. She is disappointed; I promise her next time I'll stay longer.

On the way back to Athens the bus stops in a coastal village. Cicadas churn out their heated chant in the trees. A group of old women clutching the corners of their shawls walk down the road, around the bend toward a hamlet in the distance. Down at the water we scoop small jellyfish from the crests of low waves; they glide into our palms.

"Let them live," a man calls out from one of the tables.

"Take them out," a woman answers. "They bite." She's sewing something in her lap by the water.

"Eh," the man answers her. "If you can't communicate, you bite." We start back to the bus; the woman is pulling thread and needle, thread and needle, in concentrated, abrupt movements. She barely looks up as people pass her to go back into the bus. I see a heap of old leather soles in the corner of a garden, a fig tree growing in the middle of what was once a room.

"No one sells," she says looking up, reading my mind. "These houses rot, and then the water and dampness leaks into our homes." I look around, houses, or what look like squares of rooms with whitewashed walls, are built so close together they form a maze of white diagonals that wind up the mountain side. When the head of the household dies, the homes become the property of the remaining relatives who usually can't agree on how to divide up the money from a sale. Whole lifetimes are spent fighting over inheritances until the houses are slowly claimed by time.

The bus passes fields of poppies. Thyme and oregano are growing wild, mauve buds on grey stalks, their scents waft through the open windows.

Thistle bushes claw over hills of rocks and thorn trees, stone fences zigzag for kilometers. The poet George Seferis wrote, "There is no waiting for what is alive," and I think of what surges up in me as I lie awake nights, listening to the crickets, listening to my grandmother's night breathing, wondering what it will all come to when she dies, when Corinna dies, and realize they have become my world.

Ismini is distracted in the new apartment. She hardly seems present when I talk to her. We sit on the balcony overlooking the sea, and count the boats, the sail boats and speed boats docked next to an old taverna. At night I help her undress; she says her muscles have become like iron. The black dress is loose around her waist. She clutches the back of a seat for balance as I unzip the sides of her slip. She wears no bra, her breasts are slack with age, her skin is as milk, but firm when her muscles move. Her thin, strong arms envelop me.

"May God give you all you wish for, Adrianna *mou*." She lies down on the bed, painfully raising her legs. I help lift them onto the mattress. She pulls out one of her hair combs and scratches her scalp with its teeth.

"Sleep well," I tell her, folding the sheet over her, moving the blanket down by her feet where she wants it. "Have some dreams." She laughs at this.

Yiayia gets up early, before dawn. I hear her cane scrape against the wood floor, moving toward the kitchen or bathroom. Today she is expecting Mrs. Pantazis for her first visit to the apartment. I notice she has put on one of her better dresses. I smooth the black lace around her neck, tell her I like it. She pulls at the loose fabric around her chest.

"They're all gone," she says matter-of-factly, pulling at the thin silk to show me the looseness.

"You think I'm talking about your breasts?" I say, laughing.

"Weren't you?"

I tell her I was speaking about her dress, how nice it looked on her. We laugh together, she pulls at her damp hair, just washed, pinned in a tight bun. She says it comes out of her scalp in clumps now. I'm about to go out for groceries when she says she wants to tell me something. It is going to be forty days since my grandfather's death; she has arranged to have a *Mnimosino* service at the cemetery next Sunday. I ask her why she didn't tell my parents to stay (after moving my grandmother into the new apartment they went back to their lives in the States). She shrugs, tells me she has told Corinna to come from Patras, and Maria, the cleaning lady who used to help at the Syngrou house.

"Why Maria?" I ask her.

"*Kakomira*," my grandmother says, which means 'bad destiny'.

"She worked for thirty years standing on her feet, measuring cloths to cut them. She kept two households, when I slipped on the ice and couldn't leave the house for two months, and she never complained about coming here to help."

On Sunday, the morning of the *Mnimosino*, *Yiayia* is up before any of us; I don't even wake to the sound of her cane against the floor boards. When I go into the kitchen she tells me she is not going to the cemetery for the service, but that it is at four and Corinna will be coming directly from Patras.

"You're not going?" I repeat, not believing her.

"I want to," she says, pausing, pouring my tea. "Maria's going to bring the flowers," she says without answering my question. "My legs are too swollen." I know she means this, but what she really means is that she fears what will overwhelm her when she sees my grandfather's name carved into marble over the closed grave.

There's a light rain in the afternoon. I am at the cemetery before anyone. Women at different tombs are fixing flowers, watering plants, cleaning off the marble slabs with wet cloths. I think how domestic it all is, what they are doing, what they did while their loved ones were above ground, tending to them the way they are still tending to them under ground. I am strangely calm; touch *papou's* name freshly cut into the marble slab, tell him I am here. Maria arrives with fresh flowers and starts to cry. Crossing herself she immediately addresses my grandfather. "*Aimilios…Aimilios…*where are you?" she wails. We light the *candili* wick. It crackles in oil, almost goes out so Maria cups the flame with her hand until it takes. The mandarin trees droop their fruited branches over the marble slab. I like the trees, their sweet scents waft over the graves. The priest is in a hurry. He nods to me. Maria kisses the back of his hand. He crosses himself and faces the tombstone to give a short prayer. Before we know it it's over, and the priest is moving on to another grave after Maria slips some money into his black robe. I don't say much of anything.

As we leave the cemetery, walking through rows and rows of marble surfaces propping up photographs of the dead, colored, framed pictures, black and white photographs, some smiling, some looking like they are about to say something, Maria stops in front of a picture of a middle aged woman. I notice the sadness in her eyes as if she were already regretting her short stay.

"Lito," Maria says, "she told me I was going to be the only one who would visit her." She touches the dried flowers in her vase. "She has a son too," she sighs. "But he never comes. Sometimes I even see him in the neighborhood. I tell him he should come visit his mother, and you know what he says?"

Corinna starts to throw out the dead flowers. Maria doesn't stop her. She wants to know what I think the son says. "What?" I say, still looking at Lito's face, her attractive mouth, reddened with lipstick. She is almost smiling, but her eyes seem to prevent her. Corinna's goes over to another tomb where a spread of pink and white carnations decorates all four corners of the tomb; she takes out a few from each of the four vases and brings them back to Lito, gets water from one of the taps, pours it into the vases.

"He says he didn't have time!" Maria almost spits out the sentence. "He's given the undertaker's money to make sure her grave is clean." Outside the cemetery gates Corinna opens a box of biscuits she has been carrying in her bag. She offers them to strangers who nod, chewing on the biscuits dutifully. I ask why she's brought them. She tells me she didn't have time to make *koliva*, she couldn't find the fresh parsley and didn't like the raisins she had bought. I'm thinking if *Yiayia* finds out she didn't make the *koliva* she won't talk to her again until she dies. Corinna shrugs, "It's for your grandfather's soul; I want it to be fresh. I made these." We wait for people to take the biscuits. I eat one too.

When we get back to the apartment *Yiayia* is waiting with tea ready; she is in tears. She says she kept worrying it would rain and the priest wouldn't come, wouldn't say the prayer. We tell her everything was fine. The cat's gone crazy, scratching her, playing behind the vases and dishes.

"She's doing it on purpose," *Yiayia* mumbles, "to upset me." I tell her she is making herself sick. Her eyes are wild with exhaustion. "My nerves are broken," she moans. "That's why I'm speaking the way I do. I've never spoken up in my life." She looks at me reproachfully as though I've trespassed into a space she would have happily kept locked. We drink our tea. Maria talks about seeing Lito. Corinna takes her tea into the kitchen where she sits next to the radio to listen to the weather prediction. My grandmother's words are bitter, as if they have been slowly rusting inside her.

"Nothing, nothing, absolutely *nothing* gives me any satisfaction," she says to Maria. Maria nods, her head bowed over her tea. I don't know if she actually believes what she's saying or if it's the distraught strain of her inability to express what she is feeling.

I tell her, later, that she should tell me when she needs me to stay with her, if she wants a doctor to come for a check-up. I am not always at the house now that I have started to teach part time in the evenings. I also talk of renting a small place in the center of Athens, near the school. *Yiayia* shrugs the first time I tell her, then says she thinks it is time I found a husband and didn't expect me to manage that while living with her.

"Don't tell any of your friends I live in this apartment," she says, adjusting her hair combs.

"Why?"

"Someone may come and kill me. They do it all the time. The newspapers are full of stories of old people murdered in their homes." I try not to laugh but she sees me smile, and is angry. "You don't have any idea," she snaps. "You're young," she says, dismissing me. Corinna walks into the bedroom with newspapers. *Yiayia* asks her what she owes her for the day's groceries; she pulls her wallet (my grandfather's) from inside her pillowcase. Corinna tells her she doesn't need the money now. She has the newspaper open to the election results for major of Athens.

"You see, Averoff didn't win," she says, almost smiling. "Even though he paid for I don't know how many planes to fly banners over Athens." Corinna goes on, tells us this right-wing candidate put people up in fancy hotels to get their vote, busing them in from the villages.

I add that I know a woman was running, "Virginia Tsidirou," I say.

"A Communist!" my grandmother blurts.

"She's a Centrist," I say. My grandmother claims my grandfather knew her. She says they were sent a dinner invitation to her house. I listen, never knowing anymore what is real or what imagined. Corinna says there are still parts of the city where they are going to have to vote again because a majority hasn't been achieved. Piraeus is one of the places. Corinna thinks the PASOK Socialist candidate will win. My grandmother says, "Skilitzis will win."

"Skilitizis is a Fascist," I say.

"But he did good things for Piraeus," my grandmother insists. "I remember when the place was just torn streets, garbage was everywhere. Skilitzis cleaned it up. He even had all the garbage collectors in blue uniforms. I remember them. There were glass vases in shop windows..." Corinna laughs and so does Isimini.

"He had money from the Junta," I say, not as entertained as they are, "That's why he did what he did; if he wins now PASOK won't give him anything."

Corinna chimes in that all politicians take, "that's what it means to be a politician." She adds, "No politician ever gives anything. It's always up to the people."

My grandmother nods, "And sometimes they don't give either." Corinna talks about the war when the Nazi Germans occupied Greece, that people in Patras shared what food they had.

"Not all shared," my grandmother says bitterly. "I remember when the Germans threw Aimilios on the road; he was out looking for food for us. They tried to run him over with a truck. He lay on the road all night. His nose was broken at the bridge, his fingers were twisted. I went to Maniati next door, praying to find him. We finally found Aimilios in the German hospital. I told them I wanted my husband. I was screaming. But they ignored us; they wouldn't let us in beyond the entrance. Then I found him. I waited outside until the guard turned to talk to someone, and I slipped in quickly and found him. He was in such shock. But we got him out. People said if he stayed in that hospital he would have died. I took his clothes to him the next day when there was another guard; I washed them with the ration of water

I had saved from the day before. I went to his brother's house to iron them, and took them to him clean and ironed."

"His brother Sophocles was in love then. He was going to be engaged. I begged him to go find food for Aimilios because I was going to bring him home, and we still didn't have any food." She pauses, her voice slow and tired from talking. "He didn't do it!" She hisses with some final effort, "He only gave me a box of yogurt when I told him Aimilios was going to die if he didn't have something to eat! He forgot how we had given him money, helped him when we sold our house on the island…" she pauses, grabs my hand. "Adrianna…that day I *stole*," she whispers with anguish. "I took handfuls of peanuts from his house and stuffed them into my pockets."

"You did well," I say, mesmerized. Her skin is flushed the way it got when she drank wine. She is looking straight ahead. Corinna picks up the narrative as if she is telling her own story.

"One day Kosta didn't come back for awhile. I went out looking for him. They had just sounded a bomb alarm and everyone had gone to the shelter. I was outside and couldn't find him anywhere. I saw the barricades and the warning siren was going on and on like something crazy. My heart…my god, my heart was trembling like it was going to break through my chest."

"Who is Kosta?" I ask.

"My youngest brother. He died after the war, of pneumonia," Corinna says.

"That's what life gives," *Yiayia* says. "You know," she turns to me, "these aren't tales. They are real. All this happened." I nod. She seems unable to believe the reality herself. "Ah…it's good to remember a little. Every time I opened the windows in the Syngrou house I would see Maniati. We waved to each other every morning. There were neighborhoods then, not like now." Corinna goes back into the kitchen, and *Yiayia* calls for the cat: "Let's sing Nushaki, let's sing, '*I'm a good child because my Yiayia says so… Nushaki mou.*'" When I bring the cat to her bed she bites her wrist. I grab her around the neck and slap her.

"Don't!" *Yiayia* shouts. "It's not a bite, it's a kiss."

"Well if she keeps kissing like that you're going to be scarred."

"You got to know me, Adrianna," she sighs. "But you came too late. You should have come earlier." She looks at me with tears welling in her eyes. "I'm sorry for your father; he has my character. He shouldn't have taken after me; he'll be the same way and suffer because he doesn't speak."

The cat jumps back onto the bed. I go to grab her. *Yiayia* starts to sing: '*Nusha is a good cat and yiayia loves her; Nusha is a crazy cat and Adrianna spanks her. Adrianna needs a spanking but Yiayia loves her…*' She laughs, asks if I want to go get a biscuit from the cupboard. I tell her I'm not hungry so she looks at me reproachfully. I see the Syngrou house again, the large bedroom cupboard with its three panel mirrors. The cupboard has a keyhole without

46

a key, worn from years of my grandmother pulling it open with her pinkie, shuffling through the folded linen to find something hidden behind the piles of sheets. She could pull out an old watch, a frame, richly embroidered tablecloths, a piece of jewelry, a ring missing a stone, an old bracelet without a clasp. Every summer we would visit she opened the closet and performed the ritual of unfolding a gift wrapped in cloth. Afterwards our fingers always smelled of mothballs and lavender.

Close to dawn I hear my grandmother moaning in her sleep. The windowpanes are sheathed in pink. I fall back asleep. In my dreams I'm in the Syngrou house, my grandmother is there with me, the rooms smell of tea and burning toast.

When I wake again, the light is yellow everywhere. My grandmother's voice comes from her room in bursts of conversation. For a minute I think Corinna is talking with her. She must have come from Patras early. When I go into the bedroom I see her alone sitting on the side of her bed, combing out her hair, braiding its strands.

"You don't know what I saw last night," she says, her eyes wide with wonder. "You *have to* believe it," she starts. "There were three people who came, one man and two women, talking and laughing; a woman on each side of the bed. The man told me they came to bring me money. He was counting it out in his hands. 'Let me see your face,' I asked him. 'Where are you from?' She pauses, finishes a braid. "He said, '*Ummm, ummm*' and turned away. I asked him, 'Are you from my husband?' But he turned away and made the same sound. I accused them of coming to tell me lies." I look at her earnest expression. The woman said, 'Aren't you glad we came to keep you company?' I wanted to switch on the lights to see them better, but they said 'no'."

"You were dreaming," I say finally, uncomfortable, remembering the voices in the early morning.

"I *was not* dreaming! They came to give me money, but I wouldn't take it because I didn't know where it came from. I asked the women, 'Are you from my mother? My sister?' They pointed to the icons on the wall." She turned to them, the ones that faced her bed: Saint Spiridonos, and two icons of the Virgin.

All day long my grandmother talks about what she calls the visitors. When Maria comes to visit she tells her about them. Maria is busy putting tea in a pot and spreading out the sweets she brought in a plate. "I had the same kind of dream when my son was sick. I thought people were visiting me," she says.

My grandmother is offended she doubts her. "It wasn't a dream," she says curtly. "They were in my room. And today I'm better, like they said I would be."

I interrupt her, "When is Corinna coming?"

This irritates her more, "I don't care when she comes; she'll come whenever she feels like it. The way she always does."

"I miss her," I say. She looks at me harshly, suspicion etched across her features. "She's not a good person," she snaps, and tries to change the subject.

"Why isn't she?" I persist.

"Before your grandfather died, I said to her, 'Corinna there's Life and there's Death, go kiss your brother goodbye this time, maybe it will be the last time you see him.' But she left the way she always does! Like a thief! And he died…" She starts to weep and doesn't finish her sentence. I try to defend Corinna, explain she might have found it hard to express herself. I go on, saying she was also the only girl in a family of four boys, that that couldn't have been easy.

"So what!" my grandmother snaps. "We've all suffered. She was jealous, that's been her problem her whole life. She was jealous her brothers married and had families; that's why she is the way she is."

Neither of us speaks for what feels like a long time. Maria sets out the tea, puts a sweet in a dish for each of us. She doesn't say anything either. She knows by now when not to say anything.

Finally, sipping her tea, my grandmother says, "I had nice legs when I was young. Long legs. Corinna was jealous of them." I try to control my urge to laugh. Maria smiles, but doesn't say anything. "You must always try to do your best," she says, letting go of the subject of Corinna. I nod. "I've always looked upwards so I see God, or something of him. If I looked down I would see my own face and fall." She smiles and we start laughing.

Maria stays the night. In the early evening the three of us sit on the balcony facing the moored boats. My grandmother knits. Maria reads the newspaper. She looks up from her needles, "Is this life?" she says, addressing no one. "How did we not know it would go so quickly when we were young?" Maria nods, putting the newspaper down. "I suppose this is it then," my grandmother finishes.

When I come back early in the morning from a night out, Maria is at the door, anxious and pale. "You don't have any idea what happened!" she says. She tells me my grandmother took four laxatives; Maria found her soaked. "I was ready to call the hospital. She was so white I thought she would die. I told her to take one of them because she was complaining about her stomach. When I found her she said she had only taken two, but I saw the package, it was *four*."

I go into the bedroom. My grandmother is almost hysterical. "She's calling me a *liar*! I've never told a lie in my life! *Never*! If I had taken four laxatives I would be in the hospital!"

48

"Well maybe that's where you should be," I say, terrified.

"People love me," she says suddenly. "They love me because I've always treated them well."

"Yes," I say mechanically.

"Easy words," she murmurs. "Yes…yes, the easiest word there is…" I sit with her. Maria has gone to sleep. I tell her in the morning we have to call a doctor. She nods, wants to know if I've seen the cat. I find her on the couch in the living room and bring her in.

"How do I live with myself Nushaki?" she says, petting her. "We were all right in the war Adrianna. We had our things, we even had some food." She starts to cry; her mind is cluttered, images rise and fall, stretching their shadows so she can't see beyond them. "Your grandfather…the things he did for food. Riding on a bicycle without tires so we could have eggs, so we could have a little meat…there was a farmer near Varkiza…" She closes her eyes. I tell her she needs to sleep. Maria has cooked rice. The plate is half full by her bed. I pick it up, tell her we will talk again in the morning and kiss her.

The doctor comes early and stays no more than fifteen minutes, prescribes vitamins and tells my grandmother she could have died of dehydration. She hardly speaks; she is like a punished child, thanks him for coming and asks what we owe him for the visit. Maria leaves with him. I make chicken soup, and drop a plate which shatters across the kitchen floor. This gets Ismini up.

"Your mother!" she yells, struggling to get her cane to come see which plate broke.

"Don't come! I'll bring you the pieces," I yell back irritated.

"I don't mind if it's mine but I don't want to break your mother's plates!"

"She doesn't consider them hers. She gave them to you." She shrugs and asks if I ever found the extra key she had given me to the apartment. I admit I've lost it. She says she wants to change the lock.

I tell her I can get a locksmith to do it but she won't hear any of it. "I don't want any strangers coming here. I'm trapped here. If you were away no one would even hear me if someone broke in."

"You shouldn't worry so much. No one has keys to this apartment except you and me."

"And now someone else!"

"The key fell out of my bag, probably on the bus. Who's going to know what door it belongs to?" Ismini looks at me sternly, her mouth in that straight line that swallows her lips. I'm feeling tired and impatient. I'm thinking it's time to rent my own apartment somewhere.

"I think I'm going to go to Patras on Friday and visit Corinna for the week-end." I know Maria will stay with Ismini if I ask her to come for a few days.

She is suddenly furious, pursing her lips to the point where they completely disappear; she can barely keep herself from yelling.

"*What* do you want from Corinna?"

"Just to see her. I miss her." I think of how I had promised to visit, of how she lives so mysteriously on her own.

"I *forbid* you to go there!" Ismini snaps. "Your father would forbid you too!"

"I don't have any reason not to visit Corinna," I say feeling my distance.

"That house is a mess; a real *mess*. Go if you want to eat your meals with cat hairs!"

Corinna's House

Corinna cooks two flat silver-skinned fish, tells me she bought them fresh from the market that morning. She cooks in two wide metal pans she plugs into the wall. Bottles and tins cover a makeshift kitchen table. She explains she has just spent two days making tomato sauce. The light in her house is an alchemy we enter and leave every time we go in or out. An old refrigerator sits near the door stuffed with odd things: glasses, plates, pieces of fruit. There's no stove. The ceiling is coming apart. Under a folded newspaper she keeps a pail of dry cement for the patches. When it rains buckets are placed all through the house to catch water. The floorboards are unpolished, worn white from use. We sit at a fold-out table listening to the news. Breshnev's funeral. "Averoff," an elder politician, she mentions, is going to England for a stomach operation. She cuts a pastry, lines the pieces evenly on a plate.

At night she takes out swatches of linen, shows them to me, the threaded lines sewn into feathered birds, vines. "Beautiful," I murmur.

She shrugs. "It's not hard, if you have patience." We are sitting in the old bedroom. The iron bed is the one she tells me her mother Kalliope died in, and the dresser of carved oak, inlaid with a slab of chipped marble, was carried from the island, Andros, as part of Kalliope's dowry. Dark lines widen down the side where the stone has split. The mirror is spotted from dampness. I glimpse the sky through an open corner of the ceiling. There is a photograph of my grandfather, a young man in Italian uniform. "Kalliope hardly ever left this room," Corinna says. Ismini would tell me her mother-in-law went to her bed 'sick,' though no one knew with what, and for years all she did was sew and paint from her bed. "A huge canvas," Corinna tells me, describing her favorite painting.

"It's a young girl holding a rabbit. It turned black, the weather destroyed it." She goes to see if she can find the painting, the floorboards wheeze as she walks over them. She calls me into another room where a small balcony juts out over the street. The wooden banister is rotted, the iron below, rusted. I ask Corinna if she ever painted the wood. She nods, "Yellow, but underneath it was green." She says rain washed off the yellow in two winters. She says Kalliope's painting must have been given away. She can't remember.

The house gets cold towards evening. The last light comes through the old glass panes, picking up shadowed corners, cobwebs. Corinna pulls out a gas heater from the hallway, lights the stove. A cracked flame dances from behind the grating; she lights the gas and heats up a kettle. The rooms have a smell like old colognes. The telephone rings, the only new object in the house, and the sound startles her.

It's a friend of mine, but she exclaims, "Your mother?" I shake my head. "It's your mother calling from America!" I tell her again it's a call from Athens. "Ismini?"

She says it took six years to install the phone. If you didn't know anyone in the phone company you had to wait for what felt like forever; availability went out to people who knew someone who could help them. My grandfather finally came one summer and had it connected for her. Corinna steams some greens in a pot, tells me they are good for her diabetes.

"Have you ever been bedridden?" I ask her.

"Me? In bed?" She shakes her head and laughs. She wants to know if I'll sleep in Kalliope's room where "the mattress is solid." I am the first guest she has had in years. She tends to me like she tends to her cats and plants, taking care that I have what I need: water, warmth, food. She says I can clean myself in the small bathroom, but to be careful because the pipe is cracked. The toilet is clean, the cleanest place in the house, cleaner than the kitchen with its potato peelings and old forgotten oranges in the garbage basket. I use a pail to flush. The water runs clean from the faucet but drips into a pan below the broken pipe; its ice cold refreshes me.

The bed sheets are freezing. The alarm clock with its broken face says 3a.m. forever. A green velvet bible with a broken clasp sits next to the clock, its pages frayed and tender. I recognize the slender necked vases on the dresser; the same ones were on my grandfather's desk, their pink glass pale with dust.

"If you're going to read I'll bring in a light," Cornnina says. I tell her I think I'm going to sleep, ask who gave her a pillow I see on a chair. A cheap black velvet cloth has NIAGRA FALLS written across it in garish yellows. She picks it up and smiles. "It was a gift," she says, holding it to her chest, "from America."

"I'll be going back to America," I tell Corinna. She replaces the pillow. I suddenly hug her, and get under the freezing sheets.

She sits down in the chair. "You mean you're going to leave Greece?"

"For awhile," I say, "but I'll be back."

"Who knows if we'll be alive," she says simply.

I get out of bed and kiss her. She hugs me tightly, tells me to cover myself with the blankets she's given me. "It's cold." She draws open the thin drapes to look at the misted moon. "If there are no winds and the moon is misted, it's going to be very cold tomorrow." She moves a small rug up against the door to catch the draft. The clock in the hallway sounds eleven times. "I paid one thousand drachmas for that clock. I bought it from the market," she explains. "It doesn't miss a minute. It's from Italy. A sailor brought it to Greece illegally."

"How do you know he brought it illegally?"

"One thousand drachmas," she repeats, "that's two watermelons."

52

I am still not asleep when the clock stolen by the sailor chimes twelve. Someone coughs in the street. Corinna is sleeping in her room. I hear the radio is still on. Thin cracks snake along the walls. I try to imagine my great grandmother Kalliope painting her pictures from the bed I'm sleeping in, sewing, listening to the rain, the busy household outside her bedroom, the world she kept herself apart from.

In the morning I wake to the quick, rhythmic dripping from the kitchen ceiling. Two pans gather rain water. Corinna has rags spread along the floor. The house smells of cooking fish and damp blankets. Corinna is in her stockings, her slippers broken at the toes. Stray cats roam the house, a kitten jumps onto the table, "*Babbbbyyy…*" Corinna calls to her, moving through the kitchen. She opens what goes for a refrigerator and shows me the eggs she got. "He comes every Wednesday from the village. They are special." She fondles them, gives me one to inspect.

"What will happen when the cats have babies, Corinna?"

"They are not all female, can't you tell?" She points to one, "Female cats have those orange stripes."

We take food to the table in the hallway. Corinna seems relaxed, smiles. The backless chairs and naked light bulbs reassure me that everything hasn't disappeared into time. She takes out a silver platter and puts biscuits on the plates. I step on a fishbone on the kitchen floor. She hears my *ouch* and kicks it aside. The table is set with clean cloths that smell fresh. "You must be hungry," she says.

On one of the seats are torn magazine pages advertising tours around Greece. "Have you gone on any?" I ask her, looking at the pictures of mountain villages, monasteries.

"Not last Sunday, but the Sunday before we went to a village near Diakofto. I bought honey for Ismini." She brings me a jar from the kitchen and asks me to smell it; the honey's dark and thick and smells of roses. She describes the orchards, the oranges, walnut and almond trees. For a minute Corinna looks drunk on the smells. "Were there many houses there?"

"There aren't any more old houses; the government gave the villagers money to build and now they all have marble terraces and steps."

At one o'clock, by the sailor's clock, a radio program comes on which Corinna listens to religiously. She brings the radio out from the bedroom so she can hear it while we eat. She tells me the speaker talks about, 'nice things from other times'. She says she learned about a Peloponnesian village where there are large Easter festivals; she speaks about a coastal town where people burned their boats so the Turks couldn't get away after an invasion. She carries on, mixing up times and facts. "The Italians emptied the Acropolis of everything," she says at one point, and I'm not sure if she means the Nazi Germans. "No, the Italians," she assures me, then skips to Kalliope's death, "just before the war," in 1939, and then her father's death, three years later.

"Did you always live in this house?"

She nods slowly. "I was alone with him when he died," she says. "We couldn't go anywhere. The Italians were in Patras." She gets up to get the sweets she keeps in the dresser in Kalliope's room, away from the cats and the kitchen, wrapped in silver foil. "I'll take you to see the church of Saint Andrew," she says. "It took twenty years to build. It was finally built with the ten and twenty drachma coins of people's donations." She goes on to say there was a section on the electric bill, for years, which required money for the construction of the church.

"That's not the ten and twenty drachma donations," I say.

"Of course it is! It comes from our pockets!"

In the early afternoon we walk to Saint Andrews. The mountains surrounding the town look like large mounds of charcoal against the sky. Saint Andrews is a carved monolith of white marble. As we walk in Corinna points to the carpets, "Seventy-five of them were gifts," she says. "During the big holidays, at Christmas and Easter, they roll them up so they don't get dirty."

"Wouldn't they want them down then?"

"No, no, people hold candles. The wax would drip all over them." We walk down the wide aisle to one of the pews. Against the wall, in the corner, hidden by the benches, Corinna leans over to show me where there's grating for ventilation. She makes me look closer. "You see them?" She laughs, pleased. She moves part of the carpet away so I can see the grating more clearly. "During the service when the priest is giving his service, men are downstairs in the basement *working*." Intrigued by this idea she tells me details of how the heaters work in the basement. When we leave she insists on going around to the back to show me where the steps to the basement are, where, 'the men stay beneath to keep the church warm for everyone.'

We start to walk home; the trees are filled with birds. We walk along the sea shore where old houses still line the road. Once beautiful verandahs and doorways look over weeds, fallen entranceways, rusting iron fences. "This whole road," Corinna says, waving down toward a park with swings, "was bombed by the Italians." She describes the horror of strewn rubble, bodies dismembered. As we approach the park I see children on swings. "Your grandfather found a bone plate here," she says, tapping the top of her skull. "It was so smooth he brought it home to show us." She thinks she could still find it if she looked. The sea is placid, grey, the air cool again. We walk along the train tracks, on the pebbled slope. "The train is going south," she says.

"There is no train, Corinna."

"Yes there is. Wait and see." We wait, looking toward the sea, the violet colors of the sky. The winds are picking up, making the air cold. She shows me a wild rose bush growing by the track, tells me she has some jam she made from rose petals at the house.

"It's not coming, let's go." I say. Down the road one of the street lamps has come on; a faded yellow light makes a ring of color over the track.

"Wait a little Adrianna. It will come."

"I'm cold," I say, feeling the wind cut through my clothes.

"All right then," she shrugs. "But if we waited a little longer the train would come."

On the walk home we cross the tracks another time, closer into town. Part of the pavement buckles, tiles crush themselves into a pyramid. "Look!" Corinna says, pointing to an olive tree growing close by. "It's the roots; they tore the ground apart! The cement couldn't keep the roots down."

When we get back to the house Corinna puts the kettle on for tea and gets the rose-petal jam she told me about. "It's made with tiny, tiny flowers." She opens the lid and makes me taste. I go to bring in two tea cups I bought for her at the market, still in a bag. When I give them to her to use for our tea she frowns.

"What am I going to do with these? I've given everything away. Anything that had any value I gave to your grandmother or Nitsa, your grandfather's cousin. What am I going to do with cups...we're on our way to dust now." When I insist we use them for tea she tells me she'll bring them with her to Athens and leave them at the house for me. After we finish I rinse the cups out myself, purposefully, and place them on her shelf but realize I should have known better, should have bought her something live, a goldfish, a plant.

Before we go to bed Corinna relates a story of two starving children found in a truck outside Thessaloniki. "They went eight days without food," she says.

"What happened to them?"

"Their parents were killed in a car accident."

"No one found them?"

She shakes her head, "Some aunts and uncles...that's all they had." She dismisses this, tells me the police finally found the children.

"The younger one wouldn't let the older one eat."

"Why not?"

"Grrrrrr..." she grimaces, like one of the cats.

"The children went crazy?"

"No, no!" she laughs. "Not the children, the cats!"

"I didn't know you were talking about the cats." I say, perplexed. She stares at a colored advertisement of Pyrex dishes on a piece of cardboard she has propped against the table. She tells me she found it on the road. "It's nice isn't it?" she says, the picture intact, the letters in bold red, the dishes in clear glass, stacked in their different sizes.

"Yes. It's nice," I say. The ad is in English. Corinna is more interested in the dishes than the letters.

At dawn, five-thirty, the alarm goes off. I don't hear it but Corinna comes in to nudge me. She says I have to eat something before getting the bus back to Athens. On the table in the hallway she has already wrapped eggs, tied a can of quince into a plastic bag, placed a bunch of tomatoes together so I can see them before she puts them into a bag, then shows me a jar of olives.

"I make them every winter," she says. "Myself." I see the plastic vats in the kitchen; the olives soaking in a fine, green crust. 'Almira,' Corinna calls it, the salt and juices from the fruit. She says it took months of changing the water every five days before the olives are ready to be put into jars, the bitterness bled out of them. After she gathers everything into two bags for me, we go down the rickety steps to the front door. The sun is just coming up. We wait for the first bus of the day going downtown, and then another bus to the station. The barber shop on the corner is shut, still there, since the house was built. Corinna used to get her phone calls there. The blank windows stare out over the empty street. I wonder how long before it's all gone, before this corner of the city is taken over by newer buildings.

I tell Corinna I will call her when I get to Athens. She shakes her head, "Don't spend your grandmother's money. I'll see you in ten days, after the bills come and I pay them I'll be in Athens."

56

The Harmony

We open the package Corinna sent with me, each egg wrapped in its own tissue so it won't break. "Why did she send them?" Ismini wants to know.

"For you."

She looks puzzled. "Was it dirty there?" I shake my head. There are also pears the size of my palm in the bag.

"When I could go to the market myself I bought normal-sized pears. These are giants." She puts ten chestnuts on the stove burner to heat. "Sit down," she says as I put away the jar of quince, the eggs.

"I'm afraid to take this medicine," she points to an unopened bottle on the table.

"Why!"

"Today is Sunday," she mumbles. "Don't shout."

"You're going to get sick again…"

She ignores me and sings to the cat. "*Come Nusha…we'll marry you. We'll dance and drink our fill…Come Nushaki mou, come to Yiayia…*"

"Has Maria been to see you?"

"Maria is an aristocrat, she leaves half her bread uneaten on her plate."

"Didn't she tell you to take your medicine?"

"People are meant to be with people, and that woman, your aunt, isn't normal. When anyone visits for very long she throws them out." She starts to tell the story of when my grandfather tried to get Corinna engaged to a man. The first thing she told the man when he asked her how life was in Patras was that it was just fine because, "I get up and sleep whenever I feel like it." I laugh.

"It's not funny," Ismini snaps, getting up from the kitchen table with her cane to go to the bedroom.

"Maria is leaving," she murmurs and bursts into tears.

"How can she leave? She's your friend."

"She says she can't visit so often anymore. Her husband is sick."

"We'll find someone who can take care of you."

"Your father will think it's me," she moans, crying.

"Why?"

"He asked Maria if she ever argued with me, *me*! I love *everyone*." Her face breaks into uncontrollable sobs. I hold her, sitting on the bed, rocking her against me. "He doesn't believe me," she goes on, bitterly, "He believes her."

"What happened?" I ask, thinking the care must have become too demanding for Maria, especially after the accident with the laxatives.

"Nothing happened!" she says, straightening up, pushing her hair pins back into her jumbled strands. "Maybe Maria's husband is really sick," I suggest.

"I hope I die. It would be the best thing," her face sobers and she seems to gather strength. "Maria should have talked to me first, like two women. But she waited for your father to call from America. *Papou* was right…" she collapses into fresh tears. "He said, 'where will they put you, what will they do with you when I'm gone?…'"

"You don't like this apartment," I say, suddenly realizing how foreign it must be after a lifetime in the house my grandfather built for them.

"It's a nice place," she says listlessly. "But it's not for me. I want a small, small place away from everything and everyone," her face becomes defiant. "I don't need help from anyone." She turns, bewildered. "I never get angry…if only I did…" She tells me she should let my parents put her into a nursing home. "So they can forget about me, the way they want to."

"Shhh…" I tell her to stop exaggerating, but she gives me a fierce look. In a few weeks I will be going back to the States. I wonder what that world will be like after the year here with my grandparents. I am going back to graduate school in New York. It seems very far away, yet I know once there I will look back on the year here and feel like it happened to someone else. "I'll miss you," I say abruptly, struck by how feeble the words sound and how sincerely I mean them.

"Is this the truth Adrianna?" she asks.

"Yes, of course," I say, pulling the blankets up around her shoulders. The cat moves to the bottom of her bed.

"Come *Nushaki*…" she calls, but the cat licks her paws and moves away. "She's modern too," my grandmother laughs. "I give her everything, her food, water, treat her like my child and she turns away from me." I laugh with her.

"Will you remember to go to the house," she asks before I turn off the light. "Mrs. Pantazis called; she wants some of the lime and oranges from the trees. She says there are so many but doesn't want to go into the garden herself to get them."

I nod. I haven't been back to the Syngrou house in weeks. I pass it every morning on the way to work, the closed gates, the date tree, the shuttered windows, bring back my grandfather's words, '*Who will look after this house when I'm gone?*' My parents shut it up after moving my grandmother.

"I'll go tomorrow," I say in the dark, "I wonder if the same cats are there?"

"They go next door," she answers. "Cats don't have to worry about finding food. There were even cats in the war, so many they used them to feed the soldiers in the hospitals."

Mrs. Pantazis explained to me where her house was. "Around the corner, next to the large supermarket," she said on the phone. "You'll see a small two-storied house."

The breeze is cool at twilight. Birds are clustering in the trees. I go to the back of the house where the trees are, where my grandfather once had a chicken coop and a fig tree. Now the leaves are dry and yellowed. Only the fruit hangs ripe on the branches. I use one of my grandfather's old work chairs to get to the oranges and lemons. His workshop still smells of pitch and tar. The fruit fall heavily. Old newspaper scraps flutter in the branches. The grass is overgrown, bits of trash lay scattered in the weeds; a yogurt container, a detergent label, shreds of papers. In *Papou's* lifetime everything was always watered and trimmed. A cat scampers down a tree.

I find the Pantazi house, the apartment where she lives with her husband is up a flight of crooked, cement steps. Mrs. Pantazi greets me in her winter coat pulled close around her, says she's been waiting all day for the gas truck to arrive. The heat's been off since last night when the gas ran out. I give her the bag of lemons and citrus fruit. She hugs me. "I don't know what these are called in English," she says, taking out one of the larger citrus fruits. "I'll make a wonderful sweet."

Her apartment smells of fresh linens, the sweet, stiff scent of burning wood.

"Hello?" Her husband comes in from the short hallway to greet me. He walks with difficulty, tells me to have a seat. "Your grandfather and I were dear friends," he eases himself into a chair. "Ah," he half smiles. "Those days have passed. Our houses used to be the villas of the neighborhood. Now we're like the *Karaghiosis*, the little sad houses under the gaze of the big apartments." He laughs now, and tells me an anecdote of a distant cousin of his who left Greece for America.

"'Eleni, my sweet.' Eleni is my cousin's name. 'Eleni,' I told her, 'You were such a rose when you left forty years ago. Now look what time has done to us!'" He smiles and nods with quiet glee. "Yes, this is what time has done to us…you know." He turns to his wife, Mrs. Pantazis, "In the war we had nothing to do, so we learned languages. My wife and I tried to learn English together, so I can speak a little now." I say I am amazed that so many people speak English in Greece. "It is us poor countries who learn all the languages, isn't that so? The Americans are too busy, eh?" He laughs, "They're egoistic, no?" I nod.

"How do you say that word in English?" Mrs. Pantazis interrupts. "Snow? One says 'snOw', another says 'snOOw'…tell me how to say it right?"

I laugh, pronouncing the word slowly.

"Ah you English and Americans," he exclaims, "swallow your speech. You speak from the inside of your throats. We speak from our mouths." Mrs. Pantazis brings in coffee.

"Why do you speak from the insides of your throats?" she asks.

Mr. Pantazis explains, "Don't you know Frosini? It's because their countries are cold and they have to keep their words low so their mouths stay closed."

≈

Twice I bought film to take pictures and both times something happened. Once the camera didn't work; it clicked without registering any prints and much later I realized all the pictures were blank. A week later, the week before I was going to leave for New York, I borrowed a friend's camera, possessed with the feeling that all would be forgotten if I didn't get pictures. I kept thinking Ismini will die, maybe before I got back and I would never have a physical record of our time together. Ismini was reluctant to let me take the pictures a second time. "I don't want to see my face," she kept saying. After I took the pictures, and she posed, I found out, two days later, the film had broken in the camera and again I was clicking empty prints. I started to weep; there would be no trace, and all would grow slowly distant and finally foreign. I decided for some reason I wasn't meant to have the photographs. I was being forced to keep the record in another way.

My grandmother died a year later, in the clinic where my grandfather had his prostrate operation, and Corinna passed on two years after that, in the same room and bed in which her mother, my great-grandmother Kalliope, had died.

Traffic Politics

"The spider was power, plus limitless greed,
plus an abstraction, not God, but something like God,
which perpetrates something like Babel on us,"
from "Chaos" C.K. Williams

Traffic is the sound of modern Athens and Athenians negotiate it with savvy. For anyone who drives in the city, life is consumed by lights that change too quickly (you never manage that turn or cross that street in any legitimate amount of time) and drivers who use road politics to demonstrate the stuntmanship of getting ahead at almost any cost. The average Greek, me included, lives the daily reality of traffic like a web of bad dreams (Athena taunting Arachne): will I, can I, how do I, get through this?

Athenian road life is a good reflection of the impossibility of doing anything within a prescribed plan and the madness that comes of that reflects a disposition I became a part of. No one, or so it seems to me, follows the rules. Motorcycles make their own lane somewhere down the middle of two lane roads, or more precariously, cut ahead from the right when there is no space on the left; the ribbon of asphalt in the middle of two lane streets is always used by motorbikes to speed ahead of stalled traffic and I inevitably find myself veering to avoid them bounding into me.

Making a right turn into a street, my blinkers flashing, I suddenly discover a helmeted motorcyclist blaring his horn on my right. Speeding ahead to pass me as I make the turn, he almost hits the car and proceeds to curse. I am dumb with shock; he yells a barrage of language against my not seeing him as I gradually realize *he* had no business trying to pass on a turn. When I finally do say something he has sped off, convinced I'm at fault.

Everyone in this city needs to make the lights as if *that* green light represents some concrete salvation everyone else is too slow to take advantage of; we drive like we are possessed, as if the chores and errands and destinations we are out to complete must occur within the next few seconds if there is going to be any tomorrow. After years of living in Athens, I now drive with the same desperate urgency as my fellow Athenians, matter-of-factly parking on sidewalks, abruptly pulling myself out of stopped lanes to speed down momentarily empty strips of road to gain the few minutes it takes everyone else to finally make the light before it turns red again. I think nothing of driving right of a lane that eventually curves left when I see stopped trucks lined up for the light to change. I know if I'm quick I'll pass the trucks that are slow and salvage another couple of minutes. They do add up. Every day I vow to stop being the maniac driver I despise having to share the roads with — I turn on the radio, go into reverie, recite poetry, think up lines of my own — and I'm invariably late for work.

Koroido is a term that loosely translates into English as 'sucker,' someone too unaware or stupid to realize they're being duped. Being 'caught' *koroido*, as we say, so strongly suggests humiliation, even emasculation, that we go to absurd lengths to avoid *koroidia*. My grandparents mumbled the term; my grandfather Aimilios cursed the *koroidia* of governments, but I learned the visceral power of the word in Athens traffic. What looked like pure madness began in glimmerings to suggest a fragile order. I understand the threat of being made to look stupid by the more savvy and advantaged as a form of *koroidia*. The ego displays that amount to performances of daredevil driving and language battles that result in a ticket or arrest in more regulated worlds, are here a language of urgency.

On the way back from the airport a taxi driver (on what is a new strip of highway built to accommodate airport transportation) makes a point of speeding ahead of a female driver who is going too slowly for his taste.

"You're going to kill someone!" He yells, almost killing us as he loosely holds the steering with one hand and makes the reckless point of leaning out the window so she won't miss the incensed words he hurtles her way. The woman is bewildered. I am anxious, thinking she is going to have that accident.

"Why don't you stay home with your pots and pans!" he shouts.

She shakes her head.

"Just *look* at her! The *idiot*. She's going to kill someone the way she's driving!"

"Ignore her," I say, tense.

"*Ignore* her! She's right in front of us. I can't get rid of her…"

I start to wonder why it's so important to get ahead *and* make the person you've managed to pass feel *koroido*. The feeling is that if you don't get ahead you'll be left behind, or worse, be laughed at. It is up to the individual rather than any rule or system of rules to negotiate what's viewed, at best, as arbitrary. The light always turns red too quickly; there are never enough traffic lights where you need them, and too many where you don't. The terms of *koroidia* suggest it's reckless to assume society has any individual's interest at heart. Finding the loopholes or in traffic terms, the side streets, is the difference between actually arriving where you set out for and being stopped in the unmoving lane.

On my way home one morning, after dropping off my daughter at school, I make my way up a hill to a crossroad when I become aware of a car edging up on my right. The road narrows gradually before the lights. It is yellow. I am slowing down as the car on my right speeds up. It wasn't going to make the light. The driver expects me to slow down and move left to let her cut in front so she can get ahead. I refuse. She has to slip into line behind me if I don't move left for her. She does neither. The light turns red; we're stopped at the cross section and she squeezes herself between what is left of the road and part of the pavement. I glance her way and shake my head. She immediately rolls down her window.

"Three cars can fit here," she yells.

"Why not four?" I answer.

"Unless you got your license from some correspondence school you could see three cars fit."

"I'm in my lane and you're going to be on the pavement soon," I yell back as the light turns green and I keep to my lane without budging. She has to either fall behind or run into me. She lets me go, screaming, "If *you* were *civilized* you would have made room for me!" All the way home I keep thinking why doesn't she get it (two lane roads are two lane roads). Then it occurs to me, from the moment she found the space to squeeze her car in next to mine, she assumed, wrongly, that I'd respect the fact that she was there. It wasn't about rules, it was about their inability to bring order to something more complicated. I was telling an engineer friend involved with the Athens metro excavations about the incident and he relayed an exchange with one of his workers who he'd asked not to smoke on site. The guy put out his cigarette with the comment, "Too many rules never helped anyone," adding, "In England you can't smoke anywhere but people are dying of poisoned air." Sooner rather than later stronger powers inevitably get the better of you 'Ti na kanoume, dhe variese', we say, 'What can we do...don't bother so much'.

Rembetika music, like American Blues, are the sung laments of a people marginalized by poverty and exile whose lifestyle is one of resistance to a world experienced as fundamentally unjust. The *rebetes* musicians, as Janet Sarbanes describes them, are individual*ists*. My engineer friend in the metro works goes on with dismay to stress what *aftonomistes* (individualists) Greeks are, with little if any faith in overriding systems. In the mid 1800s in the *tekes* or cafés of Smyrna and later Thessaloniki and Piraeus, the Greek *rebetes* lived their individualist lives of music, hashish and dance by defining spaces claimed on their own terms. But on the roads in Athens individualist drivers had me murmuring to myself like someone demented. A man stops his car in the middle of the road, at a fork, to ask the car behind him for directions, a car parks, with flashing blinkers, behind an already parked car, a van in a side street blocks the street as the driver briefly gestures to the row of cars behind him while he unloads a crate of bread, his engine running – in all these moments there is always the assumption that the rest of us understand the situation and, if only grudgingly, will be tolerant.

In the bus on my way to Athens on a market day, the fruit and vegetable stalls blocking off most of the street, cars and buses have to edge around each other. The already crowded street is narrowed even more by cars parked on both sides of it. Our bus is rounding the corner as another comes in the opposite direction. For about six minutes the two drivers face each other, unmoving, mumbling, each waiting for the other to backup, but in the minutes they are thinking it through, cars line up behind both of them. Eventually our driver gestures to the other one to edge his bus along ours. We are centimeters from each other, and centimeters from the sides of the parked cars. In a series of short, braking movements by the skin of their metal, the two buses manage to clear each other. It's the only time I don't witness an argument, it's also one of the few times I see two drivers negotiate something that looks impossible to resolve.

Another morning in a small electrical parts shop, a woman walks in with a remote control for her television asking for a missing part. The owner wants to know what model of television she has; she has no idea.

"Do you have the instructions?" The man goes on. She shakes her head. He continues, "Did you look under the television, there's usually a number either underneath or on its side." She shakes her head again; perhaps in her sixties, dressed in black, she's unabashed about her ignorance. It occurs to me that she's enjoying the attention as the rest of us are waiting our turn. The owner pulls out a stack of catalogues. "Here," he says, "look through these, see if you recognize the model." She shrugs. "I don't know…" At that point the rest of us start to audibly sigh.

I try to imagine this woman in the States, approached by a broadly smiling shop assistant politely asking, "What can I do for you today Madam?" The woman would show him her television control and ask for the part without knowing the model. "Sorry Madam, we need to know the model to find that for you," he'd say without missing a beat, still smiling. There would be no shop assistant extravagantly catering to her helplessness.

I see her in the supermarket, the bank, the post office, the woman who always knows how to get ahead of the line, who gets the cans at the top of supermarket shelves, who begs someone to do her a favor. Weeks later I'm back in the electrical parts shop. This time an older attendant is there, he takes a look at the broken plug for my computer outlet. The wire needs to be cut for a new plug. My car's parked on the pavement outside with the blinkers flashing. Another man's waiting when I go in. He's also parked on some pavement or blocking someone's entrance because he keeps looking anxiously out the door. The shop owner sees the wire in my hand, "What do you need?" I show him the broken snap, "The catch is broken."

"I don't know if I have any extras," he says, looking into a plastic cup of paperclips and coins where he finds an unbroken plug. "You're lucky," he now smiles, starting to adjust the plug.

The other man keeps looking tensely out the door. It takes a few seconds to fix the wire, and then he refuses to take any money. I thank him and the man who's been waiting, and rush out to my car still without any parking ticket or sign of a police officer writing one out. I'm about to back up when

I notice a car that wasn't there before squeezed in behind me. I gesture for the driver to give me room to maneuver, he nods and I smile, pleased with my fixed wire, happy the shop owner never commented on the smallness of the job, suddenly feeling like I've made good use of my morning when I drive home to the familiar sight of the glass-recycling bin pushed over on the road outside our apartment building. It's been on its side for weeks. Every time I come home I think the same thought: why doesn't anyone put it right side up? It's full of bottles and jars, too heavy for me to budge. I see it from my kitchen window every day and every time anyone of the neighbors drives into the parking lot they see it too. I think everyone's just too busy running around for their Christmas preparations to bother with it, but by the middle of January rows of empty wine bottles and jars are lined up around it. One morning I watch one of the neighbors throw a bag of bottles into the regular trash and listen as the glass shatters.

It's late February when a group of municipality workers drive up in a truck to trim the pine trees along the road, and finally put the bin right side up. The electrician in his shop and the abandoned recycling bin in my neighborhood express idiosyncratic relationships to what is, and isn't, important to give yourself to. One to one, time is taken to help out, holding up a line to find the information for a woman who walks in with an out-of-date TV control or keeping people in the post office line waiting when a village woman insists someone read her illegible slip of paper, is more important than an inert bin of bottles. '*Ti fteo ego?*' ('How is it my problem?') drivers yell when they cut ahead in traffic (almost killing me) because I'm not going fast enough for my own good. When sidewalks are dug up, then replaced with mismatching slabs of mosaic or badly mixed concrete, when roads suddenly develop massive pot holes after heavy rains, it's always, '*Ti fteo ego?*'

Very happy to find a parking space near the bank one morning I slip in to do my errands only to come back and find a car parked (with flashing blinkers) right behind me. I'm furious and honk until someone comes rushing out of a bank calling, "I know, I know, *I know*..." the beginnings of a smile on his face.

"What do you mean you *know*!" I say, livid. "Don't you have *any* respect for other people?"

"Relax...I was in the bank. I'll move."

"You should never park *behind* another *parked* car in the first place! What if I needed to get out. What if it was an *emergency*!"

"*Ti fteo ego* if it's an emergency?" he says, genuinely surprised.

I begin to scream, "You're not supposed to block a parked car!"

"*Ela, ela*..this isn't the United States. Be patient...everyone parks wherever they find a place."

"This *isn't* a parking space in *any* country!" I go on, now hysterical.

"Boy you're crazy," he says almost respectfully as he backs out, and leaves me shaking.

This is my Athenian present, the world I have come to know and find so difficult to explain to friends and family who live outside of it, a place where people make individualist contracts with necessity and interpret the rules accordingly. An American friend of mine, still in shock when I go to pick her up from the metro, is telling me a motorcyclist almost ran her over as he sped down the sidewalk, honking his horn and gesturing for her to move out of his way. "He was *on the sidewalk* on a *motorbike*, asking *me* to move." She is incredulous. I now laugh, reminded of the Greek friend who had asked the metro worker not to smoke.

"People from abroad are so used to seeing red tape around work sites that warn them to be careful that they're likely to be seriously hurt without them," he said. They don't expect traffic to spill over onto pavements or to find themselves suddenly in ditches when walking along the street. No one expects epic disasters of mundane obstacles. One of my study abroad students on a semester visit to Greece, making her way to the library on the dimly lit road, is horrified to find herself in a hole up to her waist. There are no warnings. No signs. You come to develop an instinct for the motorcyclist belting around the corner where you least expect him, you develop a sense that to keep yourself and your car intact from one destination to another, over regular potholes and unevenly patched roads, you must expect the unexpected.

On my way to work I notice a truck coming out of a parking space. He's attempting to cross over into northbound traffic as a steady flow of southbound traffic refuses to allow him to cross over. If a northbound car let the truck in things would have gone smoothly, but no one stops. The fact that the driver forces the sheer size of his truck into the flow of traffic, obstructing it, makes the drivers in the northbound lane all the more determined not to let him in. Stopped cars in the southbound lane start honking like their horns are glued to sound boxes. The look on the truck driver's face becomes stoic. He refuses to back up, stopped a good three minutes, while he waits for someone to allow him to cut in. No one does and the fact that he's made his way across a main thoroughfare, blocked traffic, and still expects someone to give him the right of way, makes things worse. Drivers vigorously shake their heads, people honk and give him the flat palm gesture (the Greek version of the finger) until, eventually, he edges enough of the body of the trunk into the northbound flow to force the cars to make way.

No solution is too extreme. I see a car jump the foot and a half of curb on the island separating the lanes so the driver can go in the opposite direction when we're stalled at a light because some government official happens to be passing by. I see someone else make a u-turn on a one-way street as a bus is coming up the road, signaling him to hurry up so they don't have an accident. But nothing prepares me for the unfortunate encounter I have with a taxi driver.

It is almost midnight. I am waiting for the red light to change to make an immediate left up a hill to a jazz club where I am going to meet a friend. About to turn I see a taxi stopped at the curb. Without blinkers or any warning signal, the taxi moves suddenly in front of me. I don't stop in time to avoid its left front light and fender hitting the middle of my right door. I pull over. The taxi driver gets out checking his broken front light. His fender is fine.

"You didn't have your blinkers on," I say, shaken, as he continues to examine his light.

"What business did you have speeding around the corner like that?" His tone is matter-of-fact.

"I was turning. I wasn't speeding. My blinker was on and you were parked."

"What do you mean I was *parked*. I left my passenger off and was leaving," he snarls.

"Without lights? No blinkers? One minute you're parked and the next you're in front of me."

"Let's call the police."

"Call the police for what!" I am amazed. "You left the curb with *no* warning. I had the right of way."

He hears something in my imperfect Greek, and seems all of a sudden to take his time. His body slouches against the car, he lights a cigarette. I now loathe him.

"Each person pays his own damage," I say getting into my car.

I decide to forget the taxi driver and the incident and fix my car once I have the time and money. But a few days later the phone rings and the voice on the other end is his. He speaks in slow, regulated sentences as he tells me he found my phone number by calling the tax office in my neighborhood. He had taken down my license plate number.

"What do you want?" I say coolly.

"You left after the accident. I can file a charge that you didn't wait for the police."

"Do you want me to pay for your damage?" I am uncomfortable. It gradually dawns on me that he has gone to the trouble to find my number and is premeditated about everything he is saying to me. I live alone with my seven year old daughter and the thought that an unknown taxi driver might be stalking us starts to terrify me.

Again he seems to have picked up something in my tone.

"I'll call you back and let you know how much it will cost."

I call my insurance company. The stipulated 48 hours has passed; it's too late to make a claim. I make the trip downtown to the insurance people to explain the situation. I am told no one has made any claim yet but I should make one anyway, for the damages to the door.

When the taxi driver calls again, he gives me a figure that sounds reasonable. I agree to give him the money to keep my premium from going up, but still refuse to accept that the accident was my fault. If we can't settle this ourselves we will end up in court, where we finally meet again.

The taxi driver calls me several times to tell me he needs to ask for more money. The figure increases twice before I yell into the phone that the court will decide what money he will get or not get, and hang up. The stony deadpan of his voice still haunts me as much as the insurance person who assured me no one had made any claim when, a year later, back from a Christmas visit with family in the States, I found a message on my answering machine to call a lawyer whose name and number I didn't recognize.

The taxi driver counter-sued me when my insurance company went to collect damages; the insurance lawyer is the one who tells me this over the phone. I'm confused and irritated. Why am I being called a year later, without any earlier warning, what if I hadn't returned in time to be in court in two days? I'm jetlagged and disoriented in what has begun to feel like a lifetime of dislocation. Back from the States whose suburban quiet and ample roads make honking grounds for a ticket, I find myself absurdly saying, "In the States you're told these things *ahead of time*." The insurance lawyer is detached and polite as he dryly reminds me, "This isn't the United States."

Omonia Square in downtown Athens on a January morning after a rare snowstorm looks strangely clean in its fresh coat of white, the crowds and cars are slow, careful as they manage the icy streets. People say sorry when they bump into you, drivers now motion to pedestrians to go ahead and cross the street while they drive slowly. It's one of the rare times I don't see the pavements overtaken by street vendors. Inside the court rooms everyone is exchanging snow stories about how hard it was to get out of their different neighborhoods. Buses aren't on regular schedules, routes have been cancelled, tire chains are suddenly impossible to find and wildly expensive.

I meet the insurance lawyer for the first time early that morning. He wants us to discuss the facts before the case is called. We sit in an open hall with people glumly chain smoking. The lawyer wants me to go over the details. I explain the accident. I explain I'd agreed to give the driver money so he wouldn't bother me, and that the amount went up each time he called me.

"Don't say that to the judge," he says.

"I didn't wait for the police," I remind him. He nods.

68

I remember that night near midnight more than a year ago, the jazz club I was on my way to, the clear, unconfused sense I had of the accident being the taxi driver's fault, his broken headlight, my indented car door, that he went out of his way to harass me. None of it upset me as much his self-satisfied swagger when he told me I was the one at fault. I don't mention any of this to the lawyer.

"I had to get home to the babysitter," I say, quicker than I realize. He nods. "Say that to the judge."

As we sit I notice a group of people arrive. They are talking loudly enough for me to overhear them. One of the men is the taxi driver. The group sit on the opposite end of the bench where we're seated. I whisper to the lawyer, listen to the driver going over the incident with his lawyer.

"...She was a foreigner...the car came out of nowhere, then she left. I wanted to wait for the police." When I told a friend the day before about the upcoming court case, he advised me to bring a witness. I told him there had not been any. He said that didn't matter, insisting that 'everyone' turns up with witnesses. Sure enough the taxi driver has a woman with him he calls his 'witness,' someone who identifies herself as a passenger in the taxi at the time of the accident though the cab was empty at the time. But today the driver is with a woman who swears in front of the judge (who also happens to be a woman) that she was in the cab when I hit him, in her words, 'out of nowhere'.

My turn comes. "I'm divorced, and live with my daughter who is seven. I was on my way home because the babysitter was going to leave at midnight. When I turned the corner the taxi, which was stopped at the curb, moved into my lane without lights. My right back door was bent and his left headlight was broken. I told him we should each pay for our damages, but he insisted it was my fault and wanted to call the police. I didn't wait because I was in a hurry."

"The taxi left the curb without blinkers?" My lawyer interjects. "No blinkers. The taxi was parked against the curb. Then it was in front of me as I was making the turn," I continue.

The driver's lawyer is asking why I didn't wait for the police if I was so sure the accident wasn't my fault. To my surprise the woman judge speaks, "She said she needed to get home to a child."

I nod, relieved. The apparent witness starts to say I was driving at some crazy speed, and turned the corner with no flash warning. My lawyer seems to pounce, asks her where she was going in the cab that night. She says "Kifissia," a northern suburb. "And where were you picked up?" he continues. She hesitates, then says "Omonia."

"So!" his tone is harsh, "You were *passing through* Metz to get to Kifissia?" An apparently absurd route.

She says, "Yes."

I am not looking at anyone, have no idea what the driver looks like at this point. His lawyer starts to yell that I left the scene of the accident. I go back into the hallway where the air is grey with cigarette smoke. People look as weathered as the walls whose color is no longer visible through the accumulated grime. I'm thinking of the smoothness with which the driver introduced his so called witness, how easily she lied, how I intuitively did the same to save my neck. There really was no reason why I didn't wait for the police except for my livid reaction to the taxi driver's goading. My lawyer seemed satisfied that things would go well but tells me a decision won't be reached for at least a year.

"That long?" I'm surprised.

"Sometimes it's a year and a half."

A year and a month later I receive a hand-written summons for a court meeting in March; another cold day, but this time it's mid February. I call the lawyer who I haven't spoken to since I saw him last January. He tells me the summons has to do with my having left the scene of the accident.

"Does this mean he wins the case?" I say, frustration welling up in me.

"We'll see what we can do," he's short. I thank him, and hang up, despondent, sure some immediate superior has been cajoled or bribed, otherwise why didn't they consider the fact that the driver's so called witness had lied, or that my justification did have some grounds to excuse my having left, or more basic still, that he moved from a curb without signaling. The lawyer told me if I lost, it would be counted as a felony.

"But the actual accident wasn't my fault!" I argue.

"The driver's lawyer is going to focus on your not having waited for the police."

"Doesn't that make two mistakes? One for each of us?"

Drivers stopping (with their parking lights flashing) in the middle of busy roads to drop someone off or who block two lane roads to make u-turns where it's not permitted, get taken for granted. I was pulling out of a parking space on a side street, my left blinker on and more than half my car already turned left and positioned into the street when I glimpse some cars coming down the street from my left side mirror, but they aren't close. I have time to move out of my parking position. Almost out, with my blinker flashing, three quarters of the way into the road, I spot a white jeep millimeters next to my left door. I assume the driver is going to stop, even that close, but the left corner of his hood folds right into my door bending the metal like an envelope. I honk, screaming. The man in the jeep shakes his head, his expression is disgusted, his hands are madly gesturing.

"*Don't* you *see!*" He is yelling from inside the jeep.

"*ME?*" I yell back. "You're coming from behind me. My light's flashing. I'm almost in the street and you *HAVE TO* ram into me!"

"I rammed into YOU!" He continues, still in the jeep, but now with the window rolled down.

"Okay," I say, trying to control myself. "Let's call the police."

He drives over to the opposite curb to let the traffic pass. I follow.

"Just give me your papers," he says, out of his jeep now and at the window of my car.

"I'll give you my papers once the police get here." I am trying to be rational, wondering how this could be happening again.

"Just give them to me, bitch," he spits.

"Oh, you do belong in a zoo," I say icily.

"If you don't *shut up* and give me the papers I'm going to…and I won't care what happens."

"What an animal. Actually you belong in a cage." I refuse to give him my papers.

"*What* did you say?" Now he's leaning into my window as I start to dial the police on my cell phone.

"I said you're an animal, and you belong in a cage." The cell phone's at my ear.

"Listen *bitch*!" he's livid. "You're not going to get very far if you don't hand over those papers. I don't have any time to wait for the police. My insurance is going to deal with this."

"What are *they* going *to deal with*? You smashed into my door when I was half way out of a parking position!"

"*You* don't have *any* right of way coming out of a parking position!" he screams. "Hey you don't even speak Greek properly." My verb tenses were getting mixed up.

"What does how I speak have to do with what you did to my car?!"

"You should go back to your village, lady. You shouldn't even own a car."

"*My village?* You must have come out of a cave!"

"Okay! I'm going to *smash* your face in if you don't hand over those papers this minute!"

"Is that how they teach you to talk in your cave?" I am strangely detached.

I take down his insurance information, and still refuse to give him mine. Once he drives off I start to cry. Then I call a friend to explain what happened; he says the man acted the way he did because he knows I don't have any hope of supporting my case. According to the law it's the cars in movement who have priority, not cars entering or leaving a main thoroughfare.

"Only if you were stopped," he says. "That's the only way you could get him to pay for damages. But you would need a witness to prove it." I am suddenly overwhelmed, crying. "Hey relax. It's only a car…" My friend is upset, but practical. "If you each pay your own damages, there won't be any problem."

"But I called *the police*!" I am now crying hysterically.

There's a brief pause. "Call them back, tell them the man drove off, and you decided to chase him."

"And?"

"And, you're going to file with your insurance so they don't need to come."

I hesitated. "You know," I begin slowly. "It was as if he hit me deliberately. I was almost out of my parking space and he didn't stop." There's another brief pause.

"The only way you'll get any compensation is if you can prove you were stopped and you'll have to go to court to do that."

I call the police, tell them I recently called but that I left the scene of the accident because the man who hit me didn't wait. The woman who takes the phone call is cheerful. "Fine," she says, "I'll let them know." I go home and cry for what feels like hours. The incident, just over a year after my experience with the taxi driver, now feels like a curse.

Turning into my street one afternoon, on the curve of the bend, the car in front of me stops without any flashing lights. I think he must be stalled. But a woman on the sidewalk is in conversation with the driver, so I think he must be asking for directions. I think he could have pulled off to the side or moved further into the street to avoid someone slamming into his rear as they turn the curve. The couple talks for what feels like several minutes, and I start to honk. The woman talking to the driver starts to yell at me. I yell back, "Not only are you so obviously wrong but you're shouting on top of it!"

She gets mad, "What's your problem?!"

"My problem?…the car is stopped on a *bend*! Couldn't he have pulled over if you're going to have a conversation?"

This makes her incensed. Passersby watch vaguely entertained. The woman, still yelling at me, finally gets into the car on the other side of the driver.

More and more I am initiated into how public space is treated like private property, the supermarket cashier holds up the line of customers because she wants to offer the sesame bread sticks she's eating to the cashier working next to her, the public health doctor about to sign my permission slip for a mamogram wants to know (because I've interrupted a conversation taking place about Christmas cookies) whether I prefer *kourambiedhes* (white-sugar biscuits) or *melomakarones* (honey-biscuits), a woman on the street waiting to cross likes the coat I'm wearing and asks me where I bought it, and how much I paid for it.

Imposing the personal is a way of asserting the self. Maybe it was the gritty circumstances of day to day life, the crowded streets, the lack of enough of them, the way you never knew if the rules would help or hinder you, that made people more stubborn about arguing their right of way, about exchanging recipes over the phone or holding up a line to discuss tastes in fashion. Yesterday, stopped behind a stopped van in front of me because a man in front of him is gesturing for the traffic to wait as a car pulls out from a parking position, we are all thinking the post office is clearing space for one of the mail trucks to unload. We gauge the minutes, trying to be patient. The man who insists we wait so the car can pull out, now coaxes in another car to park when the man in front of me, in the van, pulls over, gets out and starts to scream. The man ushering the traffic is stupefied, then smiles sheepishly, but the van driver is beside himself for having been stopped so someone can park.

'Main road disasters' are the stories of people who follow the rules in good faith, 'with the cross in their hands' ('*me to stavro sto heri*') as the saying goes, who can not, or do not, expect the rules to dupe them, who feel their declared (legally abiding) intentions will be honored by the system until reality with its detours, makes them feel *koroido*.

There was the story, among so many, of the girl whose national test scores placed her in the 'one-hundredth-and-first' position for a job teaching French literature, who was told the Ministry of Education was going to be placing everyone in the first one-hundred-and-twenty positions, who found out she was the only one in those one-hundred-and-twenty who did not get a job.

There are the unfortunate, ongoing sagas of *DIKATSA*, an illegal means by the terms of the European Union's standards for recognizing university degrees from abroad, which remain, despite their declared illegality, functional. *DIKATSA* decided which degrees of higher education (BAs and above) were recognized by the Greek state and which were not. *DIKATSA*'s administrative body preferred to pay the hefty fine the EU (European Union) consistently slapped them with rather than shut down or create a new structure consistent with the stipulated protocol of EU standards. A young woman with an M.A. from the University of Chicago is told there won't be any problem having her degree recognized. She has secured a teaching job in a private Greek high school, her children are already enrolled at a discounted tuition, when a *DIKATSA* employee tells her it will 'take some time' to 'process the papers' and to call in six to eight months. She waits nine. The woman who assured her there was no problem with her papers is no longer at the post, and the person now responsible can't find the papers. But the woman being hired by the private high school has a protocol number that verifies that her papers have indeed been processed. The woman now in charge at *DIKATSA* says without the full file her M.A. degree will not be recognized, which means she will not be given legal permission to work. She mentions her protocol

73

number again, that her degree from the University of Chicago has been officially stamped by the University. The woman apologizes, says she can't do anything if the papers of her file are lost. She mentions again that she has a protocol number to prove her file was in order. Why didn't anyone call her? Why did she have to call, nine months later, to find this out on her own? The woman at *DIKATSA* says, "*Ti fteo ego?*" ("How is this my fault?")

The woman with the degree from the University of Chicago explains she's been hired for a job she's supposed to begin in a month. "What can I tell you?" the *DIKATSA* woman goes on. The young woman is in tears. She's told to find the woman who initially advised her that her papers were complete. She wants to know how she's supposed to find her. The new woman at *DIKATSA* says, "*Den xero.*" ("I don't know.")

A few days ago a minister close to the Prime Minister is asked to step down. There's been a scandal concerning a tax rebate involving a famous Greek singer. Nightclub singers, doctors, and other high paying professionals are always in the press for dodging income taxes, and while Greek taxes are high, the ones who make the large sums are the ones who manage to give less of it to the state. The average worker barely gets by after paychecks are tax-pruned. A further irony of the story is that the singer, someone whose *rebetes* roots made him popular and then famous, celebrated Greek working class life, as he suavely dodged government taxes that subsidized civic works: 'the People' and 'the State' or in Greek terms, '*O Laos*' and '*To Kratos*' are not one and the same.

The Greeks' notorious disrespect for governing authorities goes back centuries. From the Ottomans on, government has too often been *xeno* (alien or foreign), rarely made up of '*dyki mas*' (our own). When not 'ours' there is no shame in trying to outwit and cheat what remains Other. Like the *rebetes* in the *tekes* of Smyrna and Asia Minor, civic consciousness is not applicable when you feel yourself taken for *koroido*.

How we drove our too narrow, too crowded roads was madness to the outsider, how we parked with the butt of our cars so far out from the curve that anyone turning risked hitting us, how we left cars double and triple parked on narrow one way streets, how we blew a kiss to the person shrieking about being unable to edge out of a parking space you sandwiched him into, was all a form of crazed bravado to the outsider. Yet when the municipality in my neighborhood decided to put an end to parking on the sidewalks by putting up tasteful iron bars along the two edges of the street's sidewalks, I watched bemused as people stopped and paused, walking or driving, to variously curse or shout phrases like, "*Where* are we going to put our cars *now!*" It was a real question; the tasteful wrought-iron bars look good and orderly, but now there was even less room in the city's already cramped spaces.

74

It was the same with the post office before it got its sudden face lift. Before the slick glass doors were installed and the higher counters jutted out even further into the modest standing area, we could move the old chairs and rickety table around the room to make space. And when it was warm we could slip a piece of torn cardboard under the old door to keep it open and spill out into the street. Now the counters were higher and bigger to give the tellers more room to do their jobs, but they took up standing room, and the glass doors were heavy and couldn't be propped open. Then one morning there is another addition: machines that provide numbered slips of paper.

A teller calls out, "85?" Some of us don't realize there is a new system, so when a woman jumps up with #85, the man in front of her already taking out his wallet at the counter, refuses to budge.

Another teller calls out, "You don't have #85, *Kyrie!*" But the man ignores her and the woman with her slip of paper. Someone else starts to yell that the machine isn't giving out any more slips so why is such a fuss being made. The handsome administrator who usually stood on the upper level strategically eyeing the women in line, is called down to solve the problem. He announces the machine's run out of paper. A woman ahead of me insists she's in a hurry, and doesn't have time to hold a slip of paper and wait her turn.

The new iron bars along my neighborhood sidewalks and the renovations at the post office were indications that things were changing. The 2004 Olympics were a year and a half away and the government was trying to impose structure on a world more familiar without it. People had unofficial solutions for what was officially unacceptable. A friend of mine routinely left her cell phone number on the windshield of her car whenever she had to double or triple park, and just as routinely, in the middle of dinner or drinks, it rang. She told me the drivers always thanked her for leaving her number for them.

At the crossroads next to my local gas station I notice another change. For years cars gauged their right of way, but traffic lights suddenly appear overnight. I almost have an accident as I swerve past the gas station on my usual route home, unaware that the driver coming in the opposite direction has a green light, while mine has turned red.

Another day on the local bus at that same crossroads I overhear two men discussing the change, "What do they think they're accomplishing with those lights?" one asks, while the man next to him nods.

"Now it's only two or three cars that make it through, and then it turns red." His friend shakes his head.

"And there's this backup. Lines of cars on both sides!"

"But you can cross the street more easily now," the other man suggests.

His friend shrugs. "I could cross the street before. Now if I don't do it quickly, I'll be killed."

The changes crept up on us, civil servants were confused.

"But I'm the one who's the victim," I'm barely shouting to the woman at the local tax office where I paid my parking tickets in the past. She's at a computer behind a window telling me I need to go to the post office now.

"The ticket's expired," I say. "So I can't just mail it?" She asks where I got the ticket. I tell her "Kifissia."

"Then you'll have to send it there, but go upstairs first to find out for sure."

I go to another office to wait as a woman talks to another employee. She's eating some cake as she talks to her. I wait. They ignore me; she offers the woman a piece of her cake. I finally say I need to know about where to send a parking ticket. "A what?" the woman says, still chewing.

"A traffic ticket."

She shrugs. "We don't have anything to do with tickets here."

I try to be civil. "Someone downstairs sent me here because she wasn't sure if I had to send the money to the tax office in Kiffisia or somewhere else. She said you would be able to tell me. The ticket's expired." The woman standing takes a look at the ticket and shakes her head.

"Go back to the woman downstairs. She'll have to look up on the computer where you have to send this."

I was shouting, I realized, by the frozen looks on the two women's faces. "*Why* couldn't she tell me this *in the first place!*"

The woman who had been eating the cake, swallowed, and took another bite.

"Why are you shouting?" asks the woman who stopped chewing.

"Because no one *ever* knows what they're doing! And people like me lose days and days in offices like this listening to the fact that *no one* knows their job!"

The woman put her cake down and now looked annoyed.

"*Kyria*, if you wouldn't shout you might get some help."

"*What help!*" I screamed.

People from another office on the floor came to see what was going on. "I go up and down these stairs from one person to the next...why doesn't *anyone* pick up a phone to find out where anyone is supposed to go?" A woman in charge comes up to me obviously disturbed. She tells me to calm down otherwise no one is going to understand what it is I need help with. I have tears in my eyes.

She shakes her head, "You're exaggerating," she says and asks me to go back down to the first woman I talked to, and comes with me. When the woman sees me with the supervisor she smiles.

"What's happened?"

The supervisor tells the woman to check for a record of the ticket in the computer; there is none. "I want to see if she can send it to Kiffisia where it was issued," she says.

In the end I go to the post office with the address of the Kiffisia police given to me by the supervisor who puts her arm around me and says, "Don't upset yourself like this. You even got me upset."

I thank her for taking time to help me, put cash in an envelope with the ticket, wait another twenty minutes in another line, and mail it. Some months later I get a receipt in barely legible writing with a return address that shows it's been issued from the Kiffisia police station.

I eventually learn to avoid the main thoroughfares and, like everyone else, use the backstreets more and more. There's the usual problem of cars parked on both sides of two-way and one-way streets, there's always the truck that happens to be unloading milk cartons or crates of bread, blocking the street with its flashing blinkers just at that moment when you can't afford to be late, there's someone who slows down when you're ready to speed up because he's recognized a friend passing on the sidewalk, and pauses to ask how he's doing. These instances were part of what I learned to expect, there was always a shrug or half smile, and if the delay went on too long, you honked and yelled that you didn't have all day.

So when, turning on a narrow bend I see a tired looking red Audi coming in the opposite direction, I make a tight turn toward the curb so the car has enough space to move to the right of me. It's the larger car, but the driver keeps to the middle of the road. We are suddenly facing each other. I gesture to him to back up a little and continue to the right of me, but he doesn't budge. He's about thirty with a woman in the car that I soon realize is his mother. He gestures for me to back up, but I refuse. I gesture again for him to pass me on the outside. He makes another gesture for me to move (which means backing into a driveway some distance behind). I again refuse. He gets out of his car. I roll up my windows. He starts yelling that I'm an idiot. I motion to him to move his car around mine. His mother starts to shake her head at me. He gets his cell phone and says he's going to call the police. I shrug, and turn on the radio. His mother calls me a fool. An old man carrying a newspaper and carton of milk pauses at the scene. His mother now looks like she is about to start crying, she's calling her son from the car to come back, and makes a motion toward the space, saying he could drive around me. Her son tells her to shut up and shakes his fist at me through my closed window; he's large, in shorts and sunglasses.

I start to imagine what would happen if we were to run into each other in the supermarket or the gas station. I start to wonder if my stubbornness isn't as insane as his. His mother is practically begging him to come back into the car. The old man with the milk carton and loaf of bread has stopped and is staring at us with no expression on his face. A good ten minutes goes by before the guy realizes I am not going to move, he suddenly swears at me in a stream of language which concludes with "…haven't you been fucked recently!" At that point I roll down the window.

"What?"

He's finally enjoying himself. "You probably haven't had a man for awhile lady, that's why you've lost it." He seems pleased he's managed to get a reaction from me and takes his time getting back into his car. His mother is concentrating on something in her lap. I wonder if she's crying.

"Actually," I say evenly, "It's been a while." He looks surprised, grunts something as he slams his door, and backs up like he's aiming to hit something and swerves around me. I lean over my steering wheel drained. The old man with the milk carton and loaf of bread is still there, still expressionless. I smile at him and he smiles back. It is so unexpected I smile again.

"*Kalimera*," ("Good morning") I say, slowly starting up the car.

Taking individualist initiatives was a cultural disposition. Some years ago an entire suburban community, supported by the town mayor, redirected the flow of traffic that went through their neighborhood on a main thoroughfare. When the first highway opened that circumvented the center of the city, people could drive from the north end of the city to the south by taking what was called the *periferiako* (roundabout). The *periferiako* was like a stroke of magic in a much too concrete reality. Instead of the usual hour and a half it took to inch down from the northern suburb where I lived to *Syntagma* (Constitution) Square, the center of the city, it now took about twenty minutes. If it was your smog day (only alternating odd and even license plate numbers were allowed into the center to help control the pollution), you could easily park on a nearby side street. Of course two-car families resolved this by buying one car with an odd and another with an even numbered license plate.

To get to the *periferiako* you drove through Papagos, one of the few residential areas with a majority of one family houses, a luxury in Athens where most people live in apartment buildings. The suburb, opposite the Ministry of Defense, is the residence of many military officials. The roads in Papagos are tree-lined, wide and well-built, a rarity in a city known for its lack of sidewalks and gardens. I always enjoyed driving through Papagos where I admired the houses with their verandahs and rose gardens that brought back memories of my grandparents' Syngrou house which had been recently sold to a BMW car dealer. In Papagos bougainvillea and jasmine bushes grew alongside wrought-iron balconies and marble terraces with their tables and chairs under date and lemon trees.

Even in the mornings during what would be considered rush hour, there's rarely any traffic. For once, the roads in Papagos were a pleasant exception that benefited the majority. After several months of zipping through this pretty suburban neighborhood on my way to the center of Athens, I notice something odd, something that looks like construction. Cement blocks and barricades appear on both sides of the spacious two-way road that leads to

78

the *periferiako*. I think a water pipe must have broken underground, or that electrical wires are being laid down for some sort of public lighting fixtures. The next thing I see are yellow stripes of guard tape, and then the actual road being dug up so cars are redirected around the construction.

I ask people what's going on, and soon learn that this unique breadth of asphalt is being narrowed by a consensus of local residents (vocally supported by the mayor). People become enraged. Newspaper articles appear in the mainstream press. *'What makes it possible for a local community to obstruct the flow of public traffic to an important thoroughfare?'* It was a question of clout, and there was a lot of it in Papagos; *to Kratos* (the State) was indeed the enemy of *o laos* (the people).

The mayor of Papagos declared point blank she would 'force' drivers not to use Papagos 'as a short cut' to the *periferiako*, though the so-called short-cut caters to several boroughs, and funnels streams of cars to the important highway. The result is disaster. Cars still drive through Papagos, or I should say necessarily drive through, but now instead of the swift ride past the pleasant houses and flowering gardens, we gradually find ourselves stuck in a stalled lane.

Not only are drivers back to inching along during the morning and evening rush hours, but they begin to honk loudly and continuously at the slightest delays in movement when someone stalls or the light turns green. Nothing happens to change the mayor's decision. The residents are as determined to stick to their plan, as the drivers are about using the same roads. The sheer stupidity of the action makes each group equally stubborn. So at the crossroads just before entering the *periferiako* where drivers go either right or left (but not legally across), they wait, gauge the seconds between one set of lights turning red and the next turning green, and drive across at the risk of being smashed by some too quick driver who doesn't stop immediately at the red light. After the many articles in the newspapers, the mayor finally announces that not only has the main road in Papagos been successfully narrowed, but she plans to do the same for all the roads in the suburb.

Traffic police became more visible in the streets, writing parking violations more often, but that didn't seem to change the fact that we still parked wherever we found space, and if we didn't, we still left our cars in the middle of the street with flashing blinkers while we rushed to do our chores.

A driver in the middle of the road was blocking a parking space when I gestured her to move.

"I'm waiting for someone," she said, nonplussed. "She'll be out in a minute."

"Yes, but I can't park with you there."

"I'm waiting for my mother," she added. "She's in the pharmacy; she'll be out in a minute."

I shake my head. "As soon as a car comes up behind me, I'll have to move."

Her mother actually appears at the minute the young woman starts up her car to move so I can park. But when I finish my errands, and come back there's another car in her place, so I can't get out. Two police men happen to be walking down the street, part of the government effort to regularly ticket parking violators. I run after them to come see the situation.

"We aren't traffic police," one of them says.

"But you have a ticket pad don't you?" I say.

"We can lift the car," the other one says, when the one I'm speaking to doesn't answer.

"I'm not asking you to lift it. I want you to give the driver blocking me a ticket. I can't get out."

One of them nods and pulls out his pad. The other one says he can slowly guide me out of my space so I can make it through. As the policeman writes out a ticket, a young woman who doesn't look more than twenty, runs out of a Benetton shop yelling, "Hey, it's mine. I'm in here with the baby…"

"So?" I yell back.

She looks surprised. "What does that mean?"

I go on, irritated. "You're not in a parking space! And I can't get out…"

"I was in here for a minute…" she goes on. The policeman manages to guide me out of my tight space without any scratches or indentations, and as I drive away, through my rear view mirror I can see the other policeman putting his pad back into his pocket, and the woman with the baby going back into the Benetton shop.

Some months later I'm stopped by a policewoman one morning right after Easter. I drop off my daughter at school and am relishing the still empty roads. Most Athenians are still out of town for the holiday. I am going to go pay some bills at the local electric company where we go when they're overdue. A policewoman blows her whistle for me to pull over. She asks for my car insurance, my driver's license, I.D. I hand them over. She looks through them and asks, "Is there any reason why you aren't wearing your seatbelt?"

I tell her I just dropped my daughter off at school, and that I live close by. She matter-of-factly writes out a twenty thousand drachma ticket. I'm upset. Like so much else, wearing seatbelts wasn't a consistently enforced rule. Drivers were starting to wear them more often, but just as many didn't. I'm also surprised. Unlike the policemen I'd met in my neighborhood, this woman is taking her job seriously. I'm suddenly speaking like the woman in the Benetton shop. "I'm sorry…" I stammer, "I was in a rush…"

"That's not a reason for not wearing your belt," she says.

"Look I just came back from Easter," I go on irrationally, "There aren't any traffic lights on the island."

She looks at me, writes down my license number, says, "Do I tell you how to do your job?"

"I'm not telling you how to do anything," I say, aware I am not negotiating this well. "All my papers are fine…I told you why I didn't have my belt on. I wasn't thinking. I just dropped off my daughter…" I start to break into English.

So she answers me in English, "In the United States or England would you be arguing with me?"

"In the States," I say, my voice rising, "laws can actually protect you! They're not there on alternate days because money needs to be collected by the State for some election."

She looks at me, visibly angry. "Then maybe you should go back to the United States where crime is higher than anywhere in the world and people shoot each other on the roads."

I start to speak insanely. "I wouldn't be here if I didn't think my daughter needed to be near her father!" Another policewoman approaches with her ticket pad in hand. She wants to know what's going on. "One day I'm going to write about this chaos!"

The policewoman finishes writing me the ticket. She hands it to me, saying "Yes, everyone is writing articles these days."

I crush it into a wad.

"This place needs to be razed and rebuilt!" I scream, the balled ticket in my sweating palm.

"Go back to the United States," she says dryly. "Maybe you belong there."

I uncrumple the ticket on my kitchen counter when I get home, sweat and tear-stained. I stare at my license number, the date, the fine. I'd crossed over. I am no longer on the outside watching, but in the web, Athena's *spin, spin, you foolish girl!* taunting Arachne, taunting me. I am trapped in the tangled structures others manage to dodge. I counted on the policewoman to understand how it felt to have been on an island without traffic lights, expected her to understand since it was still the Easter holiday and most of us weren't thinking in city, seatbelt terms. I'd just come out of the supermarket after dropping off my daughter, and forgotten to slip the belt on. There is really no difference between me and the woman temporarily parked, waiting for her mother to come out of the pharmacy; she expected me to understand as much.

Academic Phallicisms

"I do not believe, from what I have been told about this people, that there is anything barbarous or savage about them, except that we all call barbarous anything that is contrary to our own habits. Indeed we seem to have no other criterion of truth and reason than the type and kind of opinions and customs current in the land where we live."

Montaigne, On Cannibals

Chaos, A God

In my encounter with the Greek national university system the Fates were uncertain. Clotho, who spun out the thread of life, was fidgeting. Lachesis, who measured the thread, was undecided. And Atropos, who severed life, cutting its thread with shears, was particularly threatening. The experience became a tangled yarn, exchanged, sold, and bartered. Professors and administrators threaded yarns so, like Narcissus, they reflected their own best interests, and like Echo, those who believed them, followed. Suddenly threatened with Echo's fate — never to have the first word, I spun my own yarn.

In the labyrinthine world of Ministries the procedures to get any required paper from the State let alone meet the requirements for a position in the public sector meant one encountered Chaos, a pushy, modern god.

Newly back from the States, a Greek married to an American relayed the meeting when he went to get his wife's residency papers: "Have you ever been to the corner of Sophocleous and Piraeus Streets?"

"Is it the Ministry of Foreign Affairs?" I ask.

"It's a basement with catacombs and what look like bouncers guarding stacks of papers outside each door," he says.

Petros entertained us with stories of his first year back in Greece, particularly his mandatory year in the Greek army where he verified the much-repeated saying, 'where logic leaves off, the Greek army begins.' But that day, at the building on the corner of Sophocleous and Piraeus streets, he was told he was 'lucky' to have come that particular morning because no more residency applications were going to be taken afterwards, to which he replied, "What happens if someone comes next week?"

The person behind a desk in one of the catacombs raised his open-palmed hands to the ceiling and shrugged, "Ask the government who gives out the instructions from Chaos."

Petros answered, "And who do they get their orders from?
"From the international government of Chaos."

In the Spring of 2000, I applied for a position in the English literature department (*Philsophiki Sholi*) at the University of Athens advertised in a weekly government newsletter (F.E.K.) as a *Lectureship in American Literature and Culture*. I was then teaching at a private American liberal arts college. A position in the national university meant more time for research, better pay and more exposure to Greek students.

I needed thirty Xeroxed copies of my dissertation, twelve copies of all my publications, a lung x-ray from a state hospital and an official criminal record clearance from the police to apply for a national university position. Putting the documents together took me into parts of the city I rarely ventured through and into discussions that made Echo seem wise; repeating what Narcissus and others had to say was one of the ways of being heard and seen. The words of government documents are a canny veil for Chaos's unofficial politics, and remain as resilient as the gods and goddesses who choose to manipulate them.

No-Wonder Land

Aharnon Street, drab and nondescript like its smog-coated buildings, is located in the bowels of the city. After getting my lung x-ray I was on my way to getting it certified. The building I was looking for sat on a main traffic street dark with car fumes, nothing distinguished it but for the two rusting chairs with torn plastic cushions in the entranceway. The neglect of the building reflected the disposition of the woman who was in charge. Her nervous, darting eyes looked me over quickly when I told her why I was there. She seemed harassed, and mumbled something unintelligible. It was early June. I needed my x-ray stamped before I gave my lecture in front of the English department by the end of the month. "Get stamps," she said impatiently.

"Where?" I called after her as she abruptly turned down the hallway.

"Across the street," she yelled back.

A woman in the room with her stamps and slips of paper filled out told me to go to a shop across the street, adding helpfully, "They sell the stamps for these jobs." The heat that morning was numbing as I made my way to a tiny shop selling potato chips and fashion magazines with a large Xerox machine that took up the entire interior. The man standing behind the machine knew exactly why I had come and asked for 150 drachmas as he took my I.D. to copy. When I got back to the building with stamps, photographs, a copy of my I.D. and application form in hand, the woman in charge seemed more agitated.

"Are you the one who left your x-ray lying on a chair?" I nodded. "You have to come back July 20th for the results."

I ask why I have to wait so long.

"It's *summer*," she shoots back. "The council of doctors is off until September. I'm doing this as *a favor* because you're here. It's *a favor* for the three of you," she adds, nodding to the other two people.

"It's too late," I repeat. She looks fed up.

"You should think of these things *in advance*…You wait for the last minute and expect people to be available?"

I was at a loss at what to say; she turned to a woman who had finished filling out her forms. "Are the addresses okay?" The woman nods. I ask if I should write in my home address.

"Where are you from in Athens?" When I mention the suburb she splutters something, shaking her head frenetically. "They'll throw your application *out*! That's *too* far away! Don't you have a cousin or an aunt who lives somewhere in this area? Someone whose street name you could put down?"

I look at her in disbelief, and ask the woman who had just handed in her papers if she lives in the area. She nods and shows me her street address and number for me to copy. I write in the foreign address without any idea why the address has to be local or what someone does who doesn't have one. This had been the building I was told to come to by the University secretary. I go into another empty office with more peeling plastic chairs to hand them in. A newcomer rushes in with some papers and turns to the woman in charge. "Good morning," he says with a generous smile.

"Don't talk to me now," she snaps. I look apologetically at the man who shrugs. She turns to him.

"When you say *Good Morning* it means you want something."

I repeat that I need to come at an earlier date for my x-ray clearance.

"What do you mean?" She is now yelling. I repeat it would be too late by the end of the month.

"*What* am I supposed to do then!" she screams. "You'll have to see the director." I nod. "She'll be here at ten." It is just a few more minutes and as I sit she gestures to a room down the hallway. A woman's voice calls me in. The office is full of plants, a desk of piled papers take up a corner and a pretty woman in a pistachio-green organdy dress motions me to sit down; she's the director and can't be over thirty. She asks what the problem is. I explain I need the health verification as soon as possible.

"Come on Tuesday," she smiles.

I had been hearing rumors that my application was causing problems. Someone had been tagged for the position. The faculty who wanted her had not expected an outsider to apply. Any slip in protocol would provide the excuse to dismiss it. Little did I know it would hardly have mattered what my qualifications were. Not only was I a spinning Arachne threatened with Echo's fate, but now, introduced to the Greek term *dyki mas* (one of ours), I was Pandora who had opened Zeus' box. Chaos was ready for mischief. Becoming *dyki tous* (one of theirs) required that I make myself recognizable within terms I was ignorant of. Paul, in the Corinthians, speaks of making himself 'all things to all men' to win 'those who have no Law' (I Corinthians 9:20). I had not been taught how to make myself *dyki tous*, an initiation that enabled one to become 'all things to all men' when legal formalities were divorced of substance.

Arete, a friend in the department in Athens, like her namesake the queen of Phaeacia and wife of Alcinous, lived the 'virtue' (αρετη) her name translated into in modern Greek. She called to say the 'three-member faculty committee' (*trimelis epitropi*) formally made up of academics in the field of the advertised position to examine applications, included Circe (though not related to Homer's enchantress of Aeaea, the goddess who changed men to swine). Circe had co-authored two of a candidate's published papers.

I thought I was stating the obvious when I said, "That makes the committee biased."

"That's what they want," Arete answered, chain-smoking (I could hear her inhaling over the phone) as she described a litany of events: the chair had called out for interested members to sit on the committee. Technically all had to be specialists in the advertised position. Arete, an American Studies specialist, had raised her hand. Someone called out Circe's name. Someone else pointed out her position wasn't neutral; the point was ignored. The department secretary taking minutes seconded the query about the bias; she was ignored. Arete volunteered herself for the committee a second time; she was told she didn't have enough seniority. Another instructor was invited to sit (who had less seniority). The result was a committee composed of a theatre specialist, a philosopher and Circe who had co-authored two papers with the favored candidate, a woman named Scylla, a modern day namesake of the Homeric monster who lived in a cave opposite the pool of Charybdis in Ancient Greece.

In the midst of the usual Athens traffic, in a taxi going surprisingly slow, I was hoping to get to the police station in time to put in my request for the criminal clearance document before they closed at two o'clock. The secretary at the university mentioned it might take longer for me to get my papers since I was born abroad. If I got the x-ray formally approved and the criminal clearance in the next few weeks, my papers would be in order. I was urging the taxi driver to take short cuts and go faster.

"Don't be so anxious," he said, looking back at me. The police station where I had to go for the *Piniko Mitroo* (the criminal clearance) was on the other side of the city from Aharnon street. "You're at that critical age; if you start letting things get to you from now, you'll use yourself up in no time."

I nodded absently, too tense to answer. He turned down a side street, saying there were never cars on that street only to face a truck unloading crates of milk cartons. "Why *now!*" he breathed.

When we finally got through someone was hailing a ride from the corner. "I'm in a hurry!" the driver called out, rushing through the city so I managed to arrive in time to join a line wrapped round the corner of the main entranceway to the police station.

A mother and son are behind the counter manually going through a loose-leaf binder with pages and pages of hand-written names and numbers. The woman is shouting, "She's her mother." They are trying to find a name, a woman had come to pick up someone else's clearance. People are furious. The mother and son duo are going through the papers without much of a system beyond leafing through the messy pile as quickly as possible. I catch the boy's eye and give him my I.D. He nods and pulls out an application for me. I feel like I've sidestepped an avalanche. On my way out I almost run over a young Serbian woman with a child in her arms. She is carefully dressed, her shoes match the slightly pink beige of her skirt and her hair is tied back in a ribbon. "The office for the *Piniko Mitroo?*" she asks me.

I point to where the crowd spills into the small entranceway. "There're a lot of people," I say as she disappears into the building.

In another four days I am back at that terminal part of the city, Aharnon Street, to pick up the medical clearance for my x-ray. I am expecting to find the kind of crowd that I found at the police station, but go straight to the back of the hall where the pretty director, in a strapless black dress this morning, is in her office alone. She smiles when I knock and gives me papers to be signed in the next office. Two women in a room of badly smudged walls are sitting at their desks. A rusted fan keeps rhythmically flipping back a stack of papers weighed down with a rock. One woman is mechanically signing papers while the other staples. I go back to the pretty director who smiles when she asks me to wait.

A group of us are in a room waiting for our names and numbers to be announced over the microphone. Piles of paper are spread over a long table in neat stacks. The pretty director eventually comes out, handing out the x-ray folders alphabetically. I am wondering where the woman with the harassed, darting eyes is. Had some doctors been called back from their summers to sign these clearances or was there a group who happened to be hanging around until August? I almost ask, then think better than to push my luck; I was becoming as superstitious as everyone else: *mi to matiassis* (don't give it the evil eye) my ex mother-in-law warned. Lately I started to pay more attention to the evil eye; I was calling up older village women including my ex mother-in-law to *xematiassi* (exorcise) me so that my growing panic would break up into harmless beads of disappearing oil globules in the water dish she judiciously made her cross over. Even my friend Alicia, who was from the States, found herself attentive to the women who insisted they could *xematiassi* those of us under the eye's craggy influence:

> "Yes it's on you," Kalliope frowns,
> Dribbling amber beads of olive oil
> Down thick fingers into the water glass
> Where they amass
> In one big cyclops-blob, and do not scatter.
>
> Something, it seems, always *is* the matter.
> Vague pains, or clumsy accidents, a dim
> Nimbus on my head, a personal cloud.
> Perhaps she *is* endowed
> With second sight. I'm lifted by a loss
>
> As she thumbs my forehead with a cross;
> Anointed, for a moment, I forget
> The failed rehearsals of a mirth, and grief
> Floods me like relief.
> Yes, something's wrong, something she can *see*.

from "Evil Eye" by A.E. Stallings

My ex mother-in-law shook her head and murmured, *ehis poli mati!* (you have a lot of the Eye) which meant the eye had a strong hold over me. She pointed out the enlarging spread of oil that floated unbroken over the water surface. The menacing spirits had jelled and I was in the clutches of the worst of them. There was good reason for my splitting migraines. A published dissertation and a decade of teaching and professional involvement in the field of American Studies were assets in a world unencumbered by the power of evil eyes and the mysteries of being *dyki mas*.

The (Post) Colonial Eye

In a 1993 May issue of *The Economist*, Brian Beedham discusses the Sisyphean struggles and complexities of modern Greece. The fifteen-page supplement to the magazine graphs the sources and effects of what he appropriately titles *"A Country on the Edge."* Beedham talks of the 'huge economic imbalances' the country was grappling with due to a potentially fatal (his word) combination of character and history: "What history did to the Greeks between 1453 and 1821, the centuries of Ottoman rule when 'government' meant something alien," still translates into murky definitions of what constitutes cultural belonging. Speaking at a time when Greece was a new member in the EU (European Union, or EEC, the European Economic Community), Beedham makes the point: "… a political party [in Greece] has long been not so much the voice of an ideology," but "a system of social protection. It answers the question, 'Who looks after whom'."

It was important to belong; my ex mother-in-law assured me I was still 'hers' though I had divorced her son. I was left, like her, to raise a child on my own. She regularly reminded me without protection one never got very far. I was being 'American' when I dismissed her offer to wash and iron my clothes during my work week. I was 'very American' when I assured her I didn't need to be fed every time I visited.

"Do you know what my Greek professors say when I see them at conferences?" a young Greek scholar said to me as we were in conversation about what was happening with my application at the University of Athens. "They say, 'Let's go see our children,' *'ta pedia mas'*! Not the interesting scholar or the interesting paper, but *our kids!*"

He had recently been hired in a department outside the country, urged to leave by his own advisor at Aristotle University. "If I stayed at Aristotle they would have expected me to cajole them…they treat you like you're some sort of family member…and never forgive it if you manage without them."

I had heard so many stories. Stories woven into history and history embellished in story. From the time of the first Greek Republic after the Ottoman Turks were ousted in 1828, when Kapodistria, a Greek of the Diaspora, (and minister of foreign affairs under the Czar), was brought in from Russia, the outsider remains suspect; the outsider is the person, Greek or not, who does things differently from the *dopious* (the natives). As the story goes the *simaxi* (a group of Greeks led by *andartes* fighters: Mavromihalis, Kolokotronis, who fought against the Ottomans) were not thrilled that a Greek from abroad was brought in to represent them in the country's then capital of Nafplion. No matter how erudite, well–meaning, and ultimately Greek, Kapodistria was not one of theirs (*dyki tous*), which proved fatal.

Between the suggestion of a Nafplian that advised Kapodistria to let Mavromihalis out of jail and the advice of a visiting foreign minister who advised against it, Kapodistria made the mistake of listening to the outsider rather than heeding local gossip. Mavromihalis, an *andarte* leader from Mani (the southern tip of Peloponnesus), had been insulted at not having been picked to lead the newly freed land; he was vehement about it and consequently jailed. On his way to attend a church service one Sunday, the story has it, Kapodistria's pants were ripped by a dog trying to bite him (a bad omen). He went back to his house to change when he was shot to death by Mavromihalis' son.

Tipikotita

The call came early in late June. My papers were in. I could hear Arete chain smoking into the phone again. "*Where's* your dissertation?"

"There! Copied thirty damn times. I should have glued *Please Recycle* labels to the stack!"

"You have the name of the publisher on the front page."

"It's being published in the fall."

"They're going to discount it. It has to be *exactly* the way it was when you had it approved by the defense committee *as a dissertation*." I let a minute pass before speaking. My ex mother-in-law had insisted that once the evil eye got a hold of you it was bad tactics to 'throw oil into the fire', '*ladi sti fotia*.' I still had copies in my basement, lugged from Thessaloniki to pass out to friends before I knew it would go much beyond being two hundred typed pages held together with a spiral. I had until the end of the day to get the copies to the secretary before they would dismiss it. Within the hour I placed them on the secretary's desk with a note that said I would have more copies to her by tomorrow.

On July 4, 2000, the English Department at the University of Athens (with the exception of Arete) and the many absent professors who like the doctors were out of the city in mid summer, voted in Scylla for the lectureship position in *American Literature and Culture*, a woman whose research interests were in medieval British literature, Spanish playwrights, and Greek poetry. My ex mother-in-law who insists the evil eye is oblivious to the banalities of facts (and respectful of gods and goddesses, monstrous or not), was not surprised by the development of events.

"It's the Fourth of July," Arete announced dryly in an open letter to the Department amid loud talk and coffee drinking. "But we're not voting in an Americanist today." She was asked to get to the point; she read her letter which was later filed with so much paper when I decided to take the case to court. My doctoral advisor at Aristotle University did the same, contesting the decision and the department's procedures, the formalities of *typikotita* they lividly defended: "*Who* is *he* to get involved with *our* affairs!" they exclaimed. I was now worse off than Echo; I was called his 'lackey,' his 'slut,' forever outcast from becoming 'one of theirs' (*dyki tous*), and beginning to see my ex mother-in-law's point, the evil eye had taken on more power. Pandora's Box was open. I had thrown oil into the fire (*ladi sti fotia*)and it was raging.

"Why didn't they take you in the department at Aristotle where you did your doctoral dissertation?" One of the faculty members in the department at the University of Athens asked me before the vote. She seemed irritated by the fact that my application had added an unexpected turn to the department's unofficial decision to hire Scylla. Following a belated piece of advice to 'see the department members and convince them of your qualifications,' I went to one or two of the faculty before the vote.

The story of my failure to get the position in the department at Aristotle where I earned my doctorate was less flagrant and more camouflaged. I'd applied for a position in American literature, but again the position had been tagged for an insider, a woman who had had less publications and teaching experience, but who was nevertheless in American literature and favored by a professor who, like Homer's drunken Centaur, Eurytion, enjoyed his pleasures. Eurytion had a reputation built as much on the students who hung their underwear outside his door as on his voluminous self-publications.

I studied the woman behind her desk. She looked drained, and about my age. It occurred to me she didn't seem particularly happy ensconced in her academic prestige, letting me know with wearied heaviness what she had gone through to secure it. There were the constant contacts with senior members in the department, the jobs in other parts of Greece, the flying back and forth to maintain the contacts. She signed heavily. She looked like she could do with some affection. Leaning across her desk, she breathed, "You know I'm quite close to the people on the three-member committee," adding that if it wasn't for my application the decision would have been 'cut and dry.' I realized later she wanted me to take this as a compliment.

Ousia

On February 12, 2003 (a decade after Beedham's piece in *The Economist*), the Greek newspaper *Kathimerini* ran a piece entitled: "*Corruption and Nepotism are Tumors on the Body Politic.*" Nikiforos Diamandouros, the new European Ombudsman, in an interview with *Kathimerini*, discussed a recurring theme of 'mutual suspicion between the State and citizens.' The first sentence of the first paragraph reads: "Four huge issues are responsible for the chronically ailing Greek state services. The first is staffing policy which was based on criteria that had nothing to do with merit, and everything to do with patronage."

"If it gets to the point of having to tell them what the truth is you've lost the game," Arete said when I expressed dismay at how the process of selection was being conducted.

"You're pointing out a reality." I replied.

"They already know the reality; they don't work like that."

"You mean in terms of right and wrong?" I said.

"They know what they're doing. The point is to make it look legal."

"How do they think they're going to get away with this?"

Arete was silent. Procedures, the formal *typikotitas*, were legal terms by which *ousia*, the content or matter of a situation, was masked; Chaos had his structures. A lectureship position in British Literature at the University of Athens was being advertised at the same time as the position in American Literature. I assumed Scylla, who taught British Literature courses at the same college where I worked, would apply. I didn't realize Scylla was part of Circe's circle of enchantresses.

A graduate of the University of Athens, Scylla had been told she had to wait her turn while she unofficially worked for some of the University professors editing their papers, setting up web sites. She let me know she was going to try and get into the department this year and asked if I was going to apply for the American Studies position.

"Good luck," I said, when I saw Scylla outside the department secretary's office. She had just handed in her pile of Xeroxed publications and was skittish.

"Good luck to you too," she said as I made my way into the secretary's office. A handsome, heavy-set woman nodded to me to come in.

"What position are you applying for?" she asked politely.

I told her the American studies position as she took the stacked pile of papers. "How many people are applying?"

"Seven," she said.

I was surprised. The secretary listed the names, including Scylla's. I was now dumbfounded. "Isn't she applying for the position in British literature?" The secretary looked at me curiously.

"Who do you know in the department?"

I named several people including Arete who had been keeping me informed of the growing complications.

"*Kali Epitihia*," ("Good Luck") she said warmly. I thought of calling my ex mother-in-law. She was getting weary of my not listening more carefully. I had recently taken to wearing the evil eye around my neck as well as my wrist; I was too late.

Driving to work in a wild rage I wondered how Scylla was going to justify using the same article publications she had submitted for a British Literature position a year ago for an American position a year later. I realized why she had been so keen to see my CV. I called her out of class, asked why she was applying for a teaching job in American Literature instead of British Literature. She blushed, "There's someone favored for the British position. I'll have a chance with the position in American Studies," she answered, looking me squarely in the eyes.

"None of your work is in American literature," I said evenly.

Still pink and still looking me in the eyes, she answered, "I can learn."

"Are *you* an Americanist?" I was furious. She repeated the fact that she could learn. I repeated the fact that she had never taught an American literature course in her life. At that point she smiled, "May the most deserving person get the position."

There seemed no point to continue with the process. It was clear I would not get it no matter how many times I warded off the evil eye, or how many bracelets of evil eye beads I wore. No matter how many publications I might have in the field, or how many candles I lit in the churches and chapels I found myself absently walking into, I knew I wasn't enough *dyki tous* to warrant inclusion in this Olympus.

My doctoral advisor at Aristotle University kept repeating, "I don't know how they can legally put an unqualified person in the position." There was always the vote. The linguists as well as the literature professors had to vote. I could demonstrate I was the better candidate through the lecture I had to give. What does it feel like to prove something against odds deliberately weighed against you? The post-colonized psychology of the Trinidadians V.S. Naipaul's *The Middle Passage* describes expresses some of the reasons for marginalization: "For talent, a futility, the Trinidadian substituted intrigue; and in the exercise of this, in small things as well as large, he became a master" (Naipaul 35). "Again and again one comes back to the main, degrading fact of the colonial society; it never required efficiency, it never required quality, and these things, because unrequired, became undesirable" (Naipaul 53). Over a century after Ottoman rule modern Greece would not consider itself a post-colonized society, but the traumas of that oppression and the various oppressions thereafter, from the imported rule of the Bavarian Othon (Otto) to the building of NATO bases in the 1970s, the Other continues to be suspect.

"Tragedy! You Too. When Will You Look it in the Face?"

The lecture I was to give as part of my application process was called 'a student lecture,' but there were no students. A handful of professors were gathered in the classroom, most of them drinking coffee and talking in the back rows as I spoke. Armed with my amulets of garlic and evil eyes and the two shots of unadulterated vodka I'd had for breakfast, I got through my lecture and concluded with a quote from Grace Paley's "A *Conversation with My Father,*" about a mother who gives into smoking pot to be closer to her pot-smoking son, only to have him eventually turn against her. At the end of the story, Paley's narrator insists the woman, her character, has a chance in life.

"Anything could happen," she tells her bed-ridden father, a voice from the Old World who has asked her to narrate a story as he lays sick in his hospital bed. After he hears the story he is emphatic: the mother who has a second chance in Paley's vision of possibility remains doomed in the father's insistence that she is tragic. "Tragedy! You too. When will you look it in the face?" He says, as the story ends.

By the time I got through the lecture the chatting professors had grown quiet, some of the women in the back row looked my way. I overheard someone say I sounded *xeni* (foreign). A scribbled note to myself — *faces/ in lazy struggle/impatient to take up space* — is what I remember of the day, that and driving home depleted. The garlic in my bag (given by my ex mother-in-law), the blue evil eyes I wore around my neck and wrist and my enthusiasm for literature, had kept me vaguely hopeful that the motley group I found myself speaking to might actually listen to the talk. But the vodka on an empty stomach as I spoke in front of the chatty coffee drinkers finally got the best of me.

At my neighborhood hairdresser, owned by Anastasia, a young woman who had recently opened the shop, I went into details. I was asking Anastasia if she thought anyone could objectively judge someone's work they had helped to write. "Greece…" she said, without completing the sentence, swiftly lifting clumps of my damp hair between her fingers and cutting briskly. Anastasia, from a village in the Peloponnesus, an attractive girl in her twenties, had taken out a loan to open her own hairdressing shop. She was very proud of her SEBASTIAN products from the States and let her clients know they were environment friendly, that SEBASTIAN invested an amount of its profits for the preservation of the Amazon jungle. Today her hair had vivid purple highlights.

She listened, concentrating as I spoke. "That's what keeps us back," she finally added. "People like that."

94

I tell her I'm thinking of taking the case to court.

"Yes you should!" she exclaimed. "Standing up for what we believe is how we live with ourselves." I started to talk about what this was going to cost, the strain, what this would do to my already fragile peace of mind, my home life.

"You're fine!" she quips, briskly cutting. "If you've managed this far you're just fine." We laugh. "It's amazing," she says, checking out the cut in the mirror; my mop of hair pruned of its wild strands.

As I leave the shop she squeezes my arm and tells me, "People are magical. We accomplish unbelievable things."

The fourth of July was a day so hot no one was sitting at any of the open air tables under the canopies of a well-known fish tavern on the square in Kessariani. I was waiting for Arete who had been at the department meeting to vote; it was my last and only chance, but I knew it wasn't going to happen, my ex mother-in-law told me as much (she couldn't believe how stubbornly the oil in the dish of water refused to break up in this latest attempt to exorcise the eye). Even my horoscope warned of the influence of Mars; the wheat was going to be separated from the chaff in violent ways. There was so much chaff and so little wheat Circe warned, cajoling those in the department with tales of my ambition; of how specialized my focus was as opposed to Scylla's eclectic interests. So when Arete appeared on that blistering day in a stark white dress with a large gold cross around her neck, I knew the answer.

"Are you wearing the cross for a reason?" She smiled, obviously tired. In fact she looked exhausted. We ordered two liters of bottled water. I had already finished one by myself. It was over 40 degrees centigrade. The water fountain next to us was working. I got up and put my face in it as Arete laconically relayed the events. "They voted for Scylla," she said quietly. I nodded.

"Everyone?"

"Everyone except me."

She had typed a letter and read it aloud stating the reasons why Scylla was not the best qualified for the job; people interrupted her. Someone said, "Let's get this over with." The secretary, infuriated, directly announced the wrong person was being elected, stating that advertised positions had to be filled with candidates who had the proper qualifications. She took the minutes. It was a sweltering mid-afternoon hour. I had lost track, numbed as much by the heat as by what Arete was describing. We realized some time later we could have gone into the air conditioning. Fragments of other people's conversation drifted in and out of our talk. I thought absently of Gregory, a Greek lawyer who once said, "People in places where society is better organized can gauge the results of their actions because they can gauge what the results will be." In those cultures, Chaos had boundaries.

The results, I thought, feeling numb, left us in too much heat and vaguely hysterical; Chaos was brutal.

"Now what?" I finally said. Arete shrugged. The sweat was running down her neck. For some reason we still had not gotten up to go into the air conditioning.

"It's up to you." She meant the decision to go to court. "First it goes to the Minister of Education to get signed. Maybe you should try and stop it there." I thought of Pericles, my friend the writer who like me belonged to two worlds, raised in one, living in another. He knew people in the Ministry, related as he was to one of the major political families in the country.

"If the Minister is informed that he's signing in a person who doesn't have the qualifications, he may not sign. But you should see a lawyer." No one had any real idea what this would involve.

"So what are the qualifications of the woman who is going to be picked for the British Literature position that Scylla was really qualified for?" Arete said she was a young woman whose mother or father had given English language lessons to a number of professors in the department.

In Love With Lies

"It's not that she wasn't qualified," one of the haggard professors confided to Arete. "But she's…well, older than Scylla."

Four years earlier when I was applying for a lectureship position at Aristotle University in Thessaloniki, Eurytion who wanted the woman who was in his field, said the same thing to my doctoral advisor. I was already old at thirty-six.

"Didn't you tell them I wasn't aware this was a beauty pageant?"

Now sitting in the heat in Kessariani, dizzy from it, I went on. "At Aristotle I had to deal with a Centaur with a man problem…"

"A prick with a man problem." Arete smiled.

"Or a man with a prick problem?" We were laughing, the sweat dancing off our foreheads.

Arete put her head down on the table, I thought she was going to faint. I said we should leave. Driving home I realized Scylla had always been *dyki tous*, a graduate of the department where Circe had been her teacher and then co-authored articles with her, there had never been a question of Scylla's belonging; it had only been a question of time. It was unlucky that I had applied at the same time. In her frustration at not getting the position a year before in British Literature, Scylla blurted in the office at work, "They *promise*, they keep *promising*…" She went on about how she helped the professors with their papers, edited, researched them and how they in return, had promised her a position.

A year later, elected into a position for American Literature, Scylla got what she had been promised. Only the British position whose candidates were also giving their lectures and Xeroxing publications was left empty, announced as *agoni*. I was told the three-member committee who recommended the candidate was now afraid. Word was out that I was seeing a lawyer, one of the professors confessed to Arete that she didn't feel she could sign for the favored candidate who had not met the publication criteria.

I finally lost control.

"They elected a woman in the American Literature position who should have gone into the British position, but didn't because of a favored candidate who finally didn't get the position because they're now afraid to put her in? Meanwhile they could have filled both positions with the right people if they hadn't told Scylla to apply for something she wasn't qualified to fill!"

Arete was chain-smoking again. I gauged the tension of our conversations by how many pauses she took to inhale or exhale. She didn't say anything, exhaling at audible intervals.

"I'll call you later," I said, feeling the frustration on both sides had started to affect our friendship.

The reverberations of this on students who pay what amounts to the fee for a private education to be tutored to pass the national entrance exams and are then taught by the favored candidates of professors whose qualifications are about who they know as opposed to what they know was making me realize why almost every Greek wore some version of the evil eye, and never ceased to cross themselves when things took a turn for the good. I noticed the usual assortment of garlic, horse shoes, pomegranates and crosses dangling from rear view car mirrors, key chains, necklaces, bracelets and worry beads. Arete confessed she kept a small eye pinned inside her bra.

These freights of encroaching menace were too burdensome for the evil eye. Not only was I not one of theirs, but I was *xeni* (alien or foreign). A professor present at the student lecture that had no students had published a critique of 'the ideology of [a] one-language-one-nation' humanist tradition '[that will] jeopardize the vitality of difference' (*The Other Within* 2). Apparently difference also jeopardized vitality; I was too different. But there was some humor to the machinations of the evil eye. Once in, Scylla was initiated into the same doublespeak, criticizing candidates for not having enough teaching experience, for needing more specialization in their research, strengths she had lacked herself.

"The Greeks are *in love* with their lies!" a Greek-American politician exclaimed.

Outside the bakery I ran into Ctimene, one of my first neighbors in Metz where I lived years ago. She had moved to our new neighborhood, and sometimes we ran into each other. She seemed surprised that I was still in

Athens. Her daughter had finally passed the national exams to get into the University of Athens.

"She's living her adolescence now, at twenty," she said, describing how hellish the process had been. "She had to study so much she never went out." It had been that way for three years. There were expenses, tutors, the *frontistiria*, (paid classes that prepped kids on the range of exam subjects). Despite the free public education provided by the Greek state, tutoring had become more and more of a necessity for students to pass national entrance exams and the costs amounted to that of private schooling.

"We're always going to be fifty years behind," Ctimene said matter-of-factly. "Always."

I looked at her surprised. She described a recent visit to Italy where she experienced what it might have been like for the Greeks had they not had their history of oppressions, to be comfortable in their cultural skin, amongst their ruins, enjoying their food, their statues, the beauty of the country, all the subjects foreigners celebrate when they visit or write about Greece.

"We've had too many slaps," Ctimene goes on sadly. "Too many things have gone wrong for us. People are burnt out."

"And burnt," I say.

"Just look at how we act when we win anything," she adds, "a basketball game or a soccer match. We're ecstatic." I tell her I like these expressions of spontaneous and communal spirit, but wonder if that too won't eventually be lost.

Ctimene shakes her head and says, "No." She assures me, "It's just that everything has happened so fast. And this city wasn't built for so many people. Every day I take a cab to get to the metro I go through such anxiety with the traffic, and my day hasn't even begun." I tell her about Patmos, that one day I hope to buy a house there.

"But that's not part of the practical world," she says. "It's not part of our daily world."

"It's still good to know it exists," I add.

She nods, "But we live here."

The Japanese writer Natsuki Ikezawa invited by the Ministry of Culture to attend a symposium called *The Greek Experience* along with such illustrious guests as Seamus Heaney, Rachel Hadas and Michel Deon, described how his experiences in Greece had liberated him from the constraints of his own culture, how they provided an alternative model to that of the conditioned obedience he had been brought up with in Japan. He called what he witnessed here, 'extreme individualism' and described a quarrel in the post-office where he witnessed a person argue with the post-office teller about the price change on stamps.

"I so admired that," he said with genuine good feeling. "I admired the man's stubbornness and refusal to accept what we, in Japan, would never have argued against in public." Ikezawa made the further point of comparing how defeat can devastate the Japanese, provoking a loss of motivation.

"While the Greeks," he went on, "seem to become more passionate and determined; they aren't afraid to fight by themselves."

Interestingly a Greek writer during the question and answer session used Ikezawa's point to highlight the Greeks' heroic resistance to Mussolini's invasion during WWII when the Greeks famously obstructed Mussolini's Fascist soldiers from invading the country with their brilliant, "*Ohi.*" ("No.") More than the fact of history, the Greek writer was interested in its mythic heroism.

But Ikezawa was describing a scene in the post-office, something he respectfully called 'opera.' This was not a case of being in love with lies, but of being in love with myth. 'Lost in history,' is how Stratis Haviaras has described contemporary Greece's identity crisis, 'and found in mythology.'

If you have to resort to "stating the truth," Arete insisted, "the game is already lost." I toyed with the idea of going to the English department chair and asking directly why I had been prevented from being given fair consideration for the American literature position, why I had not been asked to withdraw my application (as so many were informed to do in other instances of favored candidacy). At thirty-six I had been considered too old for the lectureship position at Aristotle University by Eurytion whose dubious reputation and creaturely habits put him into strange positions. Six years later another battle took place at Aristotle in which a sixty year old woman applied (and was given) a lectureship with one published paper because she was the wife of a high-ranking administrator.

"These are civil servants; they do practically whatever they want to in the academy. Ministers come and go, the Party changes, but civil servants are there for life. They run the show in the public sector," Arete answered, though neither of us realized the extent to which the agilities of generations taught to keep a wary eye on anyone not *dyki tous* made 'truth' relative to the perspective of the person speaking it.

The February 12, 2003, *Kathimerini* newspaper article on the Ombudsman Nikiforos Diamandouros, quotes Yannis Michail, the man responsible for the Citizens' Advocate Committee:

"Parliament is simply cropping the weeds, not tearing them up by the roots. We don't grasp that bad administration is what forms fertile soil for corruption. If the State doesn't clean out its Augean stables, then cases of corruption will recur. But the government does not seem willing to establish the rule of law. State employees that break the law remain unpunished, due to the disarray of disciplinary procedures."

Tsifliki

Tsifliki, from the Turkish *tsiflik* that refers to a large area of land under the control of a single person, is used idiomatically in modern Greece to suggest a domain under the authority of one person, or clique. I had heard the term used when people talked derogatorily of how various domains of the public sector were run, whether it was the hospitals where doctors were given *fakelakia* (small envelopes of cash) to pay attention to patients and give priority to others, or the Ministries and national universities where 'favors' were 'owed.' A recent political scandal seemed a particularly vivid example of how entrenched the notion continues to be. The owner of the affluent Porto Carras resort hotel, a major tourist attraction in Greece's Chalkidike region, wanted to buy up acres of forested land to build lucrative housing units. The law, as it stood, did not allow for the privatization of woodland, particularly coastal regions which, since the fall of the Junta dictatorship, were to remain public property. Apparently with his high connections in government, the Porto Carras owner managed to get an amendment passed in Parliament so he could buy up the land, saying this would bring in more tourism and boost the economy.

On the eve of elections in January 2004, as soon as the amendment passed into law with the signatures of nine MPs and a deputy finance minister, havoc broke loose; the amendment or *tropologia* which allowed for the sale was considered illegal, the government deputies who signed and allowed for it were held accountable. *PASOK*, the party in power, announced they would not include the ten names on the party ticket. The MPs immediately and publicly claimed they were simply following protocol from the Minister. Three of them insisted they had not even signed, that their names had been forged. This was later admitted on national television when another MP said he had indeed forged the names without consulting his colleagues. But it was more complicated; this was regular practice, MPs routinely signed each other's names to amendments to government bills "in the belief," George Gilson of the *Athens News* reports, "that they were acting as good soldiers advancing the government's work." The more familiar procedure was to inform the person whose name is signed by phone, "but they sometimes are not even aware of the content of the legislation to which their name is signed."

The Finance Minister himself vowed to rescind the Porto Carras amendment the day after it was passed, claiming he was unaware of the Deputy Minister's intentions. Meanwhile it was the MPs belief that the Finance Minister was backing the amendment; they had acted in good faith, without reading what the law actually said. George Papandreou convinced then Prime Minister Costas Simitis to purge the party of the ten people directly involved with the signing, and institute what he named 'a new ethos'. The

Athens News article quotes him: "All I know is that this amendment concerns only one citizen of Greece and grants privileges to a single business." He was chastised by other party members for not even contacting the MPs before they were removed. The proportions of the scandal and the confusion spoke volumes about the layered strata of what was more complicated than the fact of corruption. It was never as simple as extricating the person responsible because it was never 'a person.'

Lines

I was in New Jersey visiting family when I met a Greek from Charlotte, NC who had been raised in the States and had a restaurant business. We chatted about how Athens was being ripped apart with construction for the upcoming Olympics: roads, metro, trams. "It's a mess," I said. He talked of the frustrations of trying to convince Greeks he worked with to believe in a project, complaining of the discrepancies of what he had read and seen of a past in ruins and what he faced in his workaday life.

"Whenever I propose a deal that's going to help us, the Greeks never trust that you aren't taking advantage of them." He explained his unsuccessful proposal for creating a co-op of Greek restaurants in Charlotte. "They're convinced I have something up my sleeve. They want to know what I'm getting out of it. I tell them I'm trying to save myself from paying $3000 instead of $75.00 but they think I have an angle I'm not telling them about."

Trust assumes common boundaries and in Greece those boundaries are conflicting. There is the infamous story of how the potato was introduced to the country. Imported from Europe in the 1830s as a cheap solution to famine by the Bavarian Othon (Otto), the Greeks were asked to help themselves to free potato sprouts in Nafplion. No one took them. General Makriyannis, a hero in the Greek War of Independence who taught himself to write so he could record his now invaluable memoirs of the war, suggested two guards protect the sacks of potatoes at night. The next day there wasn't a potato or potato sprout left. Chaos was fickle.

> In this city
> the rest of the world
> is where bills get paid by mail
> or phone, where
> the overworked and underpaid
> get decent pension plans,
> plenty of sleep.
> *We're here to suffer*
> someone mumbles

when the postal clerk mutters
next? chewing a cigarette.
Lined up to get our checks,
buy stamps,
people spill out
onto the pavement.
Elbowing her way in,
a woman begs
can she *please* send
a cylindrical packet.
A man with a scar-burnt face
breathes *do you think*
the rest of us are vacationing?
Someone hisses, *Be polite!*
A woman with a pastry roll of
hair murmurs
I'm taking care
of two children, but
I'm waiting my turn.
The man behind me asks,
Are we going to complain like that
when we're old like them?
His bags dig
into my rib, the door's open
because we don't all fit.
Huddled against the November air
I notice a woman
in sandals, her toenails
painted white, the man
whose eczema has spread
down his arm, the old woman
with a frayed collar and
mongoloid daughter
inching toward a clerk
desperate for sleep who takes
her letters and bills
and asks *Did I give you*
the right change?

When my decision to take my case to court became public knowledge, one of the more vocal professors spoke in superlatives emphasizing the line between 'our' vision (*to orama mas*) to provide national educations, and the threat of 'private interests' *ta xena sholia* (the foreign schools). This private nemesis to public domains of service was especially ironic when the vocal professor was a graduate of one of the *xena* institutions in Athens.

The February 12, 2003, *Kathimerini* article continues: "legislation is often obscure and fragmented, resulting in overlapping and obscure laws. And unclear laws create the conditions for arbitrary interpretations of legal provisions, with all their potential for corruption." During the application for the position at the University of Athens, the department couldn't use the fact that I worked at a private college against me since Scylla worked at the same institution. Yet when I made a legal claim, spokespersons from the department described themselves as belonging to a national institution in need of defending itself against the encroachments of those outside the university's national spirit; by not being *dyki tous* I had crossed the line into foreignhood.

"You have to go and see Pallas at the Ministry of Education, she's a law-yer for the state," my large, well-meaning lawyer urged. I had met him on a downtown side street off smog-ridden Aharnon street. He appeared in a suit, introducing himself and kissed the back of my hand before we walked through a dimly lit hallway to his office. "I just painted this place when we had the earthquake," he says, apologizing for the large cracks along the inside of his office and inviting me to sit down. Right away he mentions the importance of making myself known to people so 'a face' can be attached to my name, so I will no longer be *xeni* (foreign).

"I'll find out the times Pallas is in her office at the Ministry," he contin-ues. This was a new idea, the importance of presenting myself in person to someone in authority. Arete had urged the same thing, "Let them get to know you," she'd said when I reluctantly went to see some of the professors in the department before the vote. "Don't they have copies of all those published articles I Xeroxed?" I answered. She shrugged and repeated what I started to hear more often, "You need to become a face for people to remember you."

My lawyer, a jovial, expansive man recommended by Arete offered me coffee, and wanted to know if I enjoyed teaching at a private institution, how I ended up in Athens, and finally, how he couldn't believe I was single. I had become used to the overlap of private and public worlds in conversa-tions, the line blurred by ringing phones in the tax or post office or in some Ministry, the woman or man in charge taking their time to talk about how the kids were, what was for lunch, how his or her mother was doing after an operation, the rest of us in line patiently or not-so-patiently waiting to get a paper signed or a job done while being privy to the private tastes and recipes and family updates of an otherwise anonymous face.

"Is the problem with your position a problem of formal *typikotika* (procedure), or is it a problem of *ousia* (essence)?" My lawyer asked, handing me my coffee in a chipped mug.

"A woman who's done all her academic work in British literature was hired to teach American literature," I say, tense again.

"Did they follow procedure?" He was matter-of-fact.

"A woman who *co-authored* two of the candidate's papers was on the judging committee for the position." I go on, still raw.

"These people in the state universities treat these positions like they own them," my lawyer says, suddenly serious. "These are *government* jobs, paid for by the government!" His voice was rising.

The differences between British and American literature was apparently an issue of *ousia* (essence or content), something evaluated by what were deemed criteria of specialization, decided by professionals in the field.

"Who are the Ministers to tell us our job?" One of the professors vented when the first legal document was sent to the department; they had followed formalities. They considered it intrusive, an insult, that an administrator from the Ministry of Education suggested they didn't know how to evaluate their own candidates.

Commas and Stop Lights

A woman with greasy, loosely gathered red hair can't believe the postal clerks aren't going to cash her postal check and give her her money. She flings her I.D. at one of them saying "*Everything's* in an I.D.! *Why* do I need a police verification?!"

"Because we don't know you," the postal clerk answers nonplussed.

"But I'm giving you my I.D.," she insists.

"How do we know it's yours?" the clerk answers again.

The red haired woman won't accept what she is being told. She suggests she call a colleague in another post office. The postal clerk keeps shaking her head. Those of us in line begin to make comments.

"Don't tire yourself and everyone else; do what the clerk's telling you to do and go to the police," one of the men in line suggests. The woman ignores him. She wants to see the manager.

"We can't take the responsibility," another clerk tries to explain.

A woman in line nods. "The way things have become these days, who's going to take that kind of responsibility, and accept an I.D. that might be false?"

The red-headed woman goes up the landing to the manager sitting at a desk. There is a desperate, caged look about her as she repeats that she can call a colleague, (a *syn adelfo*, literally, an 'added brother'). The manager repeats that she needs a police verification of her identity before she can get her money. She pulls out another form of identification as he continues to shake his head.

"Something's up with her," another man says as we watch, fascinated.

"She's just stubborn," a woman offers.

"No, she's an innocent," someone adds.

"An innocent with a callous in her brain," the woman continues.

"Explain what you mean by 'commas and stop lights,'" an American scholar visiting Athens asks, half expecting me to be joking as I start to describe the way students are conditioned to pass national university entrance exams composed of texts that need to be memorized verbatim. Paragraphs of ancient Greek are chosen from whole textbooks and students are asked to reiterate passages, word for word, and comma for comma. Points are taken off, the exam possibly failed, if commas and periods are misplaced or forgotten. Paraphrasing or critical analyses of the text is secondary to memorizing the exact phrasings.

"The commas in the right place get you in," I say. "You're taught not to question them. You don't learn to respect the reasons behind the rules."

"It's the difference between performing obedience and believing in its necessity," she offers. "Does that go for stop lights also?"

I laugh despite myself as she describes how she was almost killed in a taxi that went through a red light.

"Some red lights are just slower-downers," I explain.

Commas and stop lights were meant to limit Chaos' shenanigans, but they only provoked them. "Sort of like having a wife someone else manages to give an orgasm when you thought all along she was happy enough to be your wife," suggests a young Greek talking to me. He likes his analogy. "We think we've done things the way we were taught to do them, but your girlfriend complains or your wife is hysterical and we think none of it has anything to do with our own behavior because we're sure we've done things the way we were told to do them."

I thought of the red haired woman in the post office, convinced her I.D. was more than adequate for her to cash her check, reiterating to the manager "My *husband* said I don't need anything else! And now you're telling me I have to go to the police?"

The Ministry of Education

After our Saturday meeting in his office, my lawyer wanted me to come back the following week after I managed to see Pallas, the lawyer for the state in the Ministry of Education. "With your book," he emphasized.

"But will she read it?" I want to know.

He shook his head impatiently, "The book looks impressive, just give her a copy."

I was heavy hearted about handing over a $60 hardcover research book to someone I knew would only file it. I dreamed of Pallas in the Ministry, another Athena, making it impossible for me to state my case, damning me to listening, like Echo, to my own repetitions. I was driving a go-kart on a major highway. I kept approaching the port town of Patras without ever arriving. Then I was running along a mountain path, a pair of long earrings swinging heavily from my stretched earlobes as Chaos, just behind, kept nicking the top of my spine.

I called up my lawyer's secretary, a young woman who always sounded exhausted, and asked if Kyria Pallas was someone I could approach privately. She assured me I could. The first time at the Ministry of Education, the guard told me no one was there. It was ten in the morning. I thought he was joking.

"The lawyers come after one o'clock," he said, sipping coffee.

"Why?" I was unsure if I had understood.

"Because they're in court during the day," he said, irritated.

He didn't bother to tell me to wait. Someone coming out of the building said I needed a protocol number; the offices were around the corner. I went up a flight of steps, past the determined looking faces coming down, and asked a man at a front desk where I could leave an envelope for Kyria Pallas.

"Desk B2," he said tonelessly, nodding toward an inner room. A woman in conversation with him walked back into the room, chewing something.

"Can I give this envelope to you for Kyria Pallas?"

"Pallas?" she repeated.

When I finally saw Kyria Pallas in the Ministry a week later I asked if she got the book, explaining that my lawyer had sent me. She nodded, a tall, well dressed, attractive but tired looking woman.

"I hear so many cases like this," she sighed.

"So why doesn't anything get done?"

She gestured for me to sit down, and nodded. "It all depends on if we can prove something illegal has happened." She asked the same question my lawyer had asked: Did I know if procedure had been followed? I told her I thought so. She said the Minister consults his group of legal advisors for their opinion on matters that are unclear.

"Is this unclear?"

"This could be considered criminal," she said laconically, "putting a person in a position they aren't qualified for."

Pericles who had his connections in the Ministry told me I should go see the Minister himself.

"See the Minister?" I was surprised. This was going to provoke more than a nightmare of driving on a highway in a go-kart.

He didn't see why not. I tried to imagine myself facing the Minister with my story. Friends started to give me advice. Make sure you stress the injustice. Make sure you look good. Be flirty. Be feminine. Let him know you're a single mother. My ex mother-in-law was preparing a special *philakto* talisman, a cross she sewed next to a heart, the source, she was convinced, of my misguidance. Pericles advised that I first see an aide that used to work in the Ministry of Education. The aide was on his way out of the country on a business trip, but nodded ceaselessly as I related my story, promising to find out the status of Scylla's papers.

If the Minister didn't approve the position I would not have to proceed legally. But when the earnestly nodding aide came back from his trip it was already too late. Scylla was going to get the position. My lawyer said Kyria Pallas and others in the Ministry knew of Pericles' involvement in the case and were waiting to see what would happen next.

We thought there was a chance the case would be stopped. I was on the phone with Arete who had grown increasingly bewildered. The Minister was not so easy to find, messages were left with his secretary, he had been asked to evaluate the application himself. I started to keep my cell phone on during classes. Pericles finally called the Minister directly to let him know "a woman with degrees in French literature is getting an American literature position."

"Pericles, her research is in British Literature, not French!" I almost laughed into the my cell phone; I was in the supermarket. The hope for a chance to annul the position had taken over my life. Even my daughter was using Scylla's name as a synonym to describe how nasty one of her classmates had been; "How would you like it Mom if someone you thought was a friend turned into a Scylla?"

Pericles was laughing, "It sounds better if I say French anyway."

"You're saying he probably won't even notice?"

Pericles let me know the Minister would be on the lookout; he told Pericles he just hoped he hadn't signed in Scylla's position already.

"Doesn't he *read* what he *signs*?" I was suddenly screaming in the supermarket parking lot.

"There's always a stack of stuff they have to sign. The secretaries bring them in and sort them out."

I mumbled Stephen Dunn's lines: '*Everywhere, an error/leading to an error./Everywhere the justified,*' and hung up.

I was given a phone number I was told belonged to the Minister's secretary. A woman connected me to another woman who told me to call again after two in the afternoon; no one picked up. I called the next day, a woman picked up; she was eating. I could hear her chewing as she talked. "No the application hasn't come to us yet," she said, swallowing.

"Nothing?"

"No, nothing," she repeated, reading me some names she was sifting through between more chewing and swallowing. "Zoe, Vitali," but not Scylla. I kept calling. I called everyday to make sure the secretary caught the application before the Minister signed it. Two weeks later I was given another number in the Ministry and asked again what I was probably repeating in my sleep. From somewhere inside the Ministry's bureaucratic arteries, someone called Arete at the University and insisted the papers had long been signed.

"Yes," she found Scylla's name, a woman said over the phone, breaking through the amnesia, the position had been signed for over a month. My heart sank. Then I was sick. My ex-mother-in-law coaxed me out of shock with egg and lemon soups. Of course I was sick; the menace was much greater than the heart. Like the evil eyes she judiciously exorcised for me with her oil in plates of water, she believed the mistake was that she didn't think to put a *philakto* of the entire body, a woman, next to the icon of Agios Isidoros (the Saint of many gifts).

People were saying I had to find a way to have the papers re-examined. Pericles' secretary called the Minister's secretary, livid, but was told the papers couldn't be recalled.

"I don't know anymore," Lena, Pericles' secretary, breathed rapidly into the phone. "I don't know what's going to happen to this country…everyone wants the main portion of the *pita* (the pie) and will steal it if there's no other way to get it."

Who was connected with whom and what anyone could actually do in the Ministry became more confusing. Lena was mumbling, "They beat you down, pitilessly. Pitilessly." I called my lawyer to ask where the papers went once they had been signed by the Minister; the Ministry published a government newsletter (F.E.K.) which advertised positions and promotions in the public sector. Pericles' girlfriend knew someone in the F.E.K. offices. A woman there said she had never received so many phone calls to verify a position. The University of Athens people had been pushing the case as soon as they knew I was looking into the legalities of what had happened, and had found plenty *dyki tous* in the public sector to help ensure Scylla's appointment.

"Yes, the papers signed by the Minister are here. Scylla was officially in.

"So the secretary must have known we were on this case all along," I told Pericles.

If I wanted to go any further I would have to take the case to court. Academic issues ended up at the Supreme Court. My lawyer was telling me not to worry. I had no idea how I was going to pay for any of this. He hugged me jovially. "Did I say anything about money?"

"I need to know," I said. He acted hurt that I didn't trust his commitment. I had recently convinced my father to let me cash in some savings bonds for a house I wanted to buy on Patmos, the island where my daughter and I went for the summer. Turning what my father viewed as precious dollars into pathetic drachmas, convinced him that the culture had finally unhinged me. Little did anyone know the U.S. stock market was not going to get higher than it did in those last months of the Clinton administration. I cashed in the bonds at their vanishing high point, and wondered if this case was worth having my 'Patmos-house money' disappear in lawyer fees.

"For you," my lawyer said, scribbling a tally on a piece of paper which was the sum of the fixed *paravola* (court fees).

"And your payment?"

"I like you," he said, nonplussed at my visible embarrassment. "More people need to fight." He brought me his book on the European High Court on Human Rights in Luxembourg where he represented cases. His young, exhausted secretary was answering the incessantly ringing phone. "I drove her crazy with this book," he said leafing through it, showing me his acknowledgement for all the typing she did. I broached the issue of money again.

"Whatever you want to give me," he said dismissively, and asked me to make an appointment for an evening the following week.

"Can we discuss this over the phone?" My week day afternoons and evenings had me buried in student papers and my daughter's homework questions.

He boisterously declared how much he liked seeing me — couldn't I just come by the office — which meant driving down to the center of the city where there was never any parking, and leaving my now twelve year old on her own.

"I admire you," he said, not insincerely. "The whole ministry knows about your case."

"Knows what about it?"

The Ministry knew Pericles with the political connections has spoken to the Minister, and since the Minister had endorsed Scylla's election they wondered if something else was going to happen. It was like a soccer match, sides were betting on possible outcomes. I phoned Pericles, awkward about suggesting he look into having the endorsement reclaimed from the F.E.K offices. We'd both been brought up outside the culture and, alas, respected something of the conventional boundaries instilled in us. Contesting a Minister's signature was a hard line to cross.

Supreme Courtesies

My case was filed at the Supreme Court to be discussed in March of 2001. Once my lawyer found out which judge was appointed to the case he asked me to 'go find her' the way I had stalked Kyria Pallas at the Ministry of Education, to again 'put a face to the case.' The idea of knocking on the office door of a judge at the Supreme Court seemed extreme. I called friends for advice. "No, no, go," they urged. "It's always good to have a face to connect to an issue."

"You *must* go!" my lawyer jovially insisted. "You'll make a good impression because you're pretty *and* smart. Just like Kyria Lambri."

I quickly suggested the first point didn't relate to the second to which he laughed good-naturedly and put his arm around my shoulder. "Why are you intellectuals so sensitive? The gods gave you more than one gift, some people don't get any!" I smiled, thinking the gods were stubbornly irreverent of the gifts of mortals.

It was another world inside the Supreme Court. The Neoclassic building with marble steps took you through a Doric columned entranceway where the noise of the car horns and traffic on Panepistimiou Street mysteriously disappeared. The wide hallways of thick glass windows and doors led into spacious rooms as far from the smudged walls of the Ministry of Education as the heights of Olympus were from the Athens basin. The guard told me to check Kyria Lambri's office number on a board in the entranceway. My lawyer had left a rushed message on my cell phone to say she was in her office on Wednesdays. I let my class out early to make my way downtown, beginning to feel like I was finally lost; in and out of ministries, talking to this and that secretary, this and that lawyer, my daughter bewildered by entire afternoons and evenings spent on the phone, getting increasingly distraught as time went on. Nothing got accomplished unless I managed to see people, 'to put a face' to a name, as so many kept reminding me to do.

My lawyer was right about the attractive judge assigned to my case. Kyria Lambri was fashionably dressed in dark fishnet stockings and heels. I found her amid the marble spaciousness and generous high-ceilinged rooms. She stood up and smiled as I entered her office, then let me know the case would not be heard until October, even November, there had been a pile up of cases recently, some she said, had been pending for years. You were considered lucky if your case came up after a second or third *anavoli* (delay); this would be my second, some had up to six or seven.

110

Like Kyria Pallas in the Ministry of Education, Kyria Lambri tried to reassure me. "The problem is now with us," she said, adding that she had seen, "so many of these situations." They even used the same phrases. I noticed a tiny blue eye on a thin gold chain around her neck.

"It all ends up here; it will take time, but it will be dealt with." She quoted a line from Brecht about the danger of allowing corruption to poison you. She listened as I described how Scylla's position had been pre-decided.

"Don't you know Kyria Kalfopoulou? Greece eats her children."

"What a waste," I said.

A good friend of hers at the University of Chicago was having similar problems because she wasn't *dyki tous*, and added soberly, "You don't want to become like them." I asked if she knew the George Seferis poem, "The Cats of St. Nicholas." The Captain who rounds 'the Cape of Cats' tells a story of an island devastated by forty years without rain: *'people died and snakes were born./The cape had millions of snakes/thick as a man's legs/and full of poison.'* The monastery monks of St. Nicholas couldn't work or plough their fields because of the snakes. In the end they're saved by the cats. They fight the snakes all day long, until the sound of the monastery bell calls them to their evening feed only to go back into the night to fight again. Eventually the cats destroy the snakes, but the poem tells us: *'in the end they [the cats] disappeared;/they just couldn't take in that much poison[…]/Generations of poison, centuries of poison.'*

Kyria Lambri nods, pensive, no longer smiling, and eventually asks what American writers I've studied. I mention Gertrude Stein, Toni Morrison; the movie version of *Beloved* is playing in Athens. Her face lights up.

"I adored *Gone with the Wind*!"

I laugh, "You know Margaret Mitchell wrote the book in a couple of weeks."

"If you have talent," Kyria Lambri breathed, "it can't be stopped." We both smile as I put on my jacket, and Kyria Lambri walks me to the door. "Don't worry," she repeats again, her hand on my shoulder. "I know your case and now I know you; it's in our hands; you'll have to be patient." As I walk down the marble hallway and wave back to her, I see an attractive woman in fishnet stockings, a Supreme Court judge in love with *Gone with the Wind* standing in one of the most powerful structures of authority in the country, where meeting a Rhett Butler who might appreciate her was probably as unexpected as digging up a carrot in Tara.

"What did she say?" My lawyer wanted to know when I eventually track him down and manage to find him in his office.

"She said she would read the file over the summer. If it was as obvious as I described it the position would be annulled."

"I think she respects me."

"She's very attractive," I offered. We were getting off the subject as usual.

"Lambri has her years," he answered. I wondered why I wasn't more irritated with the comment. "You're looking tired," he added, focusing back on me, "You should take care of yourself."

Knots

I am finally Arachne and Echo and Pandora cursed by the gods and goddesses whose powers I stayed oblivious to: I am in a tightening knot, and in the center a scream unravels itself. I go to meetings, prepare lunches, and know I am managing the knot, solid as a fruit pit, now part of my everyday web. In the early morning wake-up to ready for teaching, in the coaxing morning murmurs to get my daughter up, there is something *xeno* in my knotted tapestries. Arachne's fallacy is Athena's phallus(cy), a curse that damned a simple girl's talent to eternal webs.

That summer of 2001, *PASOK*, the party in government, passed an amendment; cases involving academic issues were still being dealt with by the Supreme Court except for lectureship positions now transferred to the Court of Appeals. My lawyer was trying to appease me as I moaned over the phone in tears, "This means *more* delays!" There would be another lengthy wait. A knot snapped; why had I been traipsing all over the city spending hours and days tracking people down to become 'a face.' I was lost in the threaded labyrinths.

"What do you mean it doesn't amount to anything?" My lawyer was indignant. "We're going to fight this, even if we have to take it to Luxembourg."

I didn't say anything. I was in his office with his freshly painted walls, the earthquake cracks no longer visible.

I wanted to crawl back into my life somewhere before it began to unravel. The dutiful exorcisms my ex-mother-in-law so earnestly did for me had exhausted their store of good energy, like the cats of Saint Nicholas the amulets were overdosed on poison. "I was a simple girl who lived in the country, I wasn't beautiful or rich, but I had one great talent – I could spin and weave better than anyone in the world," confesses Elizabeth Spires' Arachne. And so I believed I would spin myself out of the mess, weaving truth out of raveled spools of subterfuge. I had ignored the goddesses; Circe, Athena. They knew this land, they ruled it. I had trespassed, 'put myself in the picture as a beautiful young maiden wearing a golden crown, as if I were a goddess, too.' Scylla and Circe were immor(t)al figures, and Athena, a punishing goddess.

"You are one," Arete was fond of saying, "and they are so many." Unnerved, I insisted nothing changed without opposition, but the immor(t)als had brocaded truths more complex than the vanity of a single spinster. What was it to belong, to be dependent on the private *tsifliki* of those who appoint themselves gods and goddesses of public Olympian domains?

A young Greek woman in the American studies section at Aristotle University was going to prepare her papers for a lectureship position; it had been over five years since my own attempt had been obstructed by Eurytion. This time the young woman was an insider but not associated with the right person. Eurytion was still around though more discreet about what decorated his office door. Unknown to this young woman who had done her endless course syllabi, her earnest course preps, her long hours of grading, her path was shadowed by a mentor in the department who had resisted the various baptisms into becoming *dyki tous*, who had not become part of the department's *tsifliki*.

"It's not about qualifications," I told the devastated young woman who didn't get the position. She had done the work, the conference run-around, and was bewildered by why she had not been chosen. According to the terms of *tsifliki* she was inappropriate; her doctoral advisor had a reputation for not being open to negotiating the rules. Major negotiations involved full year paid absences given to professors who were not up for them, hiring a linguist who was being paid for an academic year of work without being present, hiring a faculty member who had a PhD from Vienna but sold herself as being from the University of California, having someone with an actual PhD from the University of California being considered 'too qualified' for 'the needs of the department.'

"It's about who is willing to do the mopping up," someone else says from a department of another branch of the national university. "You can't even talk in terms of ethics; this is about a lack of foundation at a very fundamental level."

"Doesn't this sort of thing happen in the States too?" a Greek friend asks as I go on about the cesspools of corruption.

"People can be mean and competitive," Petros answers, "and they won't share work if they're defensive, but a department will hire the best person." He was still committed to trying to live in Greece, despite his tenure at a prestigious American university, and his various encounters with Chaos; he felt if things became unbearable he could always return. But for now he was enjoying the madness away from what he called 'an antiseptic life' in the States where 'the woman at Starbucks' precipitated a minor breakdown. "After three years of picking up the same vanilla latte to take to work every morning, she asks me, 'What can I get for you this morning?'"

I remembered the restaurant owner from Charlotte, NC and his failed efforts to create a co-op. In Greece all systems were suspect. An editorial in the *Athens News* issue devoted to education mentions my case with the University of Athens, "There is no oversight body to audit the standards in higher education in Greece. Greece's tertiary institutions are simply beyond censure, except by the courts." One of the professors at the University of Athens suggested the journalist 'must be' my ex-husband.

I read the text differently. Even if I could memorize where the commas went, and gauge which red lights to actually stop at, I was weaving an unfamiliar fabric. Athena was livid that a mere mortal boasted a talent superior to the immor(t)als of Olympus.

The Story of the Wall

> "Instead of searching for an ideal Greece, […] these writers *listened*
> to the Greeks themselves. Instead of just reading Greece, they were
> hearing the Greek people, and hearing some of their contradictions,
> their ferocious generosity, their loves and prejudices – their *reality*."
> David Mason, "Reading Greece" *The Hudson Review*

One of the first things I was told when I looked to buy a house on the
island of Patmos was, "Have a good relationship with your neighbor." The
saying in Greece warns, 'Better an enemy than a bad neighbor.' In being a part
of the village or family of *dopious* (natives), I was finally made one of theirs;
dyki tous. Unlike the Greek university system where I remained a foreigner,
I managed to buy an old stone house in the village of Hora on Patmos just as
it was about to be sold to a German man. I was not *xeni* (a foreigner) Stavros
the carpenter explained on the phone to Eleni who owned it, a relative of
one of the Greek coffee families. *Ine dyki mas* (she's ours) he kept repeating
into the phone. "Our island has been taken over by Italians and French, only
y *dyki mas* can't afford to buy the houses anymore." The gorgeous village
of Hora was slowly and steadily being bought up by wealthy families from
around the world with a predominant number of French and Italian home
owners; in the millennial year of 2000 more houses in Hora were owned by
foreigners than by Patmians who had gradually sold their family inheritances
at handsome prices that allowed many to live comfortably in more modest
homes with less costly upkeep.

Eleni of the coffee family was sympathetic. She had upscale property on
several islands already and Patmos took a nine hour boat ride to get to, plus
there was no airport. "It's going to cost you more than the Mourlos house,"
Stavros said to me. "But you'll get it with the key in the door; it won't need
much work."

It was late August. We were sitting in Stavros' open *avli* (front yard)
with Fotini his wife, and their various relatives and friends. I was bemoan-
ing the fact that I had been out of luck trying to find a house on the island.
The Mourlos place was my latest failed attempt. The first house I'd found, a
small three room place which you entered into by walking through the tiny
court yard of Agia Anna, a chapel, I believed had been destined for me. My
daughter's middle name is Anna, named after my ex-husband's fiancé killed
in a car accident. My ex-mother-in-law was thrilled that the house was next
to a chapel, she said the saint had lured us there. But after the first legal in-
vestigation of the home's title, my Athenian lawyer refused to sign.

Stavros insisted there was no problem. "Not in a million years," he said
with bravado confidence. "No one is going to bother you about the house once

you buy it." The woman who owned it had had a brain concussion and was being taken care of by her sister's family, the husband of whom was negotiating the sale. My Athenian lawyer was told (by Stavros) that the house was her dowry. Since the woman never married, then got sick, nothing was officially on paper except for a hand-written note from the nunnery of *Zoodohospigi* in Hora: the house had been given to the woman's family in 1912 in exchange for a plot of land where the nuns planted olive groves.

"You're going to buy a house without a proper title," Yanni, my Athenian lawyer, explained rationally. "Before you know it you'll be fixing that nice room for your daughter and a distant niece or nephew is going to be knocking on the door to tell you part of the house is theirs."

People from the village assured me my lawyer was exaggerating since people knew the house belonged to Chrisanthi; no one was ever going to question her ownership. Stavros became impatient, "If you don't buy it, it's going to be sold in the next minute to someone else. There aren't many houses for sale in Hora any more, at least not at the price you're looking for." He was right, every summer prices went up, and the actual properties for sale had lessened considerably.

My Athenian lawyer became equally impatient; he put his wife, a *symvouleographos* (notary) on the phone to tell me he and I would end up not speaking to one another if I continued to insist on the sale; I really did want that little house below the chapel of Agia Anna with its tiny window view of the port of Skala.

"My daughter's middle name is Anna, it was meant to be," I told Stavros who judiciously nodded, and warned me to 'keep on good terms' with my neighbors the nuns who took care of the small chapel. When I explored the house with its musty odors and nonexistent bathroom, I fantasized bougainvillea growing up the sides of the wall, a hidden stairwell to the terrace where friends and I would spend evenings of endless talk and ouzo.

Stavros warned me of an architect interested in the house; I'd have to make up my mind soon. Anxious, I tried to be diplomatic about the title, explaining to my parents in the States that 'things were done like that all the time on the islands'. They were their usual laconic selves, and asked what my lawyer had to say about it. Yanni had started to doubt what he initially considered my good sense.

"What do you mean I have to ask the neighbors to verify the ownership of the house?" He was incredulous that I, a person educated in the United States, was proving myself more gullible than an untraveled villager. Stavros meanwhile kept trying to convince us both that word of mouth was as binding as anything on paper.

"So what happens when all these people die?" Yanni the lawyer asked evenly.

116

"By then years will have passed and everyone will know the house is yours," Stavros answered.

"Ten years have to pass before it's legally yours if the title's a problem," Yanni went on.

None of Yanni's legal arguments seemed to budge Stavros' view of the situation.

"It's hers," I said. "The woman who's selling it, but she's bedridden." I was on the phone with my parents again. My mother, characteristically wary, wanted details. What was she bedridden with, "Can she talk?"

"She's had a concussion, but apparently she understands. She's able to nod, and could sign something if she had to." The silence on the other side of the phone line was palpable.

"Have you seen the woman?" I could hear her exhale.

In an attempt to compromise with Yanni's logical assessment of the situation I suggested we go to Rhodes and meet the woman for ourselves. "That doesn't change the fact that her brother-in-law has no legal right to be selling her property for her," he said with what I understood as determined patience.

"But Yanni, you know that that's how things are done here. It's only been in the last 30 or 40 years that anyone actually puts down official documentation of what belongs to whom." There was the story of the now priceless plot of land in the middle of Apollonia on the island of Sifnos that belonged to my ex mother-in-law's unmarried sister who had also been told it was her dowry, but when she never married and her life ended up in care for her brother's orphaned, retarded daughter, the surviving cousins never made any gesture to legalize the property for her. As far as I knew it still sat like a carpet of sacred green in the midst of encroaching white island houses.

Chrisanthi's brother-in-law eventually became rude; I called regularly to ask for increasing amounts of paperwork. First it was a faxed copy of the note from the nuns to verify that the property was in fact Chrisanthi's. Then it was a request for her signature, a signed agreement by Chrisanthi that the sale of the house was her decision. The brother-in-law finally said, "You either want it or you don't; and if you want the house we will set up a date here in Rhodes with two lawyers, yours and mine."

Yanni told me point blank he wasn't going to represent me. "I can't have this on my conscience; maybe the chances are one in a hundred or one in a thousand, but if that day comes, and you're taken to court because someone tells you Chrisanthi was in no mental position to sell or sign anything, I'm the one that's going to have to live with it."

Stavros the carpenter kept shaking his head. "Why do you get people from Athens involved in these things?" He repeated that there were more than enough lawyers on Patmos who could have taken care of the case in a matter of days, gone to Rhodes, seen the woman, had her sign, and I would have been finished with it. I was caught in the middle of my craving, a *lissa* for the house and cautious intuition, which finally got the better of my will to fight for it; the small cottage next to Agia Anna wasn't going to be mine nor was the view of the chapel and the port from those small cottage windows. I reluctantly succumbed to Yanni's sane judgment of my willingness to gamble the authority of word of mouth for the official terms of legal documentation.

Stavros had been right; the stone cottage blessed with Agia Anna's neighboring gaze was sold in less than two months. An Athenian hairdresser bought it and transformed it into the dream home I had fantasized would be mine. Stavros never did give Yanni much credit for his shrewd assessment of the risks involved with buying property from a woman who may or may not have had full command of her senses; he stayed puzzled by Yanni's uncompromising belief that the sale was in fact an illegal transaction without the title formally signed over to the brother-in-law. Stavros summed up the truth, or *ousia*, in a sentence. "Chrisanthi gave the house to her sister and brother-in-law for taking care of her so if they want to sell it it's their right to do so."

I was back to phone calls and knocking on doors at Easter. "Did anyone know of a home for sale?" I rented from Maria, where I had rented since coming to the island with my daughter six summers ago; she and I got on her moped and drove through the narrow winding *sokakia* (small village streets) of Hora to see what was available. We saw homes in all stages of ruin and soon-to-be ruin, crumbling balustrades, arched doorways, rusting embroideries of iron latticework, stone courtyards, and wooden *dhokaria* of ceilings under terraces that looked over the Aegean. The ruins cost as much to rebuild as to buy, and most of the ready, finished homes were beyond anything I could afford: gorgeous rooms that led into more rooms that led onto rooftops with breathtaking views of the 600 year old monastery and faraway glimpses of the islands of Leros, Samos and Ikaria. I was out of luck, the small cottage next to Agia Anna, I was convinced, had been my fated home and I had lost it.

A small black-clad woman coming out of one of the homes murmured *hronia polla*, (many years) to Maria as we passed on the moped; Maria stopped to greet Calypso, also wishing her *hronia polla* and asked if she knew of any homes for sale. Calypso's thin, frail body seemed beyond exhaustion, almost beyond being; she said her brother was selling his place. We went into a tall, two-storey house with high ceilings surrounded by ruins, with faint frescos still visible along the wood ceiling. Downstairs an open courtyard looked up to sky. I suddenly saw myself having breakfasts in the courtyard; the kitchen renovated, the bedrooms filled with canopied beds. I wanted to talk to Calypso's brother, who like Chrisanthis's brother-in-law lived on Rhodes. An amicable, almost jovial man wished me *hronia polla* over the phone as we quickly began to discuss the price of the house. It was more expensive than the Agia Anna place, but bigger. I could fit my brothers and their families for vacations I told my mother on the phone when I called her from Athens. She was reticent again; had I spoken to Yanni my lawyer? Not yet. Things had been strained between us after I'd agreed to back out of the Agia Anna place.

"You're stubborn aren't you?" Yanni said laconically but not unfriendly, when I called him.

"I really want a place on the island," I answered. "I hope this one has a proper title."

It did. Yanni called the office in Skala where property titles were filed. The house had been Mr. Mourlos' wife Katerina's dowry. Also bought from the nuns in *Zoodohospigi*, but this time money as opposed to olive groves had been exchanged, and more importantly, documented. Yanni was relieved. It was early April. I let my parents know I was going to go ahead with this sale. I would need to cash in a good chunk of my dollar savings bonds. My father said it would take about a month. Yanni wanted time to investigate the title in Athens where all property ownerships were listed. Mr. Mourlos enthusiastically told me I had his word that all was legal and clear, that I should come to Rhodes (the sooner the better) so we could meet each other and drink some of his homemade wine. I suggested we sign an initial contractual agreement so that no one else might manage to make him an offer. Mourlos was loudly verbose in his assurances that the house would go to no one else, that he had given me his word, and I should know better (all I needed to do was ask anyone in Hora about his name), than to question his word. Yanni was suspicious of Mr. Mourlos' zeal; I would have to pay property taxes before the sale could take place, which meant he had to investigate them. Then there would have to be a trip to the island of Leros where all property taxes for the Dodecanese were handled. He suggested Mr. Mourlos have a representative lawyer here in Athens; he didn't. But he had a niece who was a practicing lawyer in Athens, and he could give her the power of attorney. Meanwhile I suggested Mourlos come to Patmos so we could meet. *Yes, yes*, he wanted to meet me too he said, his sister Calypso had had good things to say, that I was a young American, but my father was Greek (this absolved me of unsurpassable foreignness). I wondered how Calypso had sifted through the myriad details of our conversation. She had told me of how she took care of several *yiayias*, bedridden in their large Hora homes, old, stone, spacious places worth millions. Calypso told me a *yiayia* who had recently died promised to leave the place to her for the years of her care only to find out the *yiayia* was in debt for millions of drachmas which cost the house. I would glimpse Calypso's tiny figure slipping in and out of large porticoes, she'd smile my way, tell me she was happy 'someone good' (*kalos anthropos*) was going to buy her brother's house.

Mr. Mourlos and I never managed to meet though we talked over twenty times on the phone, negotiating how the money would be paid. Did he want a holding fee, a down payment? "No, no," he gaffed into the phone, *"Tha ta vroume."* (We'll find the way.) *How?* I wondered. Yanni was uncomfortable again, his voice short when I called with the latest details of how we would get Mourlos' niece to sign.

"But he has to sign the tax clearance," he said. I would have to make a trip to the island to gather the papers from the *dimo*, the municipality, in one of the gorgeous stone buildings in the main square of Hora. The woman there, who I'd see feeding the cats every evening, smiled. "So Mourlos is selling too," she remarked. "At least you're not a foreigner," she said handing me the papers.

"Go ahead and sign for me," Mourlos said with is usual joviality. I wanted him to clarify this, "You mean sign *as you?* As if the signature is yours?"

"Yes, yes…put in a scratch there for a signature." Yanni had agreed to take the boat to Leros to put down the two million drachma property sales tax for me. I needed a lawyer to do the paperwork. He would take a boat to Leros, and then a cab to the tax office. I'd begged him to do it for me and willingly paid his travel expenses.

When his phone call came from Leros I was relieved.

"Done," he said, "but I almost missed the tax office. The cab driver took me to the wrong town on the island, we almost didn't make it before two when the offices close."

Mourlos had given his okay to have Yanni sign for him. It was late April. We'd arranged for the signing in June. Yanni had spoken to Mourlos' niece several times. We asked again (now that the sales taxes were paid, the titles cleared) if they wanted a down payment.

Mourlos' voice on the other end of the line was casual and confident. "No, no," he repeated. "I was again insulting his integrity by suggesting that his word wasn't binding." June was a little ways away, he said, but June it would be. We'd be in touch, he said. I told him I'd have the dollars ready and the money changed into drachmas. I'd gone to the island to find a builder to see what work could be done immediately; a toilet, first and most essential. A hose ran from the tap in an open space walled up temporarily to create a partition for the toilet and shower space. It was in the hallway just as you walked in. Somehow I would have to find a way to have the toilet put somewhere at the back of the house. Yanni called me after he got back from Leros, said I should talk to a man in Skala who had rented the house at one point.

"Why?" I asked, suspicious that Yanni had a way of finding the Achilles heel to any potential sale. I started to think Stavros was right. Athenians had another way of looking at things, while village life had its own codes.

"He said something about the back walls and a bad rain that sunk them, something about an uneven floor because of those rains and the ground the tiles lay over."

I paused, not sure if I even wanted to know. After all the house was standing, inhabited; how much could walls built almost a hundred years ago sink?

The man in Skala was the person who filed property titles. When I went to get the last papers before the signing in June, I asked him about the house.

"The floor isn't even," he said. "It sits on soil."

"Isn't that how most of the houses are built?" He agreed, but reminded me of the two ruins that flanked either side of the house, half walls and fallen rocks lodged against the sides, to say nothing of the mice. I found Calypso and begged her to open the house for me. She gave me a set of keys. "The new owner," she said happily. I wanted to sit in the courtyard, stare at the sky with its chandeliers of stars, but as soon as I turned the key in the lock I could hear a mad scurrying. Terrified, I went to the bar next door to ask a friend to come in with me. He wryly asked if I was sure I wanted a house I was afraid to walk into.

"There must be mice everywhere."

Calypso was nonplussed. "Of course, no one's living in the house, but they don't come out unless you turn off all the lights and no one moves." I had a terror that mice would crawl over my body at night. I would lie awake listening for sounds I wouldn't be able to identify. My friend who worked in the bar thought I was crazy to be buying a place next to a bar. "How are you going to sleep in the summer?" He wisely pointed out, "People around here leave in August when it gets loud."

No matter, I thought, I would grow plenty of jasmine and bougainvillea vines along the sides of the upper terrace. We would sit in the courtyard with our own music. It would even be convenient to have the bar nearby; we could always go get a drink and be with people if we felt like it.

By June the papers were signed and ready. Mourlos had given his niece the power of attorney. Yanni was in touch with her. I was in touch with Mourlos who had gone to Patmos with his wife to ready the house for me, or so he said. He would fix the toilet. "So it won't give you any problems in the summer," he offered. I was going to ask a plumber to look at it for me. I wanted to use it in August, when my daughter and I went to the island. "I'll also whitewash the place for you." I felt lucky, more than lucky to have come across someone who was genuinely concerned about helping with whatever he could do to make the transition easy.

"You know this is a lucky house," he said one of the last times we talked. "We got it from the nuns, it's blessed."

I more than agreed, believing this too was meant to be, perhaps more so than the Agia Anna house. After all it was bigger, more of us would fit more comfortably. Eventually it would be gorgeous.

A week before the signing I was on the phone with Stavros asking him if he could make me some cabinets for the kitchen so we could bring a box of plates and pans. He said he'd been by the house to measure; Calypso had let him in. He liked the high ceilings. He had also seen Mourlos who was living in the house, a last time, he said, with his wife; they talked of the fact that it was going to someone who would take care of it.

The day before the signing Yanni called me in Athens. Things with the University of Athens fiasco had left me drained and bitter, but the idea of finally having a house on Patmos became my oasis of happy possibility; I'd have a place on a jewel of an island in the Aegean. I fantasized that I would eventually move, look into job possibilities abroad once my daughter was older, and have Patmos to come back to.

"I don't know how to say this to you," Yanni began over the phone. I think I instinctively touched the evil eye around my neck.

"Mourlos is backing out."

"What?"

Yanni didn't even hear. "Did you say something?" Then he heard the tears, and continued, gently. "He said they can't sell the place. His wife fainted; he had his niece call us."

A rod of heat went through me. I knew I was shouting because Yanni's voice was telling me to take it easy.

"How can anyone decide to back out of a sale the last minute?"

"I know," Yanni continued. "Marina told the niece we would sue them. Mourlos said he would pay whatever damages needed to be paid."

"Damages?"

Yannis paused; I could tell he was upset. His voice wasn't its usual even keeled tone, but he was trying to be calm for me.

I had to ask again what the reasons were; I couldn't sort out the converging thoughts, the tax money that had been paid in Leros, Yanni's legal fees for doing so much for nothing, the fact that I had cashed a stack of dollars into drachmas for a sale that was now not going to happen. I was crying. Yanni was silent; he said he'd call me tomorrow once he knew more. I called Maria on Patmos, desperately yelling over the phone.

"I know, I know," she breathed. "My mother found him in Campos where he was with a friend and asked him what he thought he was doing." He said it was a health problem, his wife had a mild stroke brought on, apparently, by the realization that she was giving up the house.

"Didn't she realize she was giving up the house two months ago?"

"I told him he wasn't being correct, that you had gone to expenses; he said he was going to pay back whatever the expenses were."

Marina, Yanni's wife, quoted one million drachmas in damages to Mourlos' niece who listened without saying much. "You realize we could sue you."

The niece realized it but she was Mourlos' niece before she was anyone's lawyer. When I called, incensed, she coolly pointed out that these things happen; matters of health were matters of health. And I pointed out matters

122

of protocol were also legal matters in cases like this. She was silent again, suggested I talk to Mourlos. I could never find him on the phone. So I decided I'd call at all times and any time of day. By the fifth day I found him and let him know if he didn't pay for the damages I was going to sue him.

"I'm a man of my word," he insisted to the end, always adding, "Ask anyone in Rhodes or Patmos…"

"I don't have to ask anyone anything; you've proved how much a man of your word you are."

After several diatribes in which my voice got so shrill it died, he told me I had had no reason to pay for his water and electricity bills, added now to the quoted amount of Marina's million drachmas of damage.

"What do you mean I had no reason? I had to pay the bills to get the title clearance otherwise I wasn't going to be able to legally have the title transferred."

"I never told you to pay my bills," Mourlos repeated, the jovial casualness gone from his voice as I became desperate with helplessness.

"Doesn't it bother you that you gave your word to someone who might have cashed in her only savings to buy a house?"

"I know, I know…and if we ever sell it to anyone, it will be to you."

"What do you mean 'if you ever'! We agreed! I've *already paid* the taxes!"

"You'll get that money back," he said matter-of-factly.

"*When?* In a year? Once it's lost more of its value?"

Yes, it would take six months to a year Yanni calculated. I would have to take a trip to Leros myself. He would put in the legal papers notifying them of the cancellation so they could start processing it right away; there were more long distance phone calls. More expense to Yanni's lawyer bill. I was beside myself.

"I'm going to tell people in Hora you've been underhanded, *then ise endaxi* (you're not okay)," I said.

"You'll see," Mourlos insisted. "Once I can, I'll give you the money back."

"What does that mean? I've paid *your* bills! I'm going to have to pay a lawyer for preparing for a sale that didn't happen I've gone to expenses to…"

"Why are you so upset?" he interrupted. "Don't you understand this is a question of health? My wife had a stroke."

"She had a stroke because of the house?"

"Yes, yes…it broke her heart to have to let it go, and the agreement we had in Rhodes to sell our apartment fell through."

I suddenly saw the missing piece of the puzzle, and it was crooked.

"You were expecting a sale?"

"Of course; the man who was going to buy our apartment promised to give us one hundred and fifty million for the building, then he didn't."

Stella, Maria's mother, had said the price Mourlos was selling the house to me for was good, even reasonable, part of why I could afford it. It occurred to me Mourlos had had second thoughts.

"Don't I need a source of income?" He said finally, "Some security in my old age?"

I hung up on him. When I talked to Stella she said she had heard his children didn't like the fact that he had decided to sell the house.

"Why didn't he tell me before the last minute?"

"He probably was going to sell it until he came to Patmos and they stayed in the house again."

Mourlos never did pay anything in damages. I paid Yanni his lawyer fees which he, in compassion, kept modest. After several more phone calls over a period of several months Mourlos deposited the amount I had paid for his electric and water bills. As far as I knew Mourlos' wife was fine. People saw her walking around in Hora, greeting people, promising to invite them over for coffee once she gave the house a fresh whitewash. It took five months to get the tax money back from Leros where Greece's most notorious insane asylum had once been located. I thought of the pictures of the mad I once saw in a magazine exposé. The town was full of decrepit, sea-eaten villas with bolted doors whose rusting locks and chains had turned various combinations of greens and reds. Nail heads rusted into the wood. But the buildings looked magnificent despite their broken plaster walls and gaping ceilings. They had an air of abandoned grandeur.

It was summer when I took the Dolphin, a hydrofoil, from Patmos to Leros. I was anxious, not sure if I was going to have to go through another charade. Any time I had an encounter with Greek bureaucracy it was devastating. But here, outside of Athens, everyone seemed to treat time and work with a sense of interminable luck. If something didn't work out there would always be another chance. The person I spoke to about the notification of my annulled sale sat with a lit cigarette in an ashtray as I spoke; he wore a slightly outmoded suit, occasionally taking puffs from his cigarette. He nodded, but didn't recognize my name or find it in any of the paper-clipped stacks of pages he had piled in front of him. I became visibly anxious. "Your office sent me a notice." I showed him a paper. He nodded.

"Maybe it's on the computer," he said as an afterthought.

"Maybe," I said, irritated.

My name was filed on the computer, and yes, I was to be given the two million drachmas on property taxes since the sale didn't take place. The teller took his time counting out the bills and gave them to me, almost reluctantly.

I was still on Leros when Stavros called to say the place we had been discussing the evening before was going to be bought by a German man.

124

"So it's gone?" I was watching the grey-blue thrash of sea against the coastline, waiting for the hydrofoil to arrive and take me back to Skala.

"We'll see. I'm going to call Eleni," he said. He kept the keys to the house. He would take me over to see it in the evening when I got back. I'd learned not to believe that things work out as simply as I could hope they would; there had been the national university fiascos, the court case with the taxi driver, Mr. Mourlos and his well-reputed word that had me on Leros collecting money I shouldn't have paid in the first place. In all the accumulated frustrations I wondered if I hadn't lost some essential peace of mind forever.

Back on Patmos, Stavros walked me over to the house whose view spanned the Aegean for as far as the eye could see. The years of layered whitewash had cracked in places, exposing stone, but the building was intact and furnished with its owner's things. Two lemon trees Stavros called his 'girls' took up a small plot of garden; *y kores mou* he said each time he went over to the house to water them, were *polyhgenes* (many generations); trees that produced more than one crop a year. I was lucky, Stavros pointed out, this house had a tiny garden, a bougainvillea whose red wildfire spread over rusting pipes that went for a trellis, and a jasmine bush that perfumed through the open kitchen window into the house. Loose wires hung from the terrace over to the outhouse (bathrooms were outside unless homeowners built modern versions inside). Most spectacular of all was the view that spanned over an endless sapphire where one could see in the distance, on a clear day, the vague outlines of the Turkish coast, the island of Lipsi and, somewhere in between, the small cluster of Fourni islets. It left me breathless and with a strange panic to want something so completely: like new love I felt a sudden *lissa* of yearning to possess what fell short of possession. I could not believe I had come upon so perfect an expression of my ideal of Greece. I was trying not to fall in love with the lemons, the sea, the rampant bougainvillea, the intoxication of jasmine, the high wood beams of a ceiling whose central spine was, Stavros proudly told me, the mast of a ship.

Stavros bargained down the price of the house for me; the cost was significantly higher than the Agia Anna house, and higher than the Mourlos house; from 20 million drachmas, I was now being asked to buy a house at 50 million drachma (about 80 thousand dollars). "But you've got the key in the door," Stavros would repeat. "You really don't have to do any work on the place." Unlike the Mourlos house, the bathroom was large, and functioning, though outside. The house had two floors, with two bedrooms, and two large sized central rooms, up and down, with a good-sized kitchen downstairs that looked out onto the lemon trees and bougainvillea.

Eleni from the coffee family was gracious and generous. She agreed to sell the house to me for significantly less money than what she would have received from the interested German. She told Stavros, to save face she would tell the German man she had decided to give the house to someone in her family. She didn't want gossip to sully her name. The German man was puzzled and wondered why she had so suddenly changed her decision since the last he talked with her she was enthusiastic about the sale. He offered her more money. Stavros was absolute; Eleni was exceptional, a person with *philotimo* (respect of friendship, or goodwill). She had agreed to forsake the extra profit so the house could go to someone who was at least partly Greek.

On the phone to her I said, "I love it, I really love it; it reminds me of my grandparents' home where I spent my childhood summers."

She admitted she had fallen in love with the house for the same reasons, had compared it to houses of the 1950s and 60s in Athens with their plots of garden and fruit trees now fast relegated to memory as these last oases of land were turned into four and five storey apartment buildings. We agreed on the price and said we would meet one another in Athens.

"You might even get some furniture out of the deal," Stavros offered. I nodded, numb with the possibility that this time I might actually, finally, buy the house, roomier and more beautiful than I had dreamed possible. Eleni had beds in the two bedrooms and an old glass cabinet in the kitchen. The kitchen needed work; the walls were painted a royal blue that also coated the outside bathroom which I assumed was meant to match the sea.

When we finally met, Eleni said she was going to take everything out of the house.

"Even the beds?" I'd hoped she would leave a few things so I could make do with what was there for a year or two.

Stavros had piled it all into a van at the port in Skala to go to the island of Syros where Eleni was renovating an old villa built by Ottoman Turks. She told me it was lucky she had put the house on Patmos in her name, "The only house I did that with." So the transfer of titles would be relatively simple. Everything else she had left to her daughters. The Greek stock market had crashed infamously. Infamously inflated (some of the shrewder investors had made quick fortunes), it suddenly deflated, leaving a small majority impoverished. A political *kobina* (scandal) Stavros had said, disgusted, as one of the few who had resisted putting his money into the gamble. Even I'd succumbed to my ex-husband's urging not to be 'so conservative.' I still think of the 4 million drachmas I lost. It was especially missed when I took out a bank loan to add an inside bathroom.

"What about that wall," I asked Stavros, the second time I went to the house. It was the only disadvantage. On the terrace, just outside the main entrance, next to the jasmine's spilling vines and above the bougainvillea's wildfire, the neighbor's wall, just to the left, was oddly low. To the right, was the Aegean's blue expanse, but at our backs were the neighbors, an Italian couple, separated from us by a strikingly low wall.

"This used to be one house," Stavros explained. "Farmakaki bought it when he came back from America, and lived here till he died. He split it so his two daughters had dowries. Each daughter got half. That half was sold eleven years ago to an Italian, but this one was sold to Eleni five years ago because Dina built a house down in Sapsila near the water."

I looked over to the wall. Our terrace floor was, I realized, a good deal lower than the neighbor's terrace which made the partition that much lower from his side. I also noticed he (or she) had seat pillows along the wall's flat top surface. They had been using it as seating to enjoy the view.

"What can we do to make it more of a separation?"

Stavros was understated. "We'll do something, but slowly. You don't want to create a problem."

"It's low," I said, envisioning a nighttime walk from the upstairs bedroom out the terrace, down the stone steps, to the bathroom, naked. "Why not put up a sort of latticework, I could have a pot of bougainvillea growing from my side that would eventually spread and cover it.

Stavros nodded, "Eleni should have done something about this a long time ago. But she didn't really care because she wasn't here very often, and then she only visited for a few days."

The more I thought about the wall, the more it bothered me. Whether we would have dinners on the terrace, or decide to sunbathe, or decide to walk out half naked or totally naked, I didn't think I should be thinking about the neighbor's view of it all. Besides, from what I saw when I put a small ladder up against the wall to see where the terrace was, anyone from their side could feasibly, and without much difficulty, jump into our terrace.

The wall was called a *mesotihia*, literally a 'middle wall'. An equal half belonged to each side, and we shared it. When I mentioned the fact of the wall to Eleni, she said she'd thought to do something about it, but never did; she hadn't wanted to upset the neighbors since they were 'good people.' Their goodness was gauged in the generous and frequent offerings of Italian meals of pasta and parmesan, passed over the wall, only to be returned filled with fruit, or lemons from the two *polyghenes* lemon trees. Apparently Kyrie Farmakaki had kept the wall in its original state because his one daughter still lived in the house, and he could more easily call over to her, and she, in turn, could comfortably lean over to chat or share the day's cooking. When it was sold, time got the better of him and he felt 'badly' about doing anything to adjust the height since the neighbors were now 'used to the view.' The latticework Stavros and I were contemplating would still allow for the view, but it would be less direct, or in Stavros' words, 'clean'; the Italian neighbors would have to stand up, (as opposed to sitting), to have their full view. I never realized how clean (*katharo*) their view had been until my Italian neighbor invited me over for wine and parmesan when we found ourselves at an awkward impasse.

"Make sure the latticework is on my side of the wall," I warned Stavros, who measured a height of approximately half a meter from the brick surface of its flat ledge; this would also make it impossible to use the wall for seating. I thought this was reasonable. I couldn't imagine anyone being happy about strangers dangling their legs over someone's private property to enjoy the view.

It was November 2000 when Eleni signed over the property to me, and I paid it off with my dollar savings now converted into drachmas. My father was unable to prevent an edge of sarcasm in his tone when he let me know he considered the sale a *vitsio* (fetish). Little did anyone know or foresee that a year later the dollar and the American economy, would take a dive and that the Farmakaki house was probably my best, and last, chance at a house in Hora. Eleni's lawyer said as much. "This was meant to go back to a Greek-American," he said, reassuring Yanni, my lawyer, that this was a worthwhile investment. Even Yanni was finally convinced I had done the right thing.

"From the plans, it looks like you're getting something decent," he approved. "You have a small garden, a large-sized bathroom, and you say the view's spectacular."

I promised Yanni I would invite him and his family for a visit. "Okay, okay," he said dismissively. "There's time for all of that, let's just make sure everything here is resolved." He had spoken to Stavros who, two houses later, had finally developed an amicable relationship with Yanni. He chided him about what he was going to find wrong this time, and when I mentioned the wall, Yanni asked Stavros about it; he dismissed it as 'part of the two houses.'

"Is it clear that the houses are separated?" Yanni wanted to know.

"Yes, yes," Stavros insisted, now enjoying Yanni's suspicion. It seemed almost too good to believe this sale was going to happen without a hitch.

I had wanted to go into Mr. Mourlos's house (his door was occasionally open), and publicly announce that the man owed me money. Yanni had sent a court appellation for damages, but the interstices of Greek bureaucracy again complicated things. If Yanni had been a lawyer on Rhodes, with legal jurisdiction there, Mourlos would have been held accountable. He was still accountable, but if I wanted to take him to court it would mean finding and hiring someone I didn't know from Rhodes and fight the likelihood that Mourlos would attempt to pay him off rather than pay me. To this day I've not met the man, though I wonder when our paths will inevitably cross in one of Hora's *sokakia* (narrow streets) and I'll finally get the chance to tell him how 'reputable' he proved to be.

Property taxes had to be paid again, and someone had to go to Leros. I was too embarrassed to even suggest that Yanni go. When I talked it over with Maria who I was still renting from in the summers, she suggested Stavros; she said he did it regularly for others, that it was nothing for him to take a morning to go to Leros, plus he knew the people in the tax office if I needed any negotiation of the objective property value. This was a relatively new installation to property sales; the *andikimeniki axia* (objective property value) was something gauged by the property's size and location in zones: zone A were houses within close proximity to the Monastery in Hora; zone B was somewhat further away; zone C meant the outskirts of Hora. I was worried about the tax, hoping to keep it down to a required minimum. Yanni estimated that I would have to pay some three million drachmas on the fifty million which the house cost. No one buying ever officially declared the actual sale price. The adage was 'better to give the money to the person selling than the government.'

Stavros went to Leros armed to negotiate with the promise that, depending on how low he managed to bargain the tax, he would get an analogous percentage.

He called that afternoon saying, "It's over," like a surgeon satisfied with the results of a tricky operation. "I couldn't get them to go any lower than a million and a half."

"A million and a half," I repeated, not sure I heard correctly.

"Yes," he assured me, and then went into details. "I told them you were one of us, a public servant working with a salary. I told them you were Greek, and only we Greeks weren't able to afford to buy property anymore. I told them in the end we're going to be taken over by foreigners, the way we were taken over in the war, the way we've been taken over by people who dictate our governments…"

"Stavros," I interrupted, "is the sum legally binding?"

"Of course! It's all on paper now, it's finished."

"How did they come to agree to such a low sum?"

"Eh," he breathed, "I told them the house was old and needed repairs, and that it wasn't in zone B, but zone C…"

"Is it in zone C?"

"It's on the border."

"How much on the border?" I was starting to have visions of a tax check that would suddenly decide I had not properly declared the location.

"That area where you are is just above the road, that's zone C. You're just a little higher than the road." I was quiet, thinking.

"I did the best I could," he continued. "I couldn't get it any lower than that."

"No, of course not," I said, confused but relieved despite the fact that I wasn't sure if it was an entirely good thing that Stavros had managed to lower the tax so much.

I called Yanni at his office to tell him the tax money had been paid so we could go ahead with the sale. I told him the amount.

"That's impossible…that's too low."

"Well, its done now," I said, uncomfortable.

"That's impossible," he repeated. "If anyone checks on the property it will be obvious that that's not an amount that represents its objective value."

I could tell he was irritated I'd allowed Stavros to get involved in the first place. Yanni had treated Stavros' opinions with humor as long as they didn't conflict with his view of the legalities.

"So what do you want to do?" I asked carefully.

"I'll call the tax office in Leros tomorrow and explain there's been a mistake."

"You can't do that," I said, quicker than I realized. Yanni didn't answer; he was waiting to hear what I was going to say. I was surprised by how definite I sounded.

"It's just going to cause a problem."

"What if someone comes to check the property?" Yanni asked without hostility.

"If they come it won't be right away, and when they come, which is usually every ten years Stavros says, I'll have kept all the receipts of the work I'll have done on the house that it will be obvious I had work done."

Yanni didn't answer me right away. I listened to his breathing, guessing that he was probably getting tired of the fact that nothing seemed to work straight-forwardly in any of my efforts to buy a house on the island.

"Okay" he finally said. "If you don't want me to call, I won't, but it's a risk and I don't feel comfortable about it."

It suddenly felt funny to me that I, the foreigner, was coaxing Yanni, the Greek, to accept what I had learned to understand as a reality of Greek bureaucracy, that you rarely took anything at face value, let alone tell 'the plain truth' since the truth I repeatedly learned was rarely plain. I hinted as much to Stavros, that Yanni questioned the low tax payment and that he wondered if he shouldn't call the tax people.

"No!" he yelled into the phone. "Call the tax people? I've taken care of it. If he calls them they'll think I was lying!" He added, *afto ine koroidia* (a sense of honor violated).

Yanni reluctantly went with my request to let sleeping dogs lie (and lie). The tax people in that small Leros office had recognized my name when Stavros went over to negotiate the tax value of the house; "Didn't she just get some money from us?" Someone had asked him. He relayed the saga with the Mourlos house, embellishing, I imagine, where he could. He told me over the phone he'd repeated the fact that *Ine dyki mas* (she's one of ours); that it was a shame 'our own' couldn't afford to buy land when *y xeni* (the foreigners) were buying up the country.

I had not experienced this sense of belonging, of actually being treated as one of the *dopious* (natives) until I was challenged for the fact of it.

130

"The Italian wants to talk to you," Stavros said, describing my neighbor's visit to his carpentry shop with his wife.

"Did you give them my number?"

"Yes, I gave them your number and told them you were a teacher." Stavros and I had agreed on the latticework; its height and design of wood cross-sections. It would be nailed into the wall on my side of the *mesotihia* (middle wall).

I never got a phone call from my Italian neighbors, but the latticework, a pretty cross-section of slats painted white to blend in with the wall, had been unscrewed from the wall Stavros had drilled it into, and thrown into my terrace. Stavros called me in Athens, incensed. "Let me take care of this!"

I was not sure I'd understood what happened. "Who threw and removed it?"

"They did! y *xeni!* (the foreigners)" His voice rose with each sentence. I was having difficulty imagining that someone would actually take something apart on someone else's property.

"I'm going to put up a brick wall and see how they'll like that! If they didn't like something tasteful and modest, now they'll have cement to stare at."

"Do they have a phone number?" Stavros had a number they had given him. They had expected me, I now realized, to call. But then if there was any question about our middle wall, or their view, they were the ones who should have contacted me.

"I'm going to go ahead and put up the bricks," Stavros repeated, ignoring my question.

"Don't do anything extreme," I said, anxious and upset.

In a day Stavros raised a brick wall on my side of the terrace at the height of what had been the latticework, about a half meter from the existing top of our middle wall. It created a back to the flat surface of the middle wall which was now on the neighbor's side of the terrace. That afternoon the police turned up at Stavros' house in Hora.

The next phone call was from the police station. "Are you the home owner of a house in Hora, Patmos?"

"Yes," I was trying not to panic.

"You've been sued by Mr. Tavianni for building without legal jurisdiction to do so."

"Did I need jurisdiction for that?" I asked, wishing I hadn't let Stavros take things into his own hands.

"Yes. Any building in Hora needs to be approved by the Archaeological authorities on Syros."

It was news to me, as much as the fact that Stavros had to get clearance from the authorities to do anything.

"You can't move a brick in Hora without permission," Maria told me. I called her right away. Stavros was her uncle.

Within a week I received an official notice from the police authorities in Skala notifying me that I had been sued by my neighbor for the wall Stavros put up which I had still not seen.

Fotini, Stavros' wife, was beside herself. "When I saw the police come for Stavros I couldn't believe what was happening…" I was on the phone to her because I couldn't find Stavros. "Why does he get involved?" she went on. "Why doesn't he mind his own business!"

The police held him for a few hours at the station in Skala; one of the officers was Maria's husband's brother-in-law. They wanted some clarification about what had happened, who had authorized the wall and why.

A month later I was there, explaining. The wall, a quick job of bricks piled up in single columns with cement slapped haphazardly between them looked like it had been built in minutes. It was ugly and now blocked my neighbor Mr. Tavianni's view. This became the reason for my first meeting with him and his wife. I knocked on his door with the police notice in hand. Mr. Tavianni and his wife had bought the house behind mine, eleven years ago; they had no children. He had a friend of his, who spoke good English, call me in Athens to say they came twice a year to Patmos and never stayed longer than a few weeks at a time, so couldn't I be more considerate about these short visits? I answered that we could have discussed it all if Mr. Tavianni hadn't sued me with a police summons.

"But you put up that partition without asking them," the friend said politely.

"The partition was on my property," I answered. "And he removed it which is considered damaging my property."

"He didn't do it," the voice on the other end informed me. "It was his gardener, the man who looks after their house when they're in Italy."

"I doubt the gardener would have done anything without Mr. Tavianni's permission," I added.

Silence again. "Well Mr. Tavianni would like to have a discussion with you when you come to Patmos."

I knocked on the Taviannis' door in mid June and a tall, slim man in his early fifties opened it with a short nod when I introduced myself. He didn't speak much English so we communicated in fragments of French. He invited me up to his terrace behind the infamous wall. I was surprised by how much wider the view of the horizon was from that more elevated height.

He offered me a glass of wine. His wife, a soft-spoken woman who was hard to read, sat down with us when Mr. Tavianni let me know he was a lawyer, adding that they lived in a town outside of Venice.

I told him my mother's family was also Italian but from Calabria; he said the south was very different from the north, almost another country.

"So what are we going to do about this?" I asked. The Taviannis' friend who had called me in Athens and spoke English joined us on the terrace.

"Our friends here, Mr. and Mrs. Tavianni, don't want to ruin a relationship with you as their neighbor," he said, in clear though awkward English.

I nodded, "I don't want to begin badly either," I said. "But a police summons isn't exactly a friendly beginning." I tried to sound lighter than I felt. Pavlo Tavianni gave a thin smile and pointed to the wall with a flamboyant expression of hurt.

"But you built this terrible thing," his friend immediately translated for him.

"It wasn't there in the beginning; there was a nice piece of latticework which was removed from my side of the wall and thrown into my property." I could feel my tone rising. Pavlo Taviannis' wife left and came back with more wine; I was grateful for another glass. The conversation wasn't going to be easy.

Pavlo nodded. I suspected he probably understood more English than he let on; he said something in Italian to his friend, who continued for him.

"It's the people taking care of your houses who got into an argument: your carpenter and Pavlo's gardener." I didn't bother to say I doubted the man would have done anything without the go-ahead from the Taviannis. Then again Stavros had taken it upon himself to protect my property since, as he put it, "You don't have any man in your life to watch out for you." On the other hand the legal repercussions of his good-intentioned wall had me sitting on the Tavianni terrace awkwardly negotiating how to come to some agreement.

"Anyone would want more of a wall," I said. "The bathroom's outside. I have a young daughter. What if we want to sunbathe without clothes?" He smiled, but only vaguely. His translator friend laughed out loud.

"The Taviannis are hardly here," he said warmly. "It's just for June, when you say you don't come, and part of August."

"I'm here in August," I said. "Anyway, whoever uses our house won't feel comfortable with neighbors who can practically jump into it."

"But that's how the houses are here," Pavlo said in French, obviously understanding what I had said. "You bought it like this. It's an old house. It's in a village. Village houses are connected so people can see into each other's terraces and gardens."

I agreed to an extent, saying I understood our houses were once one home and that the wall had not been there forever. Pavlo's wife offered that they'd had excellent relations with Eleni from the coffee family who lived there before me.

"Yes, I understand she wasn't at the house very often," I said, trying not to sound sarcastic. They wanted to know what I was going to do about the wall. I said I needed to have more of a partition than what existed. We looked at the wall. Pavlo had some Polaroid shots lying on the table. His wife smiled when she saw me notice them. I picked them up, "What are you going to do with these?" I asked.

Pavlo looked at me, saying in French that he wanted to have a record.

"For court," I said quickly. At that point Pavlo's wife laughed, nodding. She seemed to appreciate my forthrightness, while her husband was more concerned about how we were going to negotiate the wall's height. I clarified that his view wasn't gone; it had been spectacular indeed, and still was, but with Stavros' wall you had to stand to see what was once visible from a sitting position. We sat next to the wall and decided on a height somewhere between the initial one and what existed now. He said he would draw up a sketch, and that we should make it flat again, the way it had been. The Italian wine and parmesan had done their job. I was in a better mood, and left agreeing to sign something with a sketch that I found reasonable. Almost as an afterthought, I said, "And what are you going to do about this legal summons? You need to withdraw this if I'm going to sign anything."

His friend the translator said he'd go with me to the lawyer, someone local who had his office in the port. We arranged to do that the next day. After the meeting I visited Stavros and Fotini to let them know what had happened.

Stavros wasn't in his house and his carpentry shop was closed. He usually went to feed his chickens before nightfall. It was already dark and Fotini was in their kitchen, her two hands out, her wrists wound with wool strands her mother was wrapping around a growing ball she kept turning between her palms. She smiled when I walked in. "You had some bad luck," she said, "but you got the best house in the end." She nodded approvingly, a handsome woman in her eighties who looked at least ten years younger. "It's one of the nicest houses in that area. And the road is close by too, you'll be able to move your furniture in without any problem." I agreed, and said if it wasn't for Stavros I would still be looking. I wanted to talk to him. Fotini said, "He's probably with the chickens still."

I saw Stavros' coffee flask against a boulder in the large patch of land where he had his chicken coups, and kept rabbits and a goat, and behind them, a large warehouse that had piled wood planks for his various jobs. The mountain of *Prophitis Ilias* (Prophet Elias) was still visible but the stars were coming out. "Did you take care of my *kores?*" He asked when he saw me.

"The lemon trees?"

"Take good care of them, they need lots of water." *Prophitis Ilias* was now stenciled against the dusk sky. The sea gave off a metal shine under the beginning moon. "I've been working all day," he said, pointing to the coffee flask on the boulder. "That's all I've had. Coffee."

"How do you do it?" I ask him. Despite his halo of white hair, Stavros looked a lot younger than his fifty some years, part of it because of his trim figure. I'd never seen Stavros in anything but jeans except at Easter when he turned up in church with a jacket and ironed pants.

"This place is what keeps me going," he answers. "I like it here, I see all this and I keep going. While I still have my strength I want to keep working."

Below the piece of land with his assortment of animals and vegetables and the warehouse of wood planks, was a small chapel.

"It's mine," he says, "my saint. It was an old Turkish *domna*." But I see a cross. "It was always a church, but the Turks used it for storage. It's the chapel of Paleos," Stavros' last name. "I take care of it," he adds. I sat on one of the boulders as he gathered up his things, and told him about what happened with the Italian; "*o Italos*," Stavros keeps calling him, no matter how many times I call him Mr. Tavianni.

"Don't sign anything," he says, serious.

I explain I want to try to keep the peace. There was my daughter; there was the fact that I would be seeing this man and his wife for a possible lifetime. Stavros doesn't say much, he says I should wait for the report from the "Archeologists," the group who visit from Syros to decide on the legitimacy of any changes made on houses in Hora; everything had to be within the prescribed aesthetic of the architecture native to the village. Any building in Hora was *diatiriteo*; a site of historical preservation. Now that I had been given the summons, I had to get an official permit from the Archeologists to have the wall heightened. I was going to find my friend the architect in Skala who had helped me out with the plans of the Mourlos house, and then in *philotimo* (goodwill) had refused any money when he found out the sale had fallen through. Now I needed him to come to the house and make a sketch for the wall so it could be formally authorized.

"Your property is your property," Stavros repeated. "I wouldn't let any foreigner dictate what I did in my own home."

I agree, but say again that I think it's important to keep on good relations with the neighbors, though I wasn't going to leave things as they were, and tell him of the agreement on a half-way measure of height.

"Who's to say that in another year he isn't going to ask you to sign something else!" Stavros was irritated. "I don't trust him."

During the night I thought of the fact that the Taviannis wanted me to sign a paper, the idea seemed less and less comfortable. We had agreed on the height of the wall, so why did he want me to sign anything. When I went to Kosta, my architect friend in Skala, he agreed that Tavianni's insistence that I sign was asking too much since I'd agreed on lowering the wall.

"After all," he says, "you're willing to do something about it now, but if the day comes when your neighbor or one of their friends ends up on your side of the terrace that'll mean you need to make it higher."

I laughed, but Kosta didn't. Soula, his wife, who worked with him added, "You're showing him your good will by agreeing to put up a partition that's lower than what you wanted, he should appreciate that."

"You're going to sign over rights to your property to someone who served you with a summons!" Stavros was angrier the next day.

As it got closer to meeting the Taviannis to sign the agreement they were having translated into Greek, I became more and more uncomfortable with the idea. I decided if I signed anything I would have Yanni see the paper first. Small things started to bother me: the Taviannis hadn't mentioned anything about the cost of what I called 'our mutual wall', the ugly brick thing had to come down so the other wall that we agreed upon could be built. When I went with Pavlo to the local lawyer, we were told he couldn't annul the summons until the actual court day, since it had been issued from the police. They had come to the house to see the wall because it had been built without official, legal permission. Once the latticework had been removed, without permission, and once the wall had gone up, also without permission, the Taviannis had immediately involved the police without so much as a phone call. So when I saw Pavlo and his wife in Skala and they told me they had the paper ready for my signature, I said I wanted to talk more about it. Pavlo's face hardened, his wife looked at me without any expression. He asked me in French what I meant.

"I want to discuss this more because now I have to get official permission for the wall. I'm going to have to have an architect draw up the measurements and send that to Syros for the Archeologists to examine."

He listened, nodded, said he didn't understand why this would prevent me from signing our agreement. I wanted to say his chucking of the lattice-work had cost me, just to that point, a wooden partition, a brick wall, an architect, and, eventually, a lawyer, and he hadn't said a word about sharing any of the expense. His wife started to say something in Italian, he nodded, said something back. I stood there in the side street of people roaming with groceries, tearing at the heels of bread loaves, eating white pastries, the flakes and crumbs clinging to their fingers and lips. I felt a craving for something. I was also perspiring. Mr. Tavianni nodded stiffly to me, and asked me when I wanted to meet to discuss the matter further because he wanted to get in touch with his translator friend. We agreed to meet the next evening.

"Okay, so you're being nice to him," Aleko, Maria's husband, said as we sat that afternoon after lunch in Maria's living room. "But don't be caught *koroido*; did he even apologize for throwing your lattice work over into your terrace?"

I wasn't saying much, the situation bothered me more every time I thought about it. "He sees you're a woman alone and he's taking advantage of you." Maria nodded. I was staying with them for these few days I was on the island to see what I could do about the summons. I could not have fixed the house, found the workers, let alone found the house, if it wasn't for Maria and Aleko, Stavros, and Stella, Maria's mother and Stavros' sister-in-law, who always kept a bed made for me when I visited in the winter.

More than six years ago I turned up in Hora with my five year old daughter to rent a room for the month of August. Maria and Aleko were just married, and Stella was mourning the recent death of her only son who at twenty killed himself on a motorcycle that crashed into one of the low walls outside of Skala. I would sit with her over coffee, and she would ask why I wasn't married. I would tell her my ex-husband and I had realized we wanted different things; she would shake her head and urge me to 'fix my life.' Maria had told me her mother and father had been estranged, he womanized, and after her brother's death, he'd come back to the house only to disappear again, then he moved in with an Albanian woman in Skala.

"A priest told me we both wear our black clothes," Stella said. "But underneath," and she turned back the cuff of her sleeve, "is flesh that lives whether we want it to or not." She urged me to 'live everyday' completely, without regret, 'because a day never comes back.'

Six years later Stella still wore her black though sometimes she allowed herself a beige shirt or brown sweater under the heavier black jacket or sweater; I noticed she now wore scarves around her neck which weren't always solid colors, there were black polka dots or navy stripes. She was calmer, had a pragmatism I hadn't recognized before. She cleaned houses in Hora, went to Athens once every two months to do her shopping and have doctors' appointments to change her medication so she could sleep.

"Listen to Alekos," Stella added. "If the Italian wants you to keep the wall lower than you want it, he also has to compromise. If you sign something you don't know what he'll do with that tomorrow."

The next evening on the Tavianni terrace the atmosphere was a lot tenser than it had been the first evening we met. Pavlo's translator friend smiled politely but I could tell he had been rehearsed in what to say. I was nervous and determined. Pavolo's wife didn't say much of anything to me expect to ask if I would like a glass of wine.

I told the translator friend that I was willing to do what we had agreed on except sign any paper. I said signatures were binding and I couldn't do it without the presence of my lawyer. He immediately asked me why I wouldn't sign if I was agreeing to the terms of the wall. I said I was giving him my word, that that should be enough. I had no indication that he wouldn't use my signature against me at any point; he'd already given me a police summons.

"But you put up a partition without asking us," Pavlo says in French.

"Yes," I say, showing my irritation. "On my side of the wall. Anyone who bought this house would have done the same thing. I could very well decide to get permission to extend the house and you would be looking at a roof instead of the sea." At that point Pavlo's wife let out an "Oh," and shook her head, agreeing that that would be the worst of all scenarios. I told them I was going to have to get permission for anything I did, including the wall we had agreed on, and that I couldn't do it until the Archeologist group came from Syros (which was once or twice a year).

Pavlo's wife said something in Italian again. The translator friend added, "What if the Archeologists allow you to build a much higher wall."

"I've given you my word," I said. Pavlo's face was becoming gradually expressionless. I wanted to lighten up the situation. "Look my word means something. I'm not a lawyer. I guess Pavlo wants signatures on everything since he's a lawyer, but he'll have to trust me."

The translator friend seemed to appreciate this, and conveyed what I said with a smile. Pavlo's face vaguely softened. "I've always loved Italian poetry," I go on, "especially Pavese. Do you know Cesare Pavese's work?"

Pavlo now seemed genuinely caught off guard. "Pavese? Yes," he says, looking at me with some uncertainty.

"He's a great poet," I say. "He loved people tied to the land."

Pavlo asks me, through his translator friend, when I am going to make the changes on the wall. I say I would be willing to do them the next day, but now I can't legally do anything until the architect draws up the plan and submits it to the official people on Syros. He wanted to find some way we could agree to a signature; he said he may not be here when the people from Syros arrive. I tell him again I will give him my word. He says bluntly that that's not good enough. I then start to say the things I hadn't mentioned: that he had in fact begun the antagonism, that he was insisting I make changes based solely on his interests, that he was not offering to share any of the expenses. The translator friend may or may not have conveyed the extent of what I said, but I found myself suddenly in tears saying goodnight.

"Do you know he told me he had money," Stavros tells me in his workshop when I go to see him the next day.

"You never told me that," I say. He nods, cutting a plank of wood for a door he is making.

"Don't be so ready to trust him," he goes on. Stavros was proved right, but it took several weeks for me to realize Pavlo wasn't going to accept the fact that I refused to sign his paper. One day he had a local lawyer phone me to say, "Mr. Tavianni wants you to sign his paper by Monday otherwise he will go to court about the wall."

I paused, not surprised but strangely hurt. I asked the lawyer if he thought, objectively, Mr. Tavianni was being rational to insist I sign a piece of paper that would give him jurisdiction over part of my property, or at least half of a wall that was also mine. He paused, and said: "This is unofficial, and I wouldn't say this if you weren't someone from here, but yes I agree with you, if it was my property I would want a wall higher than what exists." I thanked him for being honest and let Monday come and go. When some days later I saw Pavlo on the road, he tried to avoid me, but we found ourselves face to face at a turn.

"I'm sorry," I say, "I couldn't do anything legal without my own lawyer's presence." He didn't answer and would have said nothing at all if I didn't add, "I wish you would understand, anyone…including you, would have wanted more protection for their property."

He looked at me and said, "If you want a fight, then I'll fight. And I have money." I was speechless. Pavlo's expression was stony.

"Well," I paused, unsure of what to say, "I don't have money." I was thinking he's incredible for saying what he just said. "But I have friends," I say, surprised at my response. He moved on, without so much as a nod.

When I tell Stavros about the exchange, he shakes his head. "It's because he sees that you're on your own," he says again. "They still think they own us. Next time I see him I'm going to say the Italians aren't our conquerors anymore. It's 2001, not 1943."

"I did tell Pavlo that Eleni decided to sell me the house because I wasn't a foreigner." Stavros nodded. I remembered Pavlo's response. It was the only time I saw him caught off guard and unsure of how to react for a few seconds.

Kosta the architect came to measure the wall. He said he was going to request a height substantially higher than what I had agreed on with Pavlo; he didn't think it was unreasonable to ask for. We put a ladder up against the existing brick and cement partition so he could see into the Tavianni's courtyard.

"This is an inner courtyard," he said, "it's meant to be insular. Look he has a bougainvillea and stone benches, what is he complaining about?"

I laughed. "Well, he wants the view since he's had it all these years to himself."

"He can always do something with that terrace," Kosta said, pointing to the flat rooftop of the outhouse in their small garden.

"There's still a view, he just doesn't have it from a sitting position," I said.

It took several months, into the fall, before the Archeologists from Syros finally came to Patmos to inspect the official requests for changes on the various houses in Hora. I was on the island on one of my quick weekend trips which friends viewed as a growing indication of my emotional fragility, yet the nine hour boat ride to Patmos from Piraeus was always a much-needed reprieve from Athens. I would stare at the winter sea in its slate blues, the soundlessness of the sky lulling me with its expanse and occasional gulls. On Patmos I found serenity, as though myth and rock and the facts of weather had come to define a world pure onto itself. It was always worth the trip which, during winter, meant sharing the third class seating area where I spent most of those nine hours with gypsies and smokers and the weather-beaten faces of people who work too hard for too little.

Kosta the architect was understated, "They said okay, but they didn't give you the full height I requested, which is okay. I asked for it so it wouldn't be less than what you already have."

I was relieved and thought to call Theologos, the builder I had found, so he could begin tearing down the bricked cement and start with what Kosta had designed as the traditional wall with its *koomoula*, a kind of inverted 'V' shaped along the wall top; this way no one would be able to sit on it anymore. It was what the wall had originally looked like, how the Patmian houses in Hora were built. Theologos, which literally means the word (*logos*) of God (*Theo*), always gave me advice that never failed to steer me clear of potential trouble.

"If you build the wall, we should wait for winter when there won't be people around."

"But I have the Okay from the Archeological people in Syros," I said, surprised.

"Yes, but if Petros, the gardener who takes care of the Italian's house sees us doing it he could call the police again, and they could stop it."

"How?"

"Because you still have a police summons. Until it's cleared in court you're not supposed to do anything."

"Not even with the paper from the Archeologists?"

"Don't worry," he said. I would hear the phrase often: *don't worry yourself* (*mi mou stenohoriese*). It was like a lullaby that brought back the voices of my grandparents, consoling like the island itself when its hills became the shaped veils of gradual darkness as the moon made its way into the sky. Eleni of the coffee family was right; the house in Hora was a connection to childhood, the childhood of another Greece.

In Theologos' hands the Hora house slowly emerged from its cocoon of crumbling plaster *sovas*, first in the rebuilding of the infamous wall with a stone bench placed below it, and then in the lowering of the terrace wall opposite to open up the view of the Aegean and the tiny islet of Hilomodi — a thousand (*hili*) mussels (*midia*). Underneath the 1950s flecked *mosaico* and old cement were gorgeous Patmian stones of blushed pinks and ochre. I also wanted to redo the old bathroom. It was brick as opposed to stone and badly cracked along the ceiling.

"It's the iron," Theologos said. "Once iron gets a breath of oxygen, it's done for; it will split any wall."

"Can't we re-cement?" I thought the repairs on the bathroom would be simpler than building the middle wall.

He shook his head, "You would have to take the whole thing apart; that iron inside the cement wasn't set right to begin with. Whatever you do now, since it's been exposed, is going to keep breaking through." It intrigued me how pragmatically and clearly Theologos explained the workings of his trade. If I saw skins of plaster that peeled off from my outside walls, I would tell him we needed to patch it up with paint, and he'd warn me, "Never paint over the stone with plastics."

"Why not?" I wanted to know, since plastics were a thicker, tougher paint from the thin lime wash (*asvestis*) that coated the old walls on the island. It was more economical too. One coat of plastic paint as opposed to several of lime wash, plus wiping down the plastics didn't leave your cloths or clothes filmed in white dust.

He laughed, "It's practical but it's worse for your walls, and of course cheaper than lime." He explained it took several coats of lime, which made it more costly, but it allowed the walls to breathe; the dampness could escape. Plastics were synthetic; they trapped the moisture inside which eventually accumulated, pushing through the walls and doing the real damage of cracking the plaster in chunks.

Theologos got the *mesotihia*, middle wall, finished in November. "Just before the rains," he said, only to overhear in Skala that Petros the overseer of the Tavianni house, was furious, so furious he went into Stavros' carpentry workshop and wanted to know when he had managed to build the wall, and who had given him the right to do so? Stavros told him he hadn't built anything, that the Archeologists had come to examine it and given their official permission.

The next thing we knew Stavros got a phone call from a lawyer in Athens, someone who introduced himself with a name he seemed to think Stavros should have recognized. He informed him that Mr. Tavianni was a lawyer himself, with lucrative assets. Stavros apparently didn't say much until the Athenian lawyer went on to inform him that, "Mr. Tavianni is someone with a reputation in Italy."

At which point Stavros said, "Do you know my reputation on Patmos?" The lawyer must have been unprepared because he simply said, "No." To which Stavros said, "Well, my reputation on Patmos is that I'm the best carpenter on the island."

I was laughing; Stavros was nodding to himself, a smile on his face.

"People think everyone has a price," I said.

Stavros turned away from the window shutter he was sanding. "They knew the house was for sale. Eleni told them first because she's wanted to sell it for some time. But they wanted it for nothing. They gave her an absurd price, what do they think? We're all *koroido*? That the island still belongs to the Italians?"

"Maybe they just thought since Eleni had money she would eventually give it to them for very little."

"What? For nothing!" Stavros went back to his sanding. "I don't like the attitude," he went on. "I like clean situations. Straight people. Did the Italian think he was going to get that house for free…" he repeated, shaking his head.

The Taviannis didn't give up. They didn't accept the fact that the wall was officially examined and legally permitted. The case would go to court. I went back to the police station to plead the case. Someone there knew about it. "What is he?" someone else wanted to know. "Italian," I said. The officer nodded a nod I'd learned to translate into 'don't worry.' But I did, there was reason to worry. I was in two court cases, and this made a third. I started to joke with friends that if any of the documents crossed the same desk, the person in charge would start to recognize my name.

Stavros shook his head; he was behind schedule with the front door he had promised to make for me, as he was with the kitchen cabinets, and other things which seemed less important next to everything else. "Eleni should have dealt with that wall a long time ago. And if it wasn't for me looking out for your interests, you would still be at his mercy…"

I wanted to remind Stavros I now had a police summons because of the wall, but I knew what he meant, the Italian had assumed I was going to agree to his demands. I almost did, almost walked right into a signature which, as Stavros kept reminding me, would have given a foreigner jurisdiction over my property, "And not just your property," he liked to emphasize, "but your daughter's!"

After Theologos finished with the wall, I found an electrician, a plumber, and a painter. Through the winter months to the spring of 2002, the house was pitted and redone. Maria and I sat with the Patmos yellow pages on our knees calling different people, the way a year ago we had listed the houses we thought might be for sale. Alekos would be there every time someone came to look at the work I wanted done, and give me a quote. "She's one of us," *ine dyki mas*, he would begin, "And she's a story" *inai mia istoria* in Greek, which implies more of history than story. Inevitably, Antoni the electrician would nod, as did the painter Christodolos, and the plumber Fengaros. When someone came to discuss the plastering, and didn't make the familiar nod but asked, carefully, how much the house had cost me, Alekos would advise me later to let the person go, saying it was bad taste to ask me about the price of the house when the person wasn't known (*gnosto*), someone we could call *dyki mas*. Theologos on the other hand had spoken openly. "I will

142

do the best I can for you, but I don't want to short change myself, or you." I agreed, relieved and strangely trusting of this person I had just met. When he fixed my wall, and lowered the other around the terrace to give us more of a view, he found beautiful stones, and then, at the top of the steps added another to finish it off. He told me not to buy anything, that he would find an extra stone slab from his various work sites. And old Patmian tiles too. I saw them in the courtyards and the floors of chapels. The tiles weren't made in the same way anymore, with the Byzantine cross stamped crudely in the middle of the clay brick. The beautiful terra cotta slabs that paved the steps down to the cave of Saint John the Divine that covered the walk ways of the older houses and the kitchen and dinning room floors, were now gold to imitate. Only one person made them on the island and they were approximately one thousand drachmas (four dollars) a brick 'because of the high heat that's needed to put them through the kiln,' I was told, extravagant for what were essentially bricks.

Theologos promised to find me some. "Even if they're old and stained?" I assured him the older the better. He wouldn't have enough to cover my walkway but he could find enough to cover the top of the little shed he built for me around the water pump, and some to place around the jasmine bush.

"Yesterday they gave you light," Antoni told me when I called to find out what was happening with my application for a three-phase electrical box; I'd officially switched names of ownership. The house was newly rewired. There was triumph in his voice. I saw the village of a past when ships approached, always after midnight making their way around the rock cove of an island in darkness, showing its lights along the shoreline like gradual stars. I imagined what it must have been like before electricity existed, and as it became available, decades of darkness, generations of decades, growing slowly visible after sunset.

"You have electricity now," Antoni explained after my few seconds of silence.

"In the garden too?" He had put some lights under the lemon trees, Stavros' kores, and for some reason the image of those lemon trees lit at night excited me more than the now lit house. Antoni always helped me out, whether it was a plug or an extra outlet, the job was never too small to prevent him from coming over to do it. When I wanted to hang a light fixture from the high mast beam in the living room, he brought his two meter ladder (no one else had one that high), and hung it for me. And when I had to move in furniture he told me about Kyrios Sideris (Mr. Iron): an old man in a three-wheeler who usually hauled things from one of two large storage places run by one of the two movers who brought things to the island from Athens. I didn't think it was possible, let alone realistic that Kyrios Sideris could actually manage to get a double mattress, 3 bed frames, 2 single mattresses, a couch and two chairs into his rickety three-wheeler and negotiate the narrow, unevenly paved *sokakia* to drive up to my front door.

"We can't do it in one go," he says matter-of-factly.

I explain where the house is. He says he knows the small street in front of it. Not something anyone outside the village would call a street, but nevertheless all sorts of machines passed through that narrow strip of cobbled stones, from small tractors to motorcycles.

I tell Kyrios Sideris I will wait for him at the house to help unload.

Sure enough Kyrios Sideris made his way up the hill to Hora with my mattresses and pillows and assortments of wood frames roped to his small vehicle which sounded and looked like a hybrid of a scooter and an open-backed Deux-Cheveux car. When I heard his slow, steady motor, I opened both doors to the house's *avli*. As Kyrios Sideris untied the mattresses, he let me know he had a sprained shoulder and wouldn't be much help with the actual carrying of the things into the house. "Don't you have someone here?" he asked.

I say, "No, it's just me." He seems not to believe it, and asks several times again as we hoist the things through the doorway and he reluctantly allows himself to balance the mattress end on his weak shoulder. "Don't you have anyone here to help you out?"

"No," I say again, starting to feel somewhat strange that I am in fact on my own. He seems to be trying to understand. I am young in his eyes, with a house I am moving bed frames and furniture into.

"No one to help you put these things in place?" He repeats, telling me in the same breath that he shouldn't be exerting any more pressure on his pulled shoulder muscle. His expression says, 'How can she be on her own?' This is Greece, people have families and if not immediate family, then relatives, and if not relatives then friends, no one is ever without "*dyki tous*" (their own). So when I finally say I am expecting a couple the next day to help set up the things we've moved in, he looks relieved.

"Of course, *vevea*," he murmurs, "You can't do all this on your own."

Here in the village the bonds between people are interstices wrought but not severed by the daily, where dependencies are cultivated. In line for my passport renewal in Athens a woman breaks down in front of me. She was there getting two passports, her son's and daughter's, and in the process was telling her life story. There was a question of the address on one of them. "My daughter's living with her boyfriend," she started, adding "…you're young," to the employee working on the papers who barely raised her head. "You know that people live together these days before they marry. I got the invitation yesterday. They're getting married on the 15th." At some point the woman turned to me to ask to verify one of the numbers on the I.D. "I can't tell, is that a nine or a six?" I thought it looked like a six, but didn't have

144

my glasses with me either, so the employee double checked. She finally got her passports, and when it was my turn I asked if she would mind filling in the blanks because my Greek wasn't good enough. She was reluctant. "But you speak Greek fine," she said. "I know but I don't write very well," I told her. The teller filled in the details without a word, finally saying next time I should ask a friend to do it for me.

Another time at the post office, a tattered looking man clutching a wrinkled plastic supermarket bag, had come to get his wife's pension. He was in a suit that had seen better days. "Where do I write the name?" he asked.

The teller wanted to know where his wife was. He answered that she was sick. The teller informed the man she was the one that needed to sign.

"I said she is sick," he repeated. The teller counted out the money. The old man rolled the bills into a wad and pushed them down into the plastic shopping bag.

On Patmos I learned to speak a language of vulnerability. Unlike life in Athens, vulnerability in the village becomes part of what it means to share common ground, to become *dyki tous*. In turn I was given secrets, the secrets of how people lived and thought and built edifices of meaning as literal as the tools and materials with which they built them. "*Ponao yia ta palia*, (I pain for the old)," Stavros says to me as we discuss how Theologos uncovered the old stone under the cement, how in the kitchen a Byzantine cross was found etched into the stone archway of the doorway. "That's luck," he said to me over the phone when I was back in Athens. "You're going to give your house another hundred years of life with the work you're doing on it." I meanwhile was frantic that I was not going to manage to finish what I considered basic repairs: new pipes in the kitchen, rewiring, replastering, the chipping away at the coverings of time that had already started to show the gathered greens of moisture and humidity.

I tell Stavros again I couldn't have done any of it without his help, and he says, "We can't all do the same things. I don't know books the way you do…"

"But you know things I'll never know," I say, "like how to make beautiful furniture and entranceways."

"I'm happy that you're doing good things to the house," he goes on, "and you're doing it properly, with workers who take their work seriously. None of it is sloppy because you listen to me and believe what I tell you. When a home owner lets the workers do what they know, the job gets done properly."

One evening at the small bar in Hora I sit with Niko, another builder, who is having a drink with some people. He's telling the story of a German home owner who had asked him to build a stone arch. They had agreed on 24,000 drachmas. "Then," he says, "it was an impressive sum." When the German man came in the summer and saw the finished arch he gave Niko 2,400 drachmas. He explained to him that had been the agreed upon sum.

The German acted like Niko was the one who had made the mistake. Niko shakes his head over his drink and says he could have torn it down but he felt 'pity' for the work he had done, *to lipithika*, he says in Greek, it had been *mia kali doulia* (a job done well). Niko shrugs, "I finally told him I would give it to him as a gift." Adding "It was a beautiful arch, I just didn't want to be treated like I was *koroido*." Builders who know how to work the stone properly are a handful, it is a skill passed down like so much else on the island, through family, like Stavros' carpentry secrets passed down to his two sons. Stavros' calloused, hard palms and nails, almost deformed from having been torn so many times, speak his devotion to his trade. He would tell me about the many kinds of wood he used, their shades and uses, their flexibilities, gradations of resilience and consistencies, the cost of the work always subordinate to perfecting it, and pride in that result was what was insulted with *koroidia*.

"I'm uneducated," Theologos tells me. "But I don't like being taken advantage of, if you tell me your problem, I will do what I can."

We are discussing how I will pay him for the work he has done so far. He gives me a sum written in pencil on a paper scrap; some numbers are crossed off with dates next to them, but I still owe a good amount. I'm promising to pay it off within the year, but can't give it to him in a lump sum.

"We'll find a solution," he says again, nodding "...we'll manage something; as long as a person doesn't go behind my back, I'll find a way to help." It's March and evening, a veil of moisture hangs over the sea. There's a heavy moss smell. Worms curl into themselves. Dampness glazes the wood shutters and lemon leaves. Doors and windows have swollen shut and can't be opened. We will wait until it gets warmer and the sun dries the wood and shrinks it back to size before trying to force the shutters open. Even the new nails have rusted heads. The poppies are sudden pools of red in the hills. Another boy died this winter in a motorcycle accident, he snapped his neck, was dead by the time they got him to the clinic. It happened too often. The helicopters were either unable to land because of weather or not fast enough. The horizon this evening had taken on the bougainvillea's washed pink shade, delicate like the balances of life on the island.

Stavros' father was over ninety, even Stavros couldn't remember his father's exact age. Whenever I saw Kyrio Antoni with his stick, his stooped back as curved as the wood he had with him to keep himself mobile, I would say a few words and he would shout my name loud enough to hear it himself. When I wished him *hronia polla* (may you live many years) this past new year, he shrugged and said, "Many years to you. I don't want to live more."

"But you already have," I say, surprised.

Kyrios Antoni shrugs, "I'm bored with living." It was unpredictable, how people died and others lived; it was unpredictable and intimate. You knew people personally and if you didn't, you knew their face, and if not their face, then their name, this naming of histories located me. Unlike my life in Athens I was a familiar face to the *dopious*, the world became tangible and home when I went to the bakery in Hora, the fruit and vegetable man, the grocery store in Skala. The older woman who owned the grocery store always greeted me with *kalos irthes* (welcome back). This year she tells me how things have been when I ask "*ti kanete?* (how are you)?" It had been a hard winter. The island had expected to be given a dialysis machine, and her family had counted on it for her elderly father. "Nothing's been done," she says, more stoic than resigned.

"My father's 81," she goes on. "He's lived through the war, then all the poverty. We were 8 children. Shouldn't he have a decent old age? Athens is too far for us to visit him. So we're having him brought to Kalymnos. I hope God gives us patience and strength."

I ask if she has relatives on Kalymnos, a nearby island, if there are people there to care for him.

"We're all here, but Kalymnos is close and they have a dialysis machine there. It's not Athens, we can manage to make the trip; every other day one of us will go. *Ti na kanoume* (what can we do)?" The expression resonates as I hear it again, the opposite of resignation. *Ti na kanoume?* A question rather than a statement, telling me what has already been done, asking what else there could be to do. The phrase which I've heard since childhood now sounds heroic. Despite the odds, this woman is explaining, they will manage. "We'll make the trip until we can have him brought to Patmos where he wants to be."

I wish her *couragio* (courage), take my supplies back to Hora, and remember what Stavros said so often about the necessity of doing a job right, making sure the building isn't done sloppily, why he always said my stone house was lucky, it had stood for at least a century and showed little wear.

Theologos is telling me one more time the reasons why the cement of the outside toilet's walls shows fissures and rifts. My small garden is overrun with weeds. I am pulling out handfuls, snapping the bug-eaten geraniums, listening. "It's a hard time for you with your routine and teaching," he says as I'm telling him I can't make it to the island as often as I should to oversee the work; I wanted things finished before the summer but Antonis the electrician had taken longer to do the wiring than was expected, then it was the plumber's turn and then Theologos would re-plaster, but things had fallen behind and now Theologos is saying, "It's the time when we make rose water, *antho nero*. We have to do it now while the petals are tender. And then we have to pick the greens before the mountains get dry. The ground stays moist until June, but if there isn't much rain everything dries up by then." The island's hills were briefly covered in color for the months of spring with its turmeric colored daisies and blood fired poppies, and then it all gave way to brush and thistle, and in August, oregano and thyme.

"I'll try," he says. "I'll come in the evenings after we finish with the rose water, and do some plastering." He explains after March and April it's too late to make rose water because the flowers aren't sweet anymore, and explains again why the roof over the outside bathroom will never be without cracks. He could whitewash it every year, and would do that for me in May, but the damage had been done with the initial structure; the iron, rusted from within the cement, would continue to break through it unless the whole roof was redone. "Iron that hasn't been cleaned right and gets exposed to air will rust and expand and break through anything."

Theologos let me know he had heard that the Italian (*o Italos*) was putting up his house for sale after I had been given the official okay to heighten my wall.

"I feel badly," I say to Stavros. He shakes his head, says I'm naive.

"He must be very upset about all this to want to sell his house because of a wall," I continue.

Stavros shakes his head again, "He's just stubborn. I don't feel badly for people like him. It's the one who never means harm I feel for. People like him always look out for themselves; it's other people who don't know how to."

"The Italian" never in fact sold his house; it was a rumor he spread for whatever reason. Or maybe he wanted to see if there would be any takers so he could buy something else. There was arrogance to Pavlo Tavianni from the beginning, from his assumption that I would agree to his ongoing effort to sabotage my legal jurisdiction to heighten the wall, to his refusal to compromise on anything less than his idea of what should be done. Petros who looked after the Tavianni property, to this day doesn't know Theologos, whose sister is his neighbor in Skala, built it for me.

"Petros is looking out for his interests," Stella says. "If the Italian sells the house he won't have that monthly pay he gets for the upkeep." Stella goes regularly to water the plants and the lemon trees, the *kores* (daughters or girls), when I am away. She swept and cleaned and washed, and I always felt I could never repay her enough. In those first months when there had been so many expenses, she refused to take any money so I brought her small gifts, but she gave them to Maria, or her sister Fotini. Only once she actually mentioned something she would like when I asked her to tell me what I could send her from Athens. "A blue scarf," she said, "a dark blue scarf with a plain white streak across it." I thought that would be simple enough to find, but all the times I hunted for that scarf I found blue scarves with white squares, with yellow streaks, with white and blue stripes, with polka dots, but never a scarf with a single white streak. I started to think there was something fated about my not finding the one thing Stella had ever asked for. Her life had been tragic yet she faced it pitilessly. She had lost her only son to a motorcycle accident, her husband had never been faithful, and the only man she had fallen in love with as a young woman had married someone whose family had money, and left only to come back forty years later, a man now in his sixties, when he ran into her in the cemetery. "The place where I belong," she said.

"Your hair is white," was the first thing he said when she answered, "My hair was always white." He wanted to make up for what had happened, he wanted to catch up. He began to bring presents, expensive clothes.

"I told him I clean houses," Stella said. "Where am I supposed to wear these fancy skirts and jackets?"

He wanted her to leave and live with him in Florida; he had never been happy married to the other woman. She told him she had her Maria, a grown woman who had her own children. She said she couldn't give into 'wants,' that it was too late. Still, he would see her for coffee, in the cemetery, at church; they would take walks. She told me of the years with the man she married, "an animal," of her bewilderment at why she put up with him. She tells me Maria had heard gossip in the village that her mother was seen talking to her first love, then she heard her mother on the phone. Maria wouldn't talk to her; Stella asked her what it was she had done? She told Maria, "Your father's in the port fucking a whore and you don't say a thing. But it bothers you that I'm on the phone with a man?" Maria answered that she was used to her father doing what he did. But it was different with her mother.

For as long as I knew Stella she never received in the ways she gave. She gave the gifts she was given, gave her time, gave whole days to the unpaid cleaning and washing of sheets and towels in rooms her husband rented out, gave me and anyone who rented her rooms, fresh bread, cheese, entire meals. Gave me specially cooked soups during the Lenten fast when no one was eating meat, gave me packets of home-made *tarama* and fresh eggs she tied firmly with string for me to take back to Athens whenever I left the island. Once she even gave me two frozen sword fish she had in her freezer from the previous summer when Aleko caught them. She didn't know how to stop giving. And I could not seem to find her a scarf with a single white streak, though her story became a poem.

Stella's Hands

I am in a well under darkness, listening
to what this man is telling me,
my darkness breaks: it doesn't matter to him
that I cannot change the way
I was born, on this island, in the middle
of nowhere, it doesn't matter
I cannot feel the pity of his words; they travel,
like he did, far from the wife

promised him by the archbishop (he
hardly knew her, it was me he serenaded,
Stellaki, my dark girl, in my
hand-sewn skirt, I was the one he said
he wanted). It wasn't his fault, his family
wanted her family's money,
the archbishop wanted it too.
All these years with my husband
I begged my children to have
the love I could not dream of, and then
I begged my dead son to tell me why
his father wasn't taken from me
instead of him. Instead love came
into my life, caressed my soul, filled it.
I could not give it back. It wasn't for me
to feel these things. He tells me I am
a sweet pain, says his life was dry land
without me. *Stellaki*, he says, my grandmother's name.
When I ran the uneven cobbles, the copper sky,
a beaten rust, became the color of
my husband's eyes in lust
when I grew to hate him, when I knew
marriage was worse than dying.
I forgot *Stellaki*, I learned the heavy weight of
living until it was life in pure darkness.
I knew marriage to a man who wanted to eat
the world as taste and flesh go into
the stomach, becomes bloated with taste and flesh.
I could feed his lust the way I threw slop
to the pigs, my body could kindle it
till he used it up and had to go elsewhere,
but it was my body that gave him the flame,
lit it until it was unquenched fire,
the copper flame I always saw
in his eyes. I fold sheets, iron, don't
leave the rooms he rents without stripping
the beds, airing the sheets, refolding,
squaring corners. I would clean toilets,
sponge walls. I stayed untouched
because he took what he needed
from others, doing what he always did,
making what he calls love in some room

as I poured morning coffee for a hotel guest,
swept the fallen bougainvillea from the terrace steps.

So when Lucas says *Stellaki* I think
I will see my grandmother,
but I am the grandmother now
and he is a grandfather.
In darkness all my life I never
searched these things, he says words
I have never heard, he says *I wish*
it had been another time. I become a filled sea,
unclear water floods me. He uses words
to touch my heart, I cannot listen
to these words without giving myself up.
All my life, he says, *I didn't care*
if I died. Now he wants to live. I tell him
the two of us cannot have anything
together. He has his daughters,
his wife. You picked her, I tell him,
you have her children.
You must stay close to them.
He holds my hands like they are jewelry,
tells me I never knew the worth in them.
I never knew anyone could hold my hands
like they belonged to the *Panagia*;
he says twenty-year olds have beautiful hands
but they are not *Panagia's* hands.
He found me in the cemetery
over the marble that cannot soak
my tears, over stone that covers the body
of my son. This was my life,
the rooms I clean with my hands, the marble
I clean with my tears. I am always
in the rooms or the cemetery, I never
leaned against the low walls to gossip
like my sister. I never learned anything
except for work, days worked into more work.
I won't let his whores in the rooms, they wash
the verandahs, outside where they belong.
My husband couldn't care less
who does the rooms, but without my hands
he could not have done anything.
This is the truth with people

who don't know how to take the thing
you give without stealing it, they
don't know God enters you
like the split wings of an eagle and breaks
your heart in two so you find you have halves
that will have to work to be whole again.
My life is that trial, my heart is
alive with the work.

In the middle of my soul
where nothing can grow, Lucas's eyes
planted me.
What would I have been
if I had married him? If he had taken me
away like he was meant to
instead of allowing the archbishop
to decide –
He tells me of the women he's had,
the flesh that lusts after itself
like my husband's stomach, this is thirst,
the passion that eats him, for thirty-five years
it has eaten him until he cut
a newspaper picture of a woman who had
my mouth, and carried it with him like a cross.
I tell him every day that goes by
does not come again, God does not
share everything. We could have been
perfect for each other. He buys me things
I leave unopened. A watch. Face creams.
A nightgown. Another person
would have been happy. I tell him
I never learned about luxuries.
What about tomorrow? he says.
Tomorrow, I tell him, is your wife, your children,
your grandchildren. He cries,
holds my hands like they are jewelry.
Just to see you, he says,
is my peace. He waits like a child,
excited. And the man I gave thirty-five years to,
whose children I had
and raised, whose bills I paid, is a man
who taught my son to drink until

it killed him. When I think of the suffering,
when I think I am a believer
my soul divides its burden
between my shoulder blades so I
cannot turn in either direction, right
or left, without the weight of it searing me.
When I know this is what I have had
to carry in the years which have become my life,
I want to know why God cuts the flesh
to the bone so that we living hardly know
the hurt from the joy.

"So you're going back *stin Hellatha!* (to Greece)," Stavros says, smiling. I stop by his shop to say I am taking tonight's boat back to Athens. I laugh. Stavros considers Athens a separate country. Patmos is Patmos, or Paradise, Athens belongs to *Hellatha* or the rest of Greece. I notice the man in Stavros' shop who was on the boat coming over, now covered with a work apron. I remembered him self-contained in his beige pants and shoes and dark green overcoat, on deck, and then down in the cafeteria, on his own but somehow content.

"The surgeon!" Stavros explains, introducing him to me. The man smiles quietly as he continues to concentrate on the parts he dismantled from Stavros' machinery. The shop looks like someone has swept it clean, everything is boxed, packed, covered, when I am used to stepping on a carpet of wood shavings, bumping into window and door frames that take up the work space. Stavros tells me his machines are old and one of them would cost millions of drachmas to replace. Then there was all the work that would have fallen behind if he had to make do with only one of them. 'The surgeon' had apparently billed him for a reasonable 445,000 drachmas for two tireless days of work.

"I'm satisfied," Stavros says to me as I drink coffee with his wife Fotini before heading down to Skala to wait for the boat. "Here's a man who took the ship to come to my shop. He opened up everything. Spent two full days in here checking the machines he took apart. And now I won't have to worry for at least another ten years."

I remind Stavros that I would like to have the kitchen cabinets in by summer and he nods, says now that his machines are fixed he will be able to catch up. "You can't imagine the work I have," he says, but I can. Stavros is notorious for doing a job and then leaving some unnerving detail unfinished. One person I know had twenty three window shutters to replace in a massive villa and he managed eighteen of them, but the last five took another two years to finish. Someone else I know wanted him to build a wood banister to her upper loft; the loft closets and the steps were finished, but the banister was

153

never done, so she finally had it done by a carpenter from Skala. "I had to be careful," she admitted. "You can't just give someone's job away like that."

Stavros built wonders out of his 'wood from Africa,' as he proudly called it. When I leave I chide him, "Do it for my daughter," and add, "so we'll have a finished kitchen for the summer." Stavros appreciates the comment, "Give her a kiss from us…and watch her like your eyes." It's a frequent expression, to watch over someone like your eyes, our most precious asset.

On the boat back, carrying fresh eggs from Stavros' chickens (which Fotini insisted were *real* as opposed to what sat on supermarket shelves), I also had a frozen octopus from Stella, and a bag of *tarama*.

I always got a single bed in a four-bed cabin where other women slept. I was never organized enough to insure one of the lower bunk beds (away from the ceiling air vent) was the bed I paid for, but if the boat wasn't crowded I managed a lower bunk; tonight they were taken. The *Patmos* started from Rhodes, made a stop in Kalymnos, picked us up on Patmos, and then headed for Piraeus.

A handsome body-length leather jacket hung from one of the hangers. I used the bathroom light, so I wouldn't wake anyone, took off my jeans, put the ladder up against one of the top bunk beds. Between the boat's vague tossing and the boatload of students' partying in the corridors, I slept off and on. Around eight in the morning the knock came from the purser telling us we were arriving in Athens. After the second knock, I finally get out of my bunk. The woman with the handsome leather jacket is the only person left in the cabin, combing her blond hair. We smile. She says she didn't sleep either with the noise, and asks me where I got on. I tell her Patmos. She says she got on in Kos and offers to buy me coffee upstairs.

"I won't get any real sleep till Wednesday," she says. She expected the students to calm down by around two or three in the morning but they didn't stop their partying.

"Not at that age," I say, she nods.

"I know, I have two boys, sixteen and thirteen." I tell her my daughter's thirteen. She tells me she's on her way to pick up one of her sons who is staying with his father. She is fashionably dressed, with her jeans and boots, nicely put together. Athens is becoming visible, its thick peninsula of concrete sheaved in the familiar yellow fog.

"I got away for less than forty-eight hours," I tell her. "I've even made the trip for twenty-four hours. My friends think I'm mad, but it's worth it. I'd do almost anything to get away from Athens once in awhile."

She nods, "It was a good thing I left for Kos," she says. "Life is calmer there."

"People have run out of patience in the city." I say, "They're all half crazy, me included." She laughs.

154

"I couldn't stay in Athens. I wouldn't have managed to raise my boys in the city." She tells me after her divorce she returned to Kos. "I had my mother there to help me." I tell her I stayed in Athens so my daughter would have her father close by, but that the decision may not have been the best thing for me. "I don't know if her father understands what I sacrificed," I say.

"Men here never understand," she says. "The more you sacrifice, the more they expect it and the more they want." I nod, thinking how fresh she looks, remembering her folded clothes in the morning, how she put on pajamas to sleep in. I barely remembered to put a toothbrush in my bag, and forgot my comb.

"I suppose it's all in our expectations," I say eventually, thinking of Stella again, how she expected nothing, and had given everything to a man who abused her. *I laugh. I put on a good act, and no one knows what's inside me.*

"I'm worried about my older one, I left him on Kos so I could pick up my thirteen year old here." I nod.

"The anxiety doesn't end. I guess we have to be patient," I say, smiling.

She smiles too, "Yes, but where is it?"

I nod, "Like pretending you have money when you don't."

She laughs, "Can you?"

In Piraeus we wave goodbye, I take her quiet demeanor with me. I almost forget to ask her name. "Antonia," she tells me, after I thank her for buying me coffee. I get a cab from the line-up to take me to the other side of the port where I parked my car near a warehouse on a side street of car mechanics. There's road construction going on everywhere. The taxi driver looks familiar. I hop in before he can say 'where?' the cab drivers inevitably try to double or triple up on passengers going in similar directions to get double and triple the fare. For the last two years there have been police stationed around the taxi line-ups at the airport, train stations and ports. Otherwise you waited forever for a taxi to 'agree' to take you in the direction you needed to go. If you were unlucky enough not to live somewhere where someone else was going you could find yourself waiting for hours.

I tell the driver to drop me off a little ways away, and in about five minutes ask him to stop. "How much do I owe you?"

"Two hundred drachmas," he says. When I took a cab three days ago, I paid one hundred and fifty for the same distance. I had one hundred and fifty in change and a five thousand drachma bill.

"I only have one hundred and fifty drachmas and a five thousand bill."

"*Ti fteo ego?* What am I supposed to do?" he says, irritated.

"Take the one hundred and fifty?" I suggest, "Or give me change for the five thousand."

"What's a hundred and fifty drachmas?" He says as if he didn't hear me.

I suddenly realize he's the same driver who picked me up another time and wanted to drive a second passenger a good distance out of the way from the direction we were going in. I'd been the first passenger and insisted he ask the woman to take another cab, which she reluctantly did. But for the entire twelve minute ride it took to get me home I was convinced he was going to kill us, driving faster than I had ever been driven by anyone in the city as I sat clutching the door handle.

He made a grunting sound as he braked abruptly to let me off on the busy thoroughfare. I ran to change my five thousand drachma bill at the kiosk on the corner and gave him the exact change. The sea in Piraeus was its usual dirty grey, it was Sunday so there wasn't the familiar nightmare of congestion on the roads. I was carrying a thawing octopus, fresh eggs and bag of dried *tarama* that reminded me of where I had been.

Saints and Anarchists

for Jordan/Ιορδανη, who listens with me

"You mean we have to *pay?*" Orestes, a young man in the car with me, exclaimed. It was the wrong turn. The old roads had changed. I wasn't sure how to get back home. It was night; I had just turned off a street to find myself in front of the tolls to the new highway and thought I could quickly back up. We were almost killed. There was no backing up anymore.

My car is a mess; it dies at the gas station and the gas station attendant, a man who runs the business with his family of three children recommends that I have Kyrios Yiorgos look at the car before I call the EXPRESS SERVICE people. I don't trust the idea at first, plus I pay a hefty bi-annual sum for the service and now need it. The gas station attendant shrugs. A huge truck eventually pulls up with a young man in sports-car sunglasses who has me sign a bunch of papers before he looks at the car. "It's something electrical" he finally says, "not a battery problem."

The gas station attendant looks disgusted, "You pay all this money so the experts can tell you they can't do a thing." The EXPRESS SERVICE person suggests I leave the car at the gas station until the next morning when they will send someone to tow it to a nearby service station. The gas station attendant tells me to let him call Kyrios Yiorgos. I don't want to have to wait another day to have the car looked at; the cost in money and time sounded more and more complicated. The guy in his sports-car sunglasses has me sign more papers to prove the inspection took place, then leaves. In less than half an hour an older man approaches the gas station with a car battery strapped to the back of a motorcycle that has seen better days. We shake hands; he takes a quick look at the engine before jump starting it so I can drive to his workshop down the road.

Kyrios Yiorgos' workshop is a small, perfectly ordered space. He put in his own plugs, his own switches. Wiring for the different tools used at different wattages traces the walls. He seems unhurried and never inconvenienced by my questions. His shelves are full of neatly stacked boxes of various car parts. As I watch him inspect the engine, I tell him he is meticulous. He says *y distihia mas* (our destitution) disciplined him.

"We had nothing," he says. "We needed to learn something to survive." From under the hood he adds, "We Greeks unfortunately have our *dhe variese* attitude to things."

≋

Dhe variese (never mind) had new reverberations once I understood how futile things could feel.

"Why did I even come?" a man says at the bank, holding a slip of paper with #286 on it. A new digital sign hanging from the bank's renovated ceiling indicates a teller is serving client #142. "Why do we have to pay for everything at the bank?" He goes on. I am listening to one of the tellers on the phone with someone, explaining that the piece of cake she is eating is *Yianniotiko* from the northern town of Yiannina. The man in line with me, continues answering his own question, "I'll tell you why we have to come to the bank to pay our bills, because we're losers that why, because we're the way we are, a bunch of failures. Our government, our Prime Minister, we voted for them for the past 20 years so they could complete their mandate! That's our good, progressive government, making sure we stand in line all day: the government of the many for the many." He is furious. People start to nod.

Another man answers, "We deserve it, look at us. They make us all come here to pay our bills as if we don't have anything better to do with our lives." A lot of people are gathered in the bank, it's the last days of 2002 and newly minted euros are being handed out in small plastic bags of the equivalent of five thousand drachmas. An older woman comes into the bank, her kerchief like a brown rag around her head; her face is melted wax. She is tiny and old. She gets her slip of paper with a number; it's in the three hundreds, a man sees it and tells her, "You know there are two hundred people in line in front of you." She says, "*Dhe variese*."

≋

On my way downtown I am looking for a parking space near the newly opened metro station on Mesogion street, opposite the Ministry of Defense. As usual cars are parked on sidewalks, curves, squeezed against construction sites where open spaces (with No Parking signs) for work trucks to pull in are taken over. I circle the metro station twice, my eye on the clock, thinking I'm going to miss the shops, their closing time on Saturday anywhere between 2:30 and 4:00 in the afternoon. I'm back on the road going toward the main street, beside myself with frustration when a man motions to me. "Parking?" he asks. I barely nod. He gestures to the sidewalk further down the road. How blessed I think, relieved, something unexpected. When the light turns green I drive over as he slides open a gate into an open lot. "Right there," he says, as I park in a space next to another car. "Five euros," he adds matter-of-factly. I look at him, surprised.

"Isn't that too much?"

He shrugs, "You want parking?"

158

After I lock my car and rush to the metro, I think there is something ingenious about offering parking to barely sane drivers ready to lose the last remnants of their patience. We pay the five euros. We take the suddenly prohibited left turn to Melissia off Mesogion street at the Stavros crossroads where the intersection is overwhelmed with cranes, dug trenches, pipes, half finished roads, and an eventual bridge that lurches into air, exposing steel and wire so it looks like the inside of a bitten pretzel. Under the old bridge the left turn was a given; now a sign says 'no turn'. It's the only sign. Nothing instructs us about how we can now reach Melissia. After driving toward Peania expecting a sign to help me find my way back to Melissia, driving past the Carrefour supermarket and the further shops of Peania, I realize no such turn, or sign, exists. I turn right, drive down a side road, make an eventual left, then another, to get myself back on the road going in the opposite direction.

Things aren't so simple. Once off the Marathonas road there are a series of one-way streets that wouldn't let me make any lefts; there are more one-way streets. I finally find my way back to the initial turn for Melissia, forty-five minutes later, livid. After that I do what other drivers do. I wait for the lights to turn green and make an immediate illegal left under the old bridge.

Like everyone else I learned to gauge what sidewalks and times of day are most conducive to taking the chance of parking without the risk of a ticket. I learned which turns I could or couldn't make, depending on the traffic and whether or not police stood at specific places at specific times. When I gambled wrong, I learned to insist. One morning I left the car on a sidewalk for some forty minutes and came back to a ticket neatly placed under the windshield wiper. I ran down the road to see if I could still see the policeman who had written it. Sure enough he was about two blocks away steadily writing out more tickets.

"Please...*parakalo*," I begin, the ticket in my hand.

The police man, a young uniformed officer, continues to write down the license number of the car he is ticketing. "I'm so sorry..." I continue. "I left my car for half an hour..." He hardly looks up from his pad. "Look I'm a mother on my own and can't afford this..." I say, shameless.

"I'm sorry," he says, finally looking at me, "I understand. But the law is the law." Here I was, months after I had crushed the ticket for not wearing my seat belt, in yet another encounter with traffic police.

"Can I pay this at Easter when we get our salary bonuses?"

He nods, "It doesn't have to be paid right away."

I'm relieved, grateful I have an option. A man eating a bun comes up to us as I am about to walk back to my car.

"I couldn't help overhearing you...do you have the right to be writing out tickets like this in a suburb? You're not city police." The policeman loses his quiet demeanor; a discussion ensues about a law that has been passed by the

Supreme Court that gives urban police the right to write out tickets, that the law was instigated by a city council. I nod and start to leave the man with the bun and the policeman, now in passionate discussion.

"I understand your position," the policeman says to me, interrupting his discussion with the man.

"You don't," I say politely, "but it doesn't matter." I add more gently "I'll pay it at Easter," and walk toward the bakery where the man bought his bun.

︎〜〜〜

In the fall of 2003 I had the luck to get a sabbatical from teaching and leave with my daughter for the States. The last thing I expected was to miss the heated conversations with policemen or women, the diatribes about what to do when water or electricity was suddenly cut off, all the crisis alternatives that were a part of my daily life: the choice to pay the parking ticket at Easter, the decision to boil snow when the water pipes broke during a January freeze, that I had to find a relative of the travel agent on Patmos to get the dates of boat tickets changed or adjusted.

In suburban New Jersey and the outskirts of Washington D.C., I was strangely disoriented. The roads looked vacuumed, trees and bushes had roots protected with plastic, large bay windows like blind eyes stared over perfectly cut lawns. I rarely saw people. I started to think they were only visible in the supermarkets and malls; there was no sign of them otherwise, except in their large cars and SUVs. There was space everywhere. In line people made space for you, at the front of lines there was plenty of space to wait for the next available teller. Customers were given space to sit, special spaces to voice their complaints, other spaces to write them out. The hierarchies and categories of space were specific. In the tight squeezes of mostly nonexistent parking lots in Athens, our smaller cars and living spaces a fraction of what the average American is used to, we bartered space, cajoled others to share it, demanded it, often stole it. Our lack of space made for chaos, imagination, subversion, unexpected affirmation and disaster. The two countries that made up my identity, a spacious continent and a small Mediterranean peninsula, were opposed spaces: America was in love with her spaciousness, proud and defensive of her large dreams, while Greece, passionate and crowded in her small corner, trampled her dreamers.

︎〜〜〜

Our first summer in the house on Patmos, my neighbor in Athens calls frantic with the news that our apartment had been robbed. I leave my daughter with someone on the island and take the nine hour boat ride back to Athens. The apartment is a mess of rumpled clothing, burnt matches strewn over the floor, drawers pulled out, emptied onto the beds and floor. The jewelry is gone; things I had been given from Ismini and my mother, a pair of earrings from Corinna. I am especially sorry about my mother's bracelets. Through childhood their thin gold circles danced along her arm in tinkling sounds falling in light or quick chimes as she did the chores, cooked, switched car gears. They never came off her arm. Then one year she gave them to me as a birthday present.

At the neighborhood police station I sit at an officer's desk. The station is dismal; the walls smudged in finger marks, a wall plug had sprung, hanging loosely to the floor. The officer patiently writes out my name. I give him the details: a kitchen window forced open, closets emptied. I list what was stolen, the bracelets, the ring with its tiny line of diamonds my father had given my mother in Rome, drop earrings with rubies from my *koumbari*, two gold braided necklaces. "Chokers?" he asks.

"Chains," I clarify, adding that they were braided. He says 'chains' is enough of a description.

"I won't get them back anyway." I knew the chances of finding any of the jewelry were close to impossible.

He looks up from the writing and says, "*Ohi.*"

"No?"

"Never give up hope," he says, concentrating on the writing. A young officer interrupts him, something about a woman who lost her wallet. "You're too young to get so worked up," the older officer advises him. The young officer nods absently, puts a piece of paper on his desk and leaves. "If we can help 10% of everyone who needs it we're happy," the officer says. I nod, curious about his optimism. He wants my date of birth, my marriage status, my profession. The room smells of stale cigarette smoke. I want to tell him about the time I lost my paycheck, threw it away by mistake and couldn't find it anywhere. He is surprised.

"See what happens when too much is going on," I say, referring to the commotion in the station.

"Nothing happens," he replies laconically, finishing up with the paperwork.

I never found the stolen jewelry, but the officer treated the possibility with utter seriousness, refusing to tell me it was hopeless, he even called later that day to ask me to verify my date of birth. When I chided him about the details, sure I would never see my mother's bracelets or ring or the braided necklaces again, the officer was annoyed. "Hope never dies," he said bluntly.

In the States the horizon for hope was ever-expanding, there seemed to be something for everyone. Shop assistants always had an answer to my questions. If they were out of a product, they could order it for me. If I wanted to return something they gave my money back with a smile. For some reason they never seemed frazzled. Did they have a product in *Bath & Body Works* that was both a scrub and a daily cleanser? Yes, the woman said smiling, it had just come out. She would give it to me now, even though they were still in boxes. The young, carefully made up woman at the lingerie counter wants to know if I would like to have three pairs of panties as opposed to the one I am buying. She is cheerful. "You can mix and match," she adds, "for only twenty dollars." That's still seven dollars more than the single pair I'm buying, I answer. She seems nonplussed, still smiling as she carefully folds my underwear in crisp pink wrapping. In Greece we made do with less, we grew irritated when our limitations became obvious. Our small spaces made us stubborn, the smaller the spaces, the more stubborn our imagination, and the hungrier.

"What am I supposed to do with this craving, this *lissa!*" Maria said to me on Patmos. She couldn't stop accumulating clothes, had nowhere to go in them expect to the village bar, and in winter on Patmos that was also closed. So she wore them to church. She loved receiving the catalogues from Germany and England sent to her or left behind by tourists who rented her rooms in the summer. I suggested she find a cheap roundtrip plane ticket to England or Germany during the sales. She told me she would never be patient enough to save the money, do without any shopping for a single trip she would experience only once. *Lissa* was what I felt when I craved the house on Patmos, and then when I wanted to fix it with the little money I had. "*Tha ta vroume,* (we will find it)," Theologos the builder reassured me. We would find a way. He made space for the possibility, told me I could pay him slowly. My sister-in-law in New Jersey had a hard time believing anyone would do work they weren't guaranteed of being paid for.

"I guess he doesn't really need the money," she said.

"He needs it more than I do," I said.

"So why is he letting you pay in installments?" She was genuinely perplexed, how does a stranger agree to be tentatively given money owed. I would never be able to afford to have the house done right away. I told Theologos I could give him some money, and then more at Easter and the following Christmas (with the help of our pay bonuses) pay the rest. He agreed.

"As long as you give me your word, that's fine," he said. "What I don't like is *koroidia.* There's a woman whose kitchen I fixed who acts like she doesn't see me when we pass each other in the village; I see her practically every day and she treats me like a *koroido* after I told her she could give me the money after the kitchen was finished. It's almost a year now." I tell Theologos he is going to have to tell her directly. He shrugs, says simply that she has no shame.

My American sister-in-law is intrigued, "You wouldn't find anything like that in this country," she says. "Nothing on paper? No written agreement?" I shake my head; her intrigue turns to amazement. "Wow…why would a person trust a complete stranger?"

"I'm not."

Theologos did not consider me *xeni* (foreign). Like Stavros who had done my kitchen cabinets and replaced some doors, he told me because I was *dyki tous* (theirs) he would do what he could to help. Stavros told me plainly, "I have three categories: the ship owners, the *ergasomeni* (working people), and people with nothing." I beg him to keep the costs down. You never knew. No one ever says what a job is going to amount to in exact numbers. Numbers were as resilient as the time it took to get the work done, as were the reasons for hurrying or not. Stavros did the best carpentry on the island but didn't undercharge it. When he came to the house with a handwritten slip of gird paper, the numbers all tabulated and dated, I made coffee for each of us, and sat down on the edge of my seat.

"Okay," he tells me seriously, not without ceremony. "I put you in the category between the *ergasomeni* (the workers) and someone who has nothing…" I almost cry. The price he gives me is half of what I expect, and tell him so. "I know" he adds, complimenting me on the coffee which he says he wouldn't find in the best café. He says he knows I am an *agonistis* (one who fights). I am *dyki tous* because my *agonia* (agony) is something they respect. I want to secure what Theologos and Stavros understand as my daughter's future: the house, they say over and over is the best security for my growing daughter because I am *moni* (alone), a euphemism for my being unmarried.

∿∿
∿∿

In the States my cravings are cluttered. People smile and I am not sure who or what they are smiling at. I find myself in spacious shopping malls, endless supermarket aisles with nothing to do with my *lissa* except to keep buying what I think will satisfy me. I hear Stella telling me people ate *revithia* (chickpeas) during the war. There was very little on Patmos. "*Revithia* with water helped bloat our stomachs so we could feel full. We made do with hunger. We never expected anything." In the States advertisements and the endless free catalogues that pile up on my sister-in-law's counter top urge me to expect as much as I want. My poems are fragmented with space and *lissa*.

from American Vignettes

1
Grey expanse of Atlantic cloud, the sudden
edge of America. Perfectly roofed

houses, patches of yard. A country
in full summer, rich in poverty,
second hand cars, pension plans.
There is no one to meet me, only the stores
where I buy cosmetics, saleswomen
who smile as they would at anyone.
Dawn seeps in, an x-ray through shutter slats,
an air-conditioned new day.

2
The Atlantic crashes itself over the Jersey coast;
everyone's enjoying a toast,
the shells are mostly broken
like my mother's mouth. I can still imagine it
whole, specific as her face. How clear
and apart the seasons were, inevitable
as my mother's sorrows. Now the trees
sound far and people touch
in their cars.

Before Christmas the NJ Transit to New York was so packed my daughter
and I sat apart. I was unhappily crowded between a boisterous football fan and
his friend. Opposite me was a woman who didn't know either of them. They
were chaperoning a group of middle-schoolers to a game at Madison Square
Garden: Duke versus a team from Texas. There was a lot of commotion.
We had been in the States for three months, me on the road doing readings
while my daughter bravely got through a tough eighth grade curriculum in
the Chatham Middle School.

"You're in the wrong seat," one of the boisterous men offered as I sat
glumly amidst the rowdy middle-schoolers.

"I'm in the wrong country," I answer, surprised at what I actually feel.
The woman sitting opposite me is startled.

"Where are you from?" the man continues politely.

I say, "Greece," which causes a brief pause. The woman says, "Oh, I was
there during the Kosovo war, they really don't like Americans. There were
all sorts of demonstrations."

"It's not Americans they don't like," I say, irritated. "It's their government."

"You mean the Bush administration?" offers the man who first spoke to
me.

I nod, "And almost all the foreign policy of the recent past." There is a
slightly longer pause. "The Greeks are generally hospitable," I say. We talk
of Iraq. We talk of the U.N. veto of the war. We talk of how majority voices

164

were ignored so war could be waged. We talk of why so many Europeans feel enraged, their countries called undemocratic because they will not offer money to rebuild a devastated Iraq after having refused to support the war. He nods. The woman who had visited Greece is silent. Someone else asks if the city is getting ready for the Olympics. I say I have been away, but imagine things are unfinished. "We have opposite problems," I offer. "People don't expect the sorts of opportunities available to people here, or have much faith in the idea of success." The man who asked about the Bush administration offers, "We're taught to pull ourselves up by our bootstraps, but forget some people don't even have boots."

Our train is nearing Penn Station; my new acquaintance is polite and thoughtful. "Do you talk about these things when you do your readings?"

"People ask about Greece, but most people's idea of Greece is very different from the Greece I would describe." He smiles. "What I love most about Greece are the ways we make up stories. It's not always possible to succeed in the ways people do here, but people know how to enjoy themselves." I think of Mary at the drycleaner's, how she had me fill several buckets from her house after the snow storm last January, how we treated the water like a miracle after it came back on, there was new joy in cleaning the dishes, putting on the washing machine, flushing toilets. The saying goes y *ftohia theli kaloperasi* (poverty needs to be lived well).

The conversation had become less intense when we got off the subject of current governments and what was going on in Iraq. "People are more fatalistic in Greece. Here no one wants to admit failure even when it's obvious." The man nods. We are being told to make sure we have our belongings as we pull into Penn Station and the train goes momentarily dark. We stand up and shake hands goodbye. I smile to the woman who had stopped talking. The man tells me he enjoyed our talk, I tell him I did too, the woman smiles without saying anything. I move down the corridor to my daughter who had been watching the conversation. "What were you guys talking about?" She asks immediately.

"About life here and in Greece."

"I felt like we were in Athens again...you guys looked like you were arguing." The conductor says, "Please take your child's hand as you leave the train."

The rules and protocols in the States made me nostalgic for the complications I had been desperate to get away from. I was hungry for real food, what Stella differentiated from what was found in supermarkets: the toughness of chickpeas, the coarse bulgur, the spinach with its thick stems and mud-caked roots, nonexistent in the preprocessed, de-sanitized products we bought. When I boiled *revithia* (chickpeas), they disintegrated; the spinach and lettuce came shredded and clean in cellophane bags, bulgur boiled immediately.

165

You didn't have the dirty roots or obvious grit, the yogurt was watery, the apples had waxed skins. I had to go to whole food stores, find the special section in supermarkets for organic products when I craved thick yogurt, olive oil, vegetables and fruit that tasted like vegetables and fruit. 'Designer food' my sister-in-law called it because it was so expensive. In Greece our roots showed, our hands got dirty cleaning them, our days were taken up in traffic, at the market, standing in lines, cooking. Real food took time, shrunk our spaces with inconvenience. In the States the conveniences opened up spaces, we picked up food at the last minute, ate take-out. My daughter was especially homesick. In the Chatham Middle School, she was 'the girl from Greece' who raised her hand when the social studies teacher asked the class to name some of the Seven Wonders of the World, and she said, "There are seven hours difference between Greece and the United States." He politely let her know that didn't count, to which she answered that it did for her. My nieces were intrigued with my 'Greek soup' when I made lentils, amazing my sister-in-law by asking for more, but decided I was mean not to let them have popsicles for breakfast.

I was intrigued with the fancy bottle openers (that reminded me of a surgical tool) which slipped corks out like putty, with the paper towels, thick and soft as fabric, with the myriad body products: moisturizers and cleansers with names like 'Skin Quenching', 'Skin Relief', 'Skin Solutions'. I bought large tubes of toothpaste with their promise of 'Vivid White' teeth and 'Tartar Protection'. Even Purina's 'Cat Treats' was advertised with 'Tartar Control'. Here were new world options, the self could be polished, the messy stains of old world imperfections, removed.

≈

We returned to Greece after Christmas, before another heavy snowfall, our sandals and summer beach wraps still lying around in our bedrooms, sun blocks and after-sun lotions in the bathroom, the clocks still an hour ahead. I had forgotten the dent in my car door, the skewed side view mirrors that made it impossible to see cars coming up from behind. I had forgotten I used my rear view mirror to gauge the distance of other cars and make turns. My car insurance had expired, but we were back in Athens and feeling strangely free. In the coming week I would renew my insurance (finally get new side view mirrors for the car). I had forgotten the sagas of frustration, the escapade the morning I discontinued my coverage, running up and down the steps of the four floors in the insurance building, a story I told to friends who belonged to ordered worlds.

The offices were almost empty in late July. Ending my car insurance policy until we returned was the cheapest thing to do. I went dutifully to the third floor of the *ETHNIKI* offices where policies were handled. A woman working leisurely, the phone cradled against her ear, told the person she was talking to she would call them back, and asked if she could help, then told me to go to the first floor and get some papers. There, a woman downloaded a document from the computer and told me to take it to the fourth floor where the cashier was. I would be issued the 160 euros they owed me for the remainder of the coverage period. On the fourth floor the cashier shook her head and told me I had to go back to the third floor with the paper and get the signature from the first woman whose office issued the policies. Back on the third floor to the woman who was on the phone again, I listened as she went on earnestly explaining, "Each person has their road…this year was hard, but I don't see any vacation. My son…what an ordeal…that hospital; we had to run for shots…my mother still can't walk. We'll see by September…"

I sat in a chair at her desk, put the paper in front of her. She nodded to me with a smile, rolled her eyes into the phone receiver, nodded again in response to something the caller was telling her. Only one other person was at a desk on that floor. Still talking into the receiver, she signed my slip of paper.

"You can get the money upstairs at the cashier," she said. Back on the fourth floor the cashier wordlessly handed me a bank check for 160 euros. I expected cash, the woman on the third floor had said as much. I said I was told I would get cash. The cashier spoke reluctantly, "Anything above 100 euros is issued in a check."

"I don't have time to stand in line at the bank for 160 euros," I said loudly. The cashier shrugged, told me she couldn't do anything about it. I went to the National Bank around the corner only to get a slip that said I was #309 in line. I flew back to the third floor of the insurance offices because I have no recollection of walking, of the street or the stores. Within minutes I was back in front of the woman I had started out the morning with, furious. This time she wasn't on the phone. I put the slip of paper with #309 in front of her. "Would you want to wait for three hundred people in front of you to get 160 euros a cashier could give you in cash?" She didn't answer, she picked up the phone, talked to what I assumed was the cashier.

When she put the phone down she said, "I don't know why they issued you a check, they usually give cash."

I was visibly sweating. Back on the fourth floor again, I stood at the cashier with the check in hand. She didn't look up as she gave me another slip of paper, saying I had to go get a signature on the third floor again. At one of the desks someone was reading the sports page of a local daily, at another a woman was looking out over the roof at the pigeons gathered on the chapel dome of Agio Theodori, her hands folded in her lap.

"No wonder people don't take us seriously! No one ever does anything right!" I blurted. The young man reading the sports page folded it and looked down at some papers on his desk. When he looked up, I caught his eye, "Why can't you take this down to the third floor and have it signed?" He blushed and said he was an intern from the University of Athens; it wasn't his job to take papers to the third floor.

"So what is your job?" He looked back down at the papers on his desk and started to write something. A woman appeared from behind the cashier and asked if she could see my check.

I was finally given 160 euros in cash and told to go back to the woman on the third floor, "All okay?" she smiled.

I nodded, still shaken, "Why do we have to go through so much for such simple things?"

She nodded in agreement. "Are you going away?" she asked as she signed. I told her I was going to the States for a few months. "Ah," she signed, "*Ameriki*…my grandfather wanted to go there after the war, but he didn't have the boat money…." As she took my insurance label, I suddenly realized I still needed to use the car.

"If you hit anyone it's going to be your expense," she said as I explained I had to do a few last errands. "Then risk it, but be careful," she smiled and shook my hand, "*Kalo taxidi* (have a good trip)."

We were back to our chilly apartment, the squeaking door hinges, washed clothes spread over radiators to dry on cloudy days (dryers a nonexistent luxury), back to little or no sidewalks, to the dipping, uneven slabs of pavement, to a woman who slams into me with her blue plastic grocery bags, who moves on without missing a step. Back to Kyria Katina down the street who fixes our clothes with her Singer sewing machine in the room she lives in below her grown children's apartment. I greet her with a pile of American bought pants my daughter needs hemmed. The sun is out, her door is open. She still has her basil plants on the sill though the leaves have browned. She asks where we've been, I tell her the States, and she describes the coverage of Saddam Hussein's capture. "Poor man," she murmurs, "He was reduced to an animal." I add that he deserves it all. "I feel sorry for him," she says. *Kakomiris* (bad destiny). She tells me the son she lost at twenty would have been my age. Every Sunday morning for the past twenty three years she makes the half hour trip to the cemetery to light the *candili* wick on his tomb. She is always in black, always generous. When I don't have the exact change to pay for the clothes Kyria Katina tells me, "Another time."

It took days to realize we had left the world of orderly public spaces, customer-friendly salespeople, house appliances, clothes' dryers, fancy toothpastes, shelves of cereal brands and Low-carbohydrate Lifestyle Options. We were back to cars honking loudly because they almost hit you, drivers stopping in the middle of main roads to let someone off, waiting as they continued to chat with that person, dumpsters left on street corners so you couldn't see the cars coming, but none of it brought me entirely back until the evening I almost had another accident. My car still uninsured, I decided to drive to a friend's house when a car coming in the opposite direction made a sudden U turn and stopped inches from my bumper. I faced a young man I thought would back up and complete the turn. He didn't move. I thought, *He can't expect me to back up when he's just made an illegal turn*. He didn't budge. Then he made a hand gesture to show me he considered me *malakismeni* (the Greek equivalent of jerk or someone jerking off). I still didn't move. He made the gesture a second time. This time I gave him the finger. He yelled *malakismeni* (female masturbator), pulled up to my bumper and hit it with his. I almost laughed.

"You want to kiss?" I managed, thinking no one is going to believe this, then picked up my cell phone as if to call someone, mouthed, "*Malaka* (male masturbator)," and drove off.

I was back. Back to standing in lines that aren't really lines, to spaces claimed when there aren't any, to the people who assumed what little there was of it belonged to them.

At our supermarket the cashier couldn't find the price tag on a hat that had to be checked by a floor attendant. The woman behind me pushes her cart into the tiny space between me and the counter, unloading her things in a hurry as the metal cart rubs against my hip. I tell her I'm not finished. She sighs, "You might take an hour to finish."

I look at her surprised, "Even if it's an hour, I'm still in front of you." She rolls her eyes. When the cashier finally gets the price on the hat and I pay the bill the woman is busily stacking her groceries.

"You should learn to be more polite," I say, lifting my bags.

"So should you," she answers.

In the States it would have been unthinkable to admit to an insurance officer that I was using my car without coverage. In the States I learned to speak to automated recordings, to punch in numbers for specific needs, to be told by recordings to wait for the next available person, to spend a nightmarish weekend calling every number I was given at Kennedy airport to change a flight ticket back to Greece.

"Madame," a lone teller finally says on a late Sunday afternoon, "These are the numbers I have. I'm sorry if no one was available." For forty-eight hours I have no human way to change a plane ticket in one of the largest airports in the world. I am truly alien, *xeni* without the proper I.D.s. No one discussed what happened when the system didn't work, when I.D.s were unfamiliar. You did not speak in the States about what could not be resolved, the system meant to accommodate all possible problems. "You should remember professionals built the Titanic," the American ambassador in Athens told a graduating class one June. "And amateurs built Noah's Ark." I wanted to quip, "Remember professionals built the Twin Towers, and amateurs destroyed them." The stories which empower us legitimize us, others deconstruct that legitimacy, and still others affirm attributes we do not see. In America I lacked the proper I.D. for legitimacy. I had two passports, with different last names, my father's chopped version, and the Greek original. My identity was not recognized without an American driver's license. I was not allowed to pay with checks, though I carried an American passport.

"Sorry, we can't accept this I.D.," a salesperson at a GAP department store politely informs me.

"It's an American passport," I say, stating the obvious. "It's an I.D. that would be accepted in Poland, or anywhere in the world, and you're not accepting it in New York City?"

"I apologize," the salesperson says again, now uncomfortable. "But that's store policy. We need a driver's license or two photo I.D.s." I give her my two passports and my Greek driver's license. She calls the manager.

More fragments *from* "American Vignettes":

3
I need an address on checks.
My passport is not enough.
The name I have is longer than it's supposed to be.
My father chopped it
in fear he would be sent back
to the old country where he could not
save money. Here the fat of the land
is in our pockets, our Life's Savings, a diet
of all the fat we want, but no fruits
and few vegetables. This is what
I carry, oil of the fruit from the old country,
olive, virgin. The chopped name, no longer virgin
comes from the long one —
land of the oil I cook with
I crave your taste.

It happened again at Dulles Airport. I'm at a loss at how to check in for a domestic flight when I go to the counter with my passport. "Just punch in your number Madame," I'm told. I punch in some numbers that don't work. The woman behind the counter is busy with someone else. I look like I'm about the cry. The flight is on time, and I'm late. I ask another passenger in line who points out I've punched in the Orbit Access number and not the ticket number, then moves on. I'm still at a loss, punching in what I think is the ticket number only to be told I've put in too many digits. "Use your credit card as an I.D.," another passenger suggests. I murmur that my credit card has another name (my long Greek last name as opposed to my father's chopped version). The woman looks uncomfortable and quickly moves on. Finally a man working for the airline notices that I've been at the machine for awhile and asks if he can help.

"You know if you have a computer at home you can access your ticket from there." I shake my head, "I'm traveling; my father ordered the ticket for me." He smiles, taking my slip of paper to punch in the number himself. "Oh isn't that nice of him," he says, getting my ticket for me. "See how easy that was?" He adds, wishing me a good day.

There are the stories of people who waited patiently at their desks for further instructions when the first plane crashed into the Twin Towers, having remembered that the last terrorist bombing took place on the ground floor. There are the stories of those who obediently waited for official directions, and then there were those who took the initiative to get out of the building despite what they were being instructed to do. When I religiously bought my New World phone cards to make long distance calls it wasn't once that the connection wasn't completed and shut down because I had not put the pin number in quickly enough. I was furious that despite the long instructions in tiny type on the back of the cards, I couldn't get through to my other world. What if someone has arthritis, an old woman whose hand shakes when she holds up the receiver and dials? What if the receiver slips from her hand because she has Parkinson's and has to spend a full minute picking it up again and another full minute redialing? What if she can't see clearly enough, what if she's the person who gets her card blocked 'for security reasons' after the second failed attempt to punch in the row of numbers for her PIN? American culture prepares for what it has learned to expect; no one expected planes to deliberately crash through the two tallest buildings in New York City. Ignorant as the still-seeing Oedipus of the deeper complexities of human fallibility, America was shaken, its myth of invulnerability devastated by a foreign threat for a second time after Pearl Harbor. In Greece we expected vulnerability; we accommodated mistakes, prepared for them, and treated success like a miracle.

"There's always worse," says the owner of the neighborhood café when one of his customers offers to pay less than the amount owed. The owner has a small square of paper next to the cash register with a neat list of handwritten names and numbers next to them. The customer, an elderly pensioner, tells him he wants to give him less than what he owes.

"I just don't have it," he tells the owner, half smiling, leafing through a wad of cash in his hand, deciding what amount to give. The owner looks just slightly impatient, repeats, "*Ti na kano* (what can I do)?" The customer fingers a ten euro bill. It's less than the fourteen he owes but the owner takes it, as the customer promises him, "Next time."

At the butcher I notice a woman in line who audibly sighs as she asks the butcher what time he's going to close. He says around two. She says, "I should have gone to the bakery first. I didn't realize you would have so many people at this hour." He advises her to go, says, "You still have time." An elderly woman with a baby carriage who I assume is related to the butcher but isn't, offers, "I would give you my place, but I have to get home to feed him before he starts crying." The butcher interrupts, "No, no…you need to take care of the baby…" The elderly woman, maybe the grandmother, starts to sing, "*To pondikaki ine yia ton Theodoraki (the tender meat is for Theodoraki).*" The woman worried about making it to the bakery asks the butcher why he doesn't get some extra help during peek hours so people won't have to wait so long. The butcher is nonplussed, "For half an hour a day? It's not worth it."

∞

It happened to be the day of *Theofania*, God's (*theo*) apparition (*fenomai*), what in Greece is known as *ton foton* (of light). When I hail a cab to finally go downtown to renew my car insurance, the taxi driver is sleepy and wishes me *Hronia polla* (a life of many years). The traffic is dense on Mesogion street so I tell the driver he should drop me off at the metro station. I would probably get downtown faster on the train, he agrees and offers that he would do the same if he were in my place. On the metro an elderly woman slouches against the window pane, pouting, a middle-aged woman is loudly reprimanding her, "I'm respecting your age!" she shouts.

A man standing next to me is annoyed. "…Shh! We don't want to hear your fights." Both women go silent. I am home. Back to heated opinions, uncanny empathy, callous indifference, to *Ti fteo ego?* (What fault is it of mine?) and *Dhe variese*, (never mind), to the man in the hardware store who spends five minutes looking for black backed screws to match a hook I want to put up, who refuses to take any money, back to the pushy women at the supermarket check-outs, to being looked at incredulously when I ask for frozen fruit, to being asked if I really mean *frozen?*

But something has changed. There are signs up. The new highway ATTIKI ODOS is gradually opening arteries into the city. Flashing lights warn of tolls to appear along the old roads that were being freshly asphalted. In the metro there are large Adidas advertisements of famous athletes behind thick glass and steel frames telling us 'IMPOSSIBLE IS JUST AN OPINION'.

172

'IMPOSSIBLE IS TEMPORARY.' I go to the post office to find all the tellers wearing matching blue ELTA (Greek Postal Service) shirts. I suddenly miss the woman in her strapless tops who stubbornly wore them through winter under her thin sweaters. The good looking manager who would periodically stand up, hands on his hips, to gaze out over the line of people, eyeing the better looking or more scantily clad, is now at his desk. The clerk tells me someone else will stamp my letters when I quickly glue them to their envelopes, waiting to see the seal that puts the date verifying that they will be on their way. Specific people do specific tasks. Each teller has a computer, their own stand of Olympic pins and postcards that decorate each counter. I don't see any teller glue and date the stamps herself, or get up to take a sudden break in the middle of a full post office to get coffee. I still remember the make shift table in the middle of the room that we pushed around depending on how long the line got. People still line up out the door when there's a crowd, but more and more people simply leave when it gets cold.

I am back to sympathizing with the woman at the kiosk outside the post office who ritually breathes, "*Tha skasso*, I'm going to explode!"

Today a man is there buying stamps because the line at the post office is too long. "Don't explode, we want you…" he chides, and her haggard face lights up. She smiles and continues, "Only when I explode will I rest."

"Then don't, my dear," he goes on. "Just give me two stamps for domestic mail." She smiles again.

"What do you mean he won the case?" I am incredulous, on the phone with the car insurance lawyer who I had not heard from. He didn't remember the case, or me, when I call to find out what happened in November with the taxi driver. He is officious.

"Didn't you get my fax saying I was in the States?" He now remembers, "Yes," he received it, but my absence worked against me.

"How could they decide in favor of the driver when the court had evidence that the driver had brought in a false witness and lied?" I start to suspect my absence reaffirmed my status as a foreigner (*xeni*). The local taxi driver was local, a working taxi-driver, while I had proved myself privileged enough to leave.

"Not waiting for the police at the scene of the accident is considered a felony," the lawyer says matter-of-factly.

"And what about him?" I repeat.

"There was some possibility that you might have won," he says, "because of the fact that you told the judge you had to get back to your daughter. You had a reason for leaving, but you never know how a judge is going to decide." He pauses, "You can buy off the sentence with 250 euros."

I am dumbfounded. "As someone who has seen plenty of cases, don't you think, objectively, this is unfair? What protects someone like me, an average citizen, from someone like that taxi driver who lied and harassed me?"

There is a longer pause. "It's hard to predict what a judge will do," he begins. "I've seen judges favor people another judge would put in jail."

"And that's supposed to reassure me?" I am suddenly stressing my new world vocabulary. "What *actual legal rights* do *law abiding citizens* have?" He pauses again, more briefly, then with pragmatic calm informs me that if I plan to leave Greece for good I could get away with not paying the fine.

I am back to feeling desperate. I had forgotten the dichotomies of *typiko* (formal) as opposed to *ousiastiko* (essential), breeches of law. I had forgotten how formal or *typiko* decisions became confused with issues of belonging. Space was more easily made for *dyki tous*; there was too little of it to waste on foreigners who may prove you *koroido*.

On a cobbled street in the village of Lefkes on the island of Paros, an old woman comes out of her tiny house to break up a potential fight as our bus of students comes to a standstill on the narrow street. A local driver in a red and black flannel shirt driving a sedan quickly drives past a space on the curve where he could have made room for us to pass. Instead we are stopped, face to face or bumper to bumper, as he gestures with a lit cigarette in his hand for the bus to back up. The bus driver from Wales, hired by a study abroad program to usher their students around the island, waits patiently not quite understanding why the man in the sedan isn't backing up into the small inlet just behind him. It would have been harder and more dangerous to maneuver the bus backwards. We are stopped for some minutes until the old woman comes out of her home and begins to gesture to the local driver.

"*Here*, right *here*, there's *plenty* of room," she motions loudly, calling the local driver's attention to the loop of space where he can back up. I think he might be related to her, perhaps knows her son or daughter or husband. She obviously belongs to the village, a familiar *yiayia* boldly ushering the grown man to take note of what is obvious. The spaces in villages are limited and tight, the outside world always larger. The driver wordlessly backs up.

I asked the car insurance lawyer when I would have to pay the 250 euros, he said he would look into it and let me know. But a year later a police summons arrived in the mail.

"My license is going to be confiscated!" I repeat, trying to hold back the tears. I'm standing in line a little after 9 a.m., too early for a breakdown. A friend of mine advised me not to turn up when I told her about the summons, but I turn up. "I pay my taxes, I pay the fines, and I'm the one that's unprotected," I'm saying, loudly upset. An employee is looking through papers. He pauses while the serious expression on his face never changes. He finally says, "It's your lawyer I'm angry with. He should have let you know!"

"A year ago he told me I had a fine to pay, but he never called me back after that."

"You know these things are on the computer now, you could have been stopped at an airport. The charge would come up if it was still unpaid. You could have been taken in by the police there and then and not have had any idea why."

Now the tears are streaming down my face. The woman who gave me the news says, "It's the confiscated license she's upset about." I nod. I depend on the car to take my daughter to school every morning. She calls in the supervisor who hears my story. He tells me I can turn in my license whenever it's convenient, and asks how old my daughter is. Once the supervisor leaves the police woman tells me she'll hold onto the license for 15 days as opposed to the 30 stated by law, and we can arrange to do it at Easter time when I don't have to shuttle my daughter to school. "Just be careful," she adds, "for the rest of the month that I'm supposed to have your license, don't park anywhere illegal or drive in bus and taxi lanes." I thank her and leave as the man with the serious expression reminds me to call my lawyer, "Ask him what was the point of paying for insurance coverage if he couldn't do his job properly?"

My lawyer is terse, "What can I tell you," he says several times. "I might have forgotten to tell you part of the penalty was the confiscation of your license."

"You did forget," I say, just as terse.

"What does that change?" He adds.

"What that changes is that I was caught off guard and if I had not come across someone nice enough to give me some time I would have walked out of the police station without a license!" He says something about human mistakes when I answer that humans also pay for them.

〰

Chaos still took me by surprise. "Building #12, the first floor," the lawyer had told me simply enough. But the man behind the glass partition with his glum expression and dark circles under his eyes says, "You need to see if your charge is in the computer. That's building #16 in the basement; bring the verification from there."

Xerox machines are lined up on one side, and a crowded cigarette and coffee stand are on the other. I entered a busy Hades. Further inside the smoke thickened as did the groups of people. There is a guy with a sunken eye, someone else with long greasy hair and a mesh of wrinkles that spread into a surprisingly candid smile when I ask if I am in the right place. "You're in the right place but you won't get out very quickly." Someone asks the policeman in the hallway who is rhythmically flipping his worry beads to come tell someone else to stop smoking. There are faded print outs on the

175

walls saying 'No Smoking', and 'No Cell Phone Conversations'. One lawyer is on his cell telling a client, "I'm in this endless line for you! *Endless!* Cursing you...yes, *yes* you'll get the pardon." A person asked to put out his cigarette says, "Are you kidding?" Meanwhile the man behind the glass at the computer lights a cigarette. The policeman goes back to flipping his worry beads in the hallway. A young man ahead of me says, "I swear I'm going to come in here in a wheelchair tomorrow." There is another sign that informs people with special needs that they are given priority. A woman next to me is telling me she thinks she already paid for her fine but didn't keep the record. I suggest if she's paid, they must have a record on the computer; she laughs and says, "Now that they want to collect money from us there won't be any records."

It took two days of waiting and the car fine was still unpaid. The second day I arrived early, but again there was a crowd. The line had lost its shape, but we'd agreed amongst ourselves who was behind and in front of whom. One woman had been there since 8 a.m. It was now almost 10:30 a.m. This was her third day, she'd had to get a stamp on the second floor in building # 1, and then pay, and then come back to Hades, to wait again for the final stamp on her release. "Can't they have one person doing all this instead of having us run around to different buildings?" I ask.

The woman smiles, she has a cold, but isn't in a bad mood, "They want us to get the exercise," she says. By the time her turn comes, close to noon, her smile has slipped and she is talking about how much her feet are hurting her. I suddenly see a new face, a middle aged man with a beret smiling as the woman pushes her coffee stained paper under the window ledge to the man with the computer. She apologizes for the coffee stains and he shrugs. The man with the beret has managed to put his paper in after the woman, but a young man next to me with spiked hair and a two-tone leather jacket tells him it's not his turn. The man opens a wallet with a row of white tablets. "I have one artery," he says soberly. "Do you want to change places with me?" The guy says, "How do you know what my position is or whether I'm going to live past 30?" and lets the man with the beret have his way. "Not even a thank you?" I say, once the man with the beret hurriedly makes his way out of the crowd. He looks at me with unadorned contempt and says, "Would you have accepted it?"

When I finally pass my paper to the man at the computer it is almost 1p.m., closing time. "You're not on the computer," he tells me matter-of-factly.

I ask him to repeat himself. I don't hear, dizzy with the hours of standing. "You have to go to building #1 to get this paper verified because you're not on the computer yet." Numb, I trip over the crowd to run to building #1 before closing time. But the cashier mechanically tells me I owe double what I had been told at the police station. I don't have the money with me. I am silently crying. "Don't act like that," he says from behind the glass. "Don't you see this?" I now see a faded cardboard strip propped against the window that says there is a 92% surcharge on all felonies as of the first of the year. "How long do I have to pay this?" I mumble. "As long as you want," he says indifferently.

Outside the gates of Hades I notice a cripple selling Kleenex packets, a gypsy woman spreading embroidered cloths on the pavement, a man in a mismatched tweed jacket loudly hawking a book: "The story of a Revolutionary! Read about a true Greek hero!"

〰️

"No one's where they should be. The botanical graduates are in banking. The teachers become shop assistants until they're placed in public schools. Some of them wait years. The people who get the positions they want have their families in Athens gearing them up for those positions long before they even graduate. Qualifications are a lot less important than how well you've managed to make the necessary contacts. I don't know what anyone's waiting for in this place. What can you hope for when people are put into positions according to who they know or how willing they are to boost the egos of the ones who have power over them?" My colleague was one of many beside themselves with frustration.

The formal, *typiko*, procedures of how the country was run lagged behind or crushed the essence, *ousia*, of so much potential: he was telling me his story. He had come to teach in the private sector because after having ordered books for a course he was to teach in the fall at the University of Athens, his class had been given to a woman who had managed to convince the professor to let her teach it. He was never notified of the change. He came back from a leave in States only to find himself unemployed. "I was on a temporary contract," he explains. "Everyone has one in the beginning, and then you're supposed to graduate to a full time position once you do all the grunge work."

"Everywhere in the world people try to facilitate each other," he goes on, still overwhelmed by his disappointment five years later. "It's the establishment, not the average Greek that wins out in the end, moneyed families from other places like Egypt or from the provinces who fall into positions because of who they know in Athens."

It is pouring rain when I stop for a woman at the bus stop. I don't know why I stop; I pass the stop every time I go to work, and it wasn't the first time I'd seen a person waiting forlornly for transportation. She is dressed in the dark-colored skirt and blouse that seems almost uniform of women in their late 50s who work as domestic help. I ask if she wants a ride to the main road where public buses pass more frequently, she thanks me and gets in. In the course of our short ride she tells me she makes this journey everyday from

177

Korydalos, a working class neighborhood where one of the high-security prisons is located. She says she starts her days at 4 a.m. and returns home between 6 and 7 p.m. She explains how she gets a bus to Omonia Square and walks to Platia Kannigos Square, and from there takes another bus to Kifissia.

"God didn't let me down or abandon me in the twenty years I've been working," she smiles, telling me proudly of her granddaughter who she helped educate, whose books last year cost 300 euros which she managed to buy for her. "Babiniotis says she's a genius," she tells me with more pride, and adds, "She corrects the professors' papers, and they ask her advice." Babiniotis, a Rector at the University of Athens, might very well have recognized this young woman's bright exception, but I am cringing, remembering my colleague and my own disastrous interlude with the Greek university system. Neither he nor I had proved ourselves enough *dyki tous* to warrant inclusion in what this woman's hard work had helped her granddaughter become a part of.

A Greek psychiatrist I know is fierce. "If the country is ready to sacrifice the health of its people do you think it's going to care about their educations?" He describes the situation in the hospitals as dire, doctors and surgeons with expertise in their fields overlooked because an individual without credentials, or less of them, is given the job. There are the notorious *fakelakia* (envelopes) of cash that are slipped back and forth between patients and doctors so certain patients are given priority and assured of receiving the surgery they need. "It's a *prosfora* (offering)," one doctor explains to an incredulous client, "for the health care we provide."

Cronus and Oedipus. As Kyria Lambri at the Supreme Court reminded me, Greece ate her children, and like the young Oedipus remained blind to the causes of what plagued her city. A new American Studies position was being announced at the University of Athens. The department was not happy with Scylla, too opinionated, too dictatorial with the students, too stubborn, publishing in the wrong field (not an American studies scholar to begin with), too much like her Homeric namesake for anyone's good. But her time for promotion was coming up, and the department wanted to find a formula, some *typikotita*, to put her in her place. A Greek woman I know at one of the private colleges was invited to come speak to the department members.

"Who is this guy Markopoulos?" she asked me over the phone. Someone she had never met in the English department at the University called her up at home.

"There are so few of us in American studies here, we should get to know each other's work and do more conferences," he said, introducing himself. She mentioned, in the course of the conversation, my name, as someone involved in American Studies; there'd been a pause. She suggested it had been a mistake not to have hired me. He apparently admited there have been mistakes, but wanted to invite her to come to his office and chat informally, to bring her CV and have some of the others in the department, including Circe, casually drop by to ask some questions.

"In other words they conducted an interview," Arete breathed rapidly into the phone. Though a full professor in American Studies, Arete had not been invited to drop by to chat with the potential candidate.

"Maybe they have another name for this too," I offer.

"This is a public service job, the offices at the university are considered public grounds, and here they are interviewing someone for a position that hasn't even been advertised yet." I am surprised she is so surprised after all that has happened; the boundaries of protocol, whether legal or not, are dependent on the relative ideas of *ousia* and *typikotita*: essence was subjective and private, formalities were public.

"Why have you never applied for a position with us?" asked one of the professors who dropped by to chat with the potential candidate. My friend answered that she was under the impression positions are tagged in advance for favored candidates, to which the vocal professor who was fond of Che Guevara, became emphatic, "No, no…we're very just," she assured her , adding that no such favoritism existed. Circe agreed that everything was done with *typiko* formality while informally pointing out that my friend should try to have more publications on her CV.

In the midst of the earnest detailing of the questions and answers of the professors gathered in one of the offices of the University of Athens, I ask my friend to stop. She assumed I'd find the story amusing. "You don't understand," I finally say, when she's taken aback by my increasing agitation. "They'll never see me the way they see you, they'll never admit that they made a mistake when they hired Scylla for the American Literature position."

"I'm still not sure that I'm even going to apply," she goes on. "I told them I'm happy where I am and have a lot of respect from the administration and the students…"

I know it will be unavoidable; I would have done the same had I been given the option. Anne Carson discusses the changing contexts of *xenia* in ancient Greece: the 'ritualized friendships' of a Homeric time, Odysseus – who takes for granted the 'complete dinner' and 'full livelihood' of a community that 'felt responsible for another's well-being' – is compared to a later period when the ancient poet Simonides must negotiate his *xenitia* (one of exiled or alienated status) in cash payment for commissioned poems. Simonides is "both *xenos* and employee, both friend and hireling, of his patron," Hieron, a tyrant, whom he is invited to share dinner with. (Carson 22)

"Why have you never approached us before?" my friend is asked again by the department professors.

Carson pinpoints a shift in the social context of the word's usage: "For alongside 'guest' and 'host' the Greek word *xenos* denotes 'stranger,' 'outsider,' 'alien.'" My friend's deliberate distancing from the department threatened to unmask the perversions of belonging, of what it took to become *dyki tous*; their question is more urgent than what one might assume. 'Why would you want to remain alien, a stranger?' Those who already belonged emphatically assured her the rules of *typikotita* were adhered to. Procedure as it was interpreted and manipulated was meant to protect *ousia*. But if unfamiliar and therefore unpredictable, *ousia* might disrupt rather than serve the social conventions of *typikotita*. Prometheus stole *ousia* in the form of fire from the gods and then, intoxicated with the power, was not sure how to handle it. The civil service, national universities, hospitals and ministries, were filled with the swollen *ousia* of people who were less than capable, and some who were dramatically incompetent. *Ousia* was fickle when unharnessed, *typikotita* was meant to rope it in, otherwise there was unbounded *lissa*. The fire ate you up.

When Greece won the European Cup in soccer just before the August Olympics it became a public victory for the country, "It's the year of Hellas!" exclaimed one TV commentator. "Tonight everyone has the right to joy! Greece is here! Even if Greece wasn't favored, we won! All over the world people are rejoicing. The Greeks of the world are rejoicing! Wherever Hellenism lives…Thessaly, Thessalonica, Macedonia…wherever there are Greeks in the world this is a great moment," goes on another. More passionately still, another exclaims, "When the Greek soul is united it creates miracles! This winning lets us, *o laos* (the people), celebrate ourselves." And more somberly, "the potential of this race is great…if only we could believe and embrace it!" The private desires of a nation had become a public victory, people including my daughter spilled out into the streets, into the squares and main thoroughfares, into fountains and buses (bus drivers obediently complying) to stop traffic and dance in the streets. The Greek flag waved from balconies and cars for weeks.

"This was a tight *parea* (group of friends)," notes another commentator, the term meant to suggest that the victory was more the result of kinship than team work and talent. The *ousia* of near familial loyalties had become the heart of the defeat of *xena* (foreign) teams.

At dinner with friends, one of whom was a professor in the educational math department at the University of Athens, a conversation takes place about the usual dysfunction of the public sector. Our friend is incensed about how a seemingly obvious mistake sabotaged an entire project with valuable information for students in a class he is teaching. "It was a packet of the newest research put together by different members of an EU research board that worked with computer programming technology. We had put months of work into it and were going to distribute it in our classes but it had to be first approved by the Ministry of Education." Apparently someone in the Ministry put the wrong date on the packet. Instead of February, the month it was put together, he had written May; it was rejected as having been submitted too late for approval. The fact that the students were denied the advantage of up-to-date research, the fact that valuable time had been invested by valuable contributors, all became secondary to the mistaken date on the packet. Our friend shrugged, unconsoled, *ousia* had not worked in tandem with *typikotita*.

Athens in the first months of 2004 was a physical metaphor of the new and old converging, of *ousia* and *typikotita*, content and procedure, vying to finally catch up with each other for the Olympics. My neighborhood was a microcosm of what was going on in the larger city, the main street ripped up for new piping, and while they were at it, the town Major had decided to finally widen the pavements so the aged and people pushing strollers didn't have to walk in the road to bypass broken or nonexistent strips of sidewalk that were usually straddled by parked motorcycles and cars. For months the already narrow road was cluttered with bobcats hauling brick slabs and cement chunks and the always busy flow of traffic going up and down in both directions. To negotiate the cars, a worker would periodically stop one direction so the opposite direction had the right of way. Inevitably, between the stopped flow in one direction and the bobcat's maneuvering across the street, drivers tried to take advantage of the stalled interval to keep moving. Inevitably, drivers in the stopped lane would begin honking, indignant that cars in the opposite lane weren't respecting the bobcat's necessary maneuver across the street.

One morning is particularly hellish. Besides the bobcats there is a cement truck parked on what little space is left on the ripped up sidewalk. A restaurant had decided to renovate amidst the chaos. Cement is being funneled to the roof. People are honking. It is rush hour, and a local bus is also coming up the road. I pull to the side with the rest of the cars waiting for the bobcat to finish its maneuvering, but the more impatient drivers coming down in the opposite direction are trying to pass the bobcat before the bus got so close that they would have to wait for it to pass — another three minute delay. Two drivers, honking madly, swerve around the bobcat and side step the bottleneck. The cars stopped on my side are furious. The bus is now behind us and about to push its way through the little road left. Suddenly a man carrying a bunch of brooms appears out of nowhere, balancing some six brooms across his shoulders, gingerly weaving his way between the cars. He is right in front of the car in front of me, which suddenly has a clearing to move. We are sweltering in the heat. I think the broom vendor is going to be hit. No one is going to have any patience for someone who so obliviously steps in front of a group of drivers insane with frustration.

But the car in front of me lets the man pass, without any fuss. I am amazed. It is the last thing I expect to see. He doesn't even honk which I imagine, at the very least, would have scared the poor guy and had him dropping all his brooms. We lose our chance to pass the construction before we are kept stopped for another bobcat maneuver.

These are the unexpected spaces made to avoid casualties, in this case a broom vendor. These were not scenes familiar to a first world where efficiency is uncompromising, the wide roads and visible signs suggesting a system secure in itself. In Greece we hardly believe we can catch up; our systems are insecure, contradictory, conflicted. Despite the massive construction projects for the upcoming Olympics, despite the new tunnels and impressive arteries of roadway that made up *ATTIKI ODOS*, we half expected the worst, we learned to swerve around the broom vendors and dumpsters, ignore the cars that bolted ahead of turning lanes to make the lights, ignore the mistakes.

I am surprised to be heading toward a toll. The road is the usual road I take to head south, but the route had changed in the time we were away. All I have is some loose change. I forget that I left my wallet in another bag, and start to panic. The young man at the booth greets me with a smile. "I don't know if I have the right amount," I begin. I count out a euro eighty; the toll sign says two euros for cars. He takes the coins I slip into his hand, counts them out individually, nods and says, "I'll cover it for you," and lets me through.

≈≈

It is voting day in Greece and I have to find the new school building in Nea Smyrni, a neighborhood south of the city where my grandparents' Syngrou house had stood, where they had lived their lives and were now buried, where my Greek I.D. was issued and where I am registered to vote. The locations are now available online. We can download maps, but they are illegible. After two decades of the Pan-Hellenic Socialist Party (*PASOK*) in power, it looks like New Democracy (*Nea Democratia*) is going to win.

It had been years since I was in Nea Smyrni, the Syngrou house was long gone, a BMW car dealer bought the lot, tore down the house and put up a huge neon sign that stayed lit all night. The only thing that remained of the old house was the date tree my grandfather planted. Professionally trimmed and cut except for some healthy sprouting branches at the top, it stood tall and leafless in the midst of a wide cement sidewalk.

"Where is the Evangeliki Sholi?" I ask a young man at the kiosk. I stop for directions to the voting center. He shrugs, hardly looking up from a magazine he's reading. I'm lost and ask if he knows if the school is near the cemetery. He shrugs again, annoyed that I am still there. I finally say, "If you were as interested in your clients as you are in your magazine you might have some business."

He puts the magazine down and looks at me with hostility. "If you asked nicely I might help you."

Back in the car, driving toward what I vaguely remember is the direction of the cemetery, I realize I have no idea where I am and try another kiosk, this time an elderly man smiles from behind a pile of gum, candy bars and playing cards. "Do you have any idea where the Evangeliki Sholi is?"

"We'll know in a minute," he says as if he was expecting me. I realize I'm not the first to stop for directions. He unfolds a tattered map, taped all along its middle, puts on his glasses and points to a corner, slipping the map around for me to see. "It's right here. You go down that road," he turns to show me a street to the left of the kiosk, "and you're almost there." He was right. I found the center in a few minutes, managed to vote and leave quickly.

It is early evening. I am driving in front of the Nea Smyrni cemetery where Ismini and Aimilos are buried, it's been years since I visited my grandparents' graves.

A woman selling carnations at the cemetery gates wants to wrap them in cellophane. "I'm taking them in there," I say, pointing toward the gates. She smiles, handing them to me with their wet stems. It's almost closing time, nearly empty. The stands of church candles are lit and visible in the chapel's dark interior as I pass down a narrow walkway. Plants smother the grave sites, real and plastic flowers, small shrubs near the various tombs, lemon trees. There are benches on some plots, small mausoleums decorated with marble planters; one has an aluminum door, a pergola of climbing vines. One grave site has a motorcycle embedded in its wall, below it is the picture of a young attractive man: Thomas Michailidis, 1963-1987. Whole family portraits decorate others. I read the family name, ZAROS, and then below, *IKOGENIAKO SPITI* (the family house); there is an 83 year old woman, a 91 year old man, a 46 year old woman and a 62 year old man.

I feel tears sting my eyes as I approach my grandparents' tomb. "Who will remember us?" *Papou* would say at the dinner table in the Syngrou house. "People are egoistic."

I stare at their names carved into white marble: Aimilios Kalfopoulos, Ismini Kalfopoulou, the hyphen between the dates of their lives. On the morning of *Papou's* funeral, I kept hearing his voice, 'Who knows where we are going Adrianna?' The church was thick with the scent of Easter lilies, their perfume almost suffocating as he lay sternly in his casket, dressed in his best suit. Ismini knelt against him, shrunken with grief. I couldn't stop the tears. In that tiny chapel an odd group of people had gathered to say goodbye, faces I had not seen before and some I had forgotten, the mysterious gardener who had come to prune the date tree, a tall, elegant woman with a black turban. Maria. Mrs. Pantazis who stood at the back with a handkerchief crushed against her mouth, a woman who dragged herself in with a three-legged aluminum walker and stoically leaned against it instead of sitting down. People kept calling "Aimilios," as if in conversation with him.

"So you are no longer aliens, or foreign visitors (*xenoi kai paroikoi*): you are citizens like all the saints, and part of God's household," quotes Julia Kristeva of the apostle Paul's *Ecclesia* (the Greek word for church). The Pauline church is a 'new alliance', 'a community of foreigners', what would bring together 'local Churches' into a universalist vocation (Kristeva 81). In that small chapel we were gathered strangers listening to the priest chant the last rites. Behind the stand of candles were the lit faces of aged women, one whose eyes glowed like wet gems in her shattered face. I wanted to find a large *lambatha* candle, not the thin wax stems that were piled up on a wood stand for a few cents. I asked a woman who was locking a door at the back of the church. Without saying anything she unlocked the door, nodding me into a room with some pails and mops, a priest's black robe neatly ironed on a hanger, a vat of *koliva* covered with cellophane on a table. She briskly picked out a long white candle, thicker than the small stemmed ones and pushed it into my hand. I was about to ask her what I owed when she brusquely shoved me out the door as wordlessly as she had ushered me in.

A wail like a sound across time cut through me. Ismini lurched over the casket as four men started to lift it to their shoulders. Mrs. Pantazis rushed forward to let her body collapse against hers. I was suddenly next to her, crying as our small procession made its way to the gravesite.

Afterwards we went to the cemetery *cafenion* where people drank cognac and ate sesame biscuits, murmuring, *zoi se mas* (life with us).

I put the carnations in the plain marble urns, light the *candili* wick behind a pane of glass on the tomb. Someone must come by occasionally because there's oil in the bowl so the flame can take. A woman passing from another grave nods my way. I smile, not sure if I know her, she nods again without pausing. *"Torn between two worlds [...] split less between two countries than between two psychic domains [...]. Foreigners could recover an identity only if they recognized themselves as dependant on a same heterogeneity that divides them within themselves..."* (Kristeva 82) Paul speaks of his *Ecclesia*, of how he managed to unify the Jews and Greeks under 'a new creation.' Split and foreign I returned to Greece, was embraced then split again, foreign all over living among a people equally split; I came upon a scar, a history of cuttings. "God is meant to gather his people in an embrace," an architect on Patmos said to me. Explaining the rounded dome of Greek Orthodox churches, he said, "We are meant to bow our heads as he too bows down to hold us." We were sometimes crushed, sometimes desperate for the haughty spires of Cathedrals where one looked upwards into infinity, God too high to reach.

Exile is chilling. It leaves you too much space; you take it with you, you don't realize you have been denied yourself until someone treats you as foreign, alien in your own skin. I touched my skin differently in the States, newly moisturized and quenched, smoothed with 'Gentle Polishing Pearls' by *Caress* I could, as the ads urged 'Grin and Bare it'.

4

I'm excited I can do things to my face,
inject a chemical, help it look younger, it's an idea
like the beauty of being here. The deer are stunned
by the highways. Distance is there to catch. Cut roots.
Go fast. Lift the lawns. Houses are carried
across the country on the backs of trucks.
Greek village donkeys carry hay this way.
A friend tells me he stayed in Greece
because his parents set the temperature at 71
all year round, his childhood had no seasons.
Now he suffers from the heat, wishes
he could afford more shirts. I promise to send some
from Target. My brother-in-law's T-shirts
burned his Jersey house down, stacked so high
the fabric touched the closet ceiling bulb,
caught fire like lit leaves, like my mother's eyes,
a motherland heart break, consumed.

"Never mind, bring me the money tomorrow, or whenever you come by again," my neighborhood pharmacist tells me in Athens when I explain I need to run home to get the rest of what I owe her for the things I bought. "I will never forget how I had to find medicine for my baby one night in France. I wouldn't wish anyone in that position. I promised myself I would never do what that woman did to us." She describes a cold fall night when she and her husband arrived in the foreign country, their one year old feverish and coughing, this long before the appearance of the euro. Nothing was open to change their drachmas, but they had dollars with them. The pharmacist refused to take the dollars or give them medication for the baby without payment in francs.

〰

I wake one morning to a sound like the moan of a low flying bird, "*Avgaa, Avgaa...*" The *paliadjidhes*, often gypsies who scavenged anything from refrigerators to plastic chairs to odd furniture, called out their wares with the same drawn out chant. I see an older woman in torn market shoes, a plastic bag over her head to protect it from the rain as she speaks into a microphone looped around her shoulder, the wires attached to a metal carriage she pushes along. "*Avgaa, Avgaa...*" she moans on into the microphone so the sound becomes a lament. I see, in the metal basket, the stacked cartons of fresh eggs she is hawking. At first I think she's a bag lady half mad with dejection until through the drone of words I make out what she is saying; she has an intricate system of attaching the microphone to what I guess is a battery in her basket. Even the plastic around her head is carefully arranged to protect her from getting too wet. The eggs are stacked in rows of threes, the cartons held together with several rubber bands. She walks at a slow but steady pace. I don't see any takers though she pauses at certain houses as if she knows them or expects someone to come out. Eventually a middle aged woman coming down the road with bags of groceries greets her, dropping her groceries on the pavement to buy a carton of eggs. Something is said between them and the egg lady digs out some coins from a pouch under her shirt. They don't spend much time in conversation as she hands over the eggs, then moves on pacing her chant.

On the newly opened *ATTIKI ODOS*, now composed of long bands of freshly asphalted highway that pretzeled over and around Attica, or Attiki, it seemed like we could finally catch up, make it on time to wherever it was we were going, get through most of what we planned to get done. There was still the orange fencing where roadwork was incomplete, there were still bulldozers. Trucks parked haphazardly here and there, people assuming their right of way where, suddenly, no u-turns were allowed. But the new roads were almost finished, just in time for the Olympics. "*Kalo Dhromo* (good road or trip)," a woman in uniform, with matching hat and jacket, wishes me as I pay my 2-euro toll to make my way to Koropi, a town near the sea where I am supposed to meet relatives for lunch. Someone behind me screams, "*Ela! Ela!*" as I ask the woman in uniform what exit to take. I think to gesture to the man shouting behind me to shut up, but the light turns green and the bar lifts for me to pass.

We were like children who had climbed up to the highest diving board at the swimming pool but weren't quite sure how to dive. Most of the cars were small, a lot of drivers found themselves needing to suddenly veer left, too close to the exit lane and cars getting off, or too far left and needing, dangerously, to get further right to exit. You could tell when someone had missed their exit, the car momentarily slowed down until someone speeding from behind honked maniacally and the hesitant driver quickly picked up speed again. There was no getting off once you got on, unless you took an exit. I drove through reams of road construction, through new tunnels, kilometers of arrows warning of momentarily narrowed road. All the gas stations and cafés seemed to be on the other side without any access from the road. I was terrified I was going in the wrong direction, there were no signs. I finally turned into a dirt path to ask a gas station attendant where Koropi is, he spoke to me with an Albanian accent. I explained I wanted to get to the row of tavernas where men in aprons call out to the passing cars to come in for food. He nodded, told me I was going in the right direction. The hills were the same dusty green, the vineyards were still vineyards, but ribbons of just finished highway now crisscrossed the land alongside the olives and above the orchards; it was all familiar but also unfamiliar. My daughter said, "I feel like I'm in the States, Mom." Next to the highway were large stock houses, a new Holiday Inn.

"At least the pensioners don't have to wait anymore," one of my relatives tells me at lunch. We actually manage to find the taverna in Koropi, tucked as it is behind orange fencing that zoned off the construction. "People used to get their pensions three years after they retired."

"So what did people do in those three years?"

She shrugs, "Families helped." Her own husband has had several strokes, he is looking at us from the other end of the table. He curses me for saving him," she smiles. "He tells me 'why didn't you just let me die…it's because of you that I'm still alive.'"

I laugh, "Instead of thanking you."

She lights another cigarette and shrugs good-naturedly. "I was hoping for a change, that's why I voted for the right wing party this time." *Nea Democratia* (New Democracy) had won the majority vote and finally ousted *PASOK*, the party founded by Andreas Papandreou in 1974. "I think most of us voted right just for the change. We need it. Who knows," she mused, "after awhile they might become corrupt too. But it's good that pensioners now get 70% of their money right away."

"And the rest?"

"The government said they would give them the rest over a period of time, two to three years. It's better than nothing. Before people had to wait two to three years to begin to get anything."

I nod. "What do you think of these roads?"

"I used to take friends to the airport to go to London and they would be in England before I made it back to Kifissia because of all the traffic. Now we can actually get to places and arrive without sacrificing the whole day."

Everyone was talking about the new roads and the Olympics, now just a few weeks away. It was late July. Athens was in a frenzy of preparation. The Olympic symbol suddenly appeared painted in the middle of a fresh Olympic lane for shuttle buses and cars transporting athletes and VIPs to the venues;

the new tram was zipping up and down the southern suburb of Alimos, and through parts of central Athens. The metro map had added stations: there was the expansive marble and steel interior of the brand new Halandri station, there were the added stations of *Agios Dimitrios* and *Agios Antonios*, and a super train seemed to appear out of nowhere alongside the highway to and from our Elefetherios Venizelos airport. The city had changed, and it felt like it happened overnight. We could hardly believe it: every day there was another addition. Fluorescent yellow lines coated the curbs of sidewalks and pavements to indicate no parking was allowed, people were in the streets handing out handsome maps of the Olympic Transportation System, the recordings that announced station stops in the metro were repeated in English, there were periodic announcements throughout the stations that 'No Eating Or Drinking' was allowed. I also noticed something I had never seen before. Above the station ticket booths, taped to the glass were pictures of Missing Children: one face in particular stayed with me. You couldn't tell if it was a boy or a girl because the child's head was shaved, until you read the name, an Albanian girl whose large unblinking eyes stared out into the world with terror and wonder.

"At least we'll have the roads," Anastasia agrees when I go to get a haircut. I ask if she has tickets for any of the games.

"I'm too tired," Anastasia answers. "The kids are already at my mother's in Peloponnesus, and Dimitri and I are going as soon as I close the shop on the first of the month." I admit I haven't bought tickets either, but am having my doubts about not trying to see a few events. It will be something my daughter will remember all her life. "They should have kept us more rested," she adds, "if they wanted us to have enough energy for the games." She wasn't the only one who felt drained from the stress of what the preparations had taken out of those of us living with the daily reality of a city torn apart. First it was the metro, new bridges, widened thoroughfares, and then the construction for *ATTIKI ODOS*, the new turnoffs and tunnels redirecting traffic zones, whole swatches of the city rerouted to accommodate the works in progress. Besides the physical difficulties of getting around, there were the financial costs; electric and water bills seemed to have suddenly inflated *pagia*, public service charges, sometimes as much as the actual electricity consumed. Prices in the supermarkets and grocery stores had skyrocketed. But we had gorgeous marble and iron sculptures by famous Greek artists suddenly appear on street corners; two new marble fountains with more sculptures in the middle of Ermou street just below Syntagma Square. The ruins, Hadrian's Gate, and the Agora in Plaka were swathed in lighting at night; the scaffolding around the Acropolis was mysteriously invisible. Our roads were decorated with pastel colored banners, all shades of blues, yellows, greens and mauves that announced the 2004 Athens Olympics with the olive wreath. The Olympic slogan, 'Catch the Light' waved from flag poles. I saw more people in the streets, more people smiling. My daughter pointed out a woman in her wheelchair being pushed by a much younger woman. "Mom, she looks like she hasn't seen the sun in years." In complete black, thin as a dried branch, her white skin was translucent as she lifted her face to the light.

"At least we'll be left with the roads and the stadiums," Anastasia repeated. "Let the visitors come and enjoy the city and the games. We need to get some rest."

Lenten Epilogue

Whatever you hold in your hands
so carefully, with so much love,
yours so totally, my companion,
you must give away
in order for it to become yours.
Yannis Ritsos, *Mode of Acquisition*
(translated by Edmund Keeley)

I packed the wrong clothes for the trip unaware that I was on a pilgrimage, that the weather would be freezing, much too windy and damp to take off my coat let alone expose my neckline. It was time to go to Patmos again, it was the long weekend of what in Greece we call 'Clean Monday' (*Kathari Dheftera*). Next week the Lenten fast begins. I was carrying gifts for Stella, Maria, Maria's children, Kyria Fotini and, as always, things for the house. My bags were heavy. "Take the bus, and then the metro," Zoi says to me when I go by for coffee the morning I decide to leave. "Don't get mixed up with the traffic, parking…money for taxis. The #407 on the street below your house will take you straight to the metro. Change in Syntagma for Omonia, and from there get the train to Pireaus."

I did exactly what she said. I walked to the street below mine. The only one waiting there, embarrassed when a woman lugging her garbage out of an apartment gave me a look that made me feel like I was in the wrong place. "Does the 407 pass regularly?" I ask, almost apologetic.

"Yes, Yes!" she is emphatic, throwing her garbage into a bin. "Where do you want to go?"

"To the metro station."

She shakes her head affirmatively. "It will take you *right there*." It did, and so painlessly I was almost joyful. No parking anxiety, no hassling with insane drivers.

The sun bled a diffuse, fading color over the evening sea. A couple of people loitered on deck, but most were in the ship's salon smoking and talking noisily as four televisions blared from different channels in each corner. I'm surprised to see so many people, especially with the bad weather predictions. I find a seat before we leave port, order coffee. The same guy in his torn white waiter's jacket is selling crossword puzzles, playing cards, *dramamini* (pills for the queasy). Every time I'm on the *RHODOS* he's onboard, though he is starting to look much older which makes his drone, "crosswordpuzzlesplaying cards*dramamini*," sound vaguely mad. Today I take a better look at him, see twenty or thirty key chains pinned to his chest swinging in tandem as he strolls through the seating area looking for takers. Kleenex packets wrapped with rubber bands and tiny backgammon sets are stacked inside a wicker basket kept together with duck tape around his arm. People nod his way.

On deck I watch the last of the sun slip behind the bottom horizon, and realize the old man had disappeared once the ship left port. There was the occasional steamship or ferry that appeared like a smudge in the distance. I ate my hard boiled eggs, thinking if one slipped in the suddenly gusting wind I'd have to resist the urge to jump after it. The sea below was almost black, and the wind turned cold. I wanted a drink. Lots of young men in military uniforms gathered at the bar in the smoke filled salon. I noticed one man sitting by himself at the table next to mine, odd in his aloneness. People kept gathering into bigger and bigger circles around the small tables. The empty seats around my table were asked after. "Can I take this?" I nod. A little later the next one goes, then another. I left my coat and bag on one so I felt less bereft among the talkative people. The young soldier sitting alone was looking at me, he almost smiled. I looked down to my book, drank more Campari, wished I weren't so shy. The next time I looked up he was asleep.

The cabin's dark smells of trapped cigarette smoke. Three women are asleep in bunk beds. I get into mine but can't sleep. I haven't been to the island for over a year, since I left Greece for the States. I'm excited and uneasy. Too warm in the cabin to sleep, the air's stale and keeps me awake until the purser knocks around 1:30 in the morning. We're nearing Patmos.

It's windy outside, the sea's a fabric of darkness. Patches and patches of tearing white froth split along the sides of the ship. As we near port I see the houses of Skala, the port, sporadic along the single shore road, their lights a loose necklace with gaps of darkness, like the lives on the island and the sudden deaths.

A young man is standing next to me in the belly of the ship as the iron tongue of the gangway opens to sky. There's the sound of rolling chains, the slowing slap of waves. Several nuns in their black habits wait to get off, a priest, the person who runs the waterskiing club in the summer. I don't see any of the soldiers on their way to a further place. The young man is attractive in his loose black jeans, heavy vest and trendy oblong-shaped glasses. His nose and ears are pierced. I like his height and build, stocky with good posture, comfortable in his skin. He holds the door open for me as we make our way further into the belly of the ship. I wonder if we'll run into each other on the island. But the last I see of him is a handsome self-contained figure disappearing down the night road as I climb into one of two waiting taxis. Thomas, the young driver, recognizes me. "Hi," he says. "What brings you here in February?"

As the taxi climbs the hill up to the village of Hora, I watch the ship pull soundlessly back into the night, lit like a piece of jewelry. It starts to rain. Stella is up waiting for me, the portable heater is on in the bedroom. We hug each other. "Tell me your news!" she laughs as we hug again. "Tell me, tell me…Oh, you've lost weight. How about me?" She lifts her sweatshirt smiling.

"You look the same," I say.

She's disappointed, "No! You haven't taken a good look. I've lost!"

We laugh, but Stella wants me to eat something. All I want is tea though the smell of bread and biscuits reminds me of how hungry I am. I want to hear Stella's stories and give her the gifts I've brought. "Eat something," she urges, opening a Tupper of homemade biscuits, "You need a full stomach to sleep."

I sleep badly, hungry, cold, listening to a hungry rain. On the ship I imagined I would go to the monastery in Hora. In bed I waited for sleep to swallow me, but wake exhausted with fragments of Stella's news in my head. Her husband had knocked on her door after finally moving out to live with the Albanian woman who bartended for him. He was drunk, wanted to know who gave her the earrings she was wearing, the new chain around her neck. "I gave them to myself," she said. "Stella gave them to Stella because now it's Stella's turn to live."

"When he was gambling did he think about where I was going to get the bread for lunch? When he's fucking his whores does he think about what I'm doing to raise his children?" Now he has a fancy speedboat, says he keeps his woman because she's trustworthy, but knocks on Stella's door in the middle of the night.

"Who would have thought," Stella says to me the night before, eating biscuits over tea, "that I wouldn't want to see his face again?" I also thought my lover would be ravenous to see me after I came back from the States. Desire bleeds like a setting sun when the object of desire is gone. I am flooded when I tell Stella, "I really want to love someone."

"No," she answers, shaking her head, serious. "It hurts too much."

As the rain drums through the night, as I finally get up in the cold room, I am thinking *it hurts too much*. "Don't you want to devote yourself? To feel like someone will devote himself to you?" I insisted. Stella shook her head.

"It passes," she said, "after awhile it passes. And you'll want your freedom again. I told my husband enjoy my arms around you because when they're gone it will never happen again. And that's what happened. You have no idea what it's like to hold a hollow body." She says it's too late for her, says she can never be in love again, "What I wanted when I was young I don't want anymore." Stella described last night's half moon as a sunken eye, murmuring, "If only we could shine like that when we hurt."

Marko comes to prune the jasmine and bougainvillea. "How long has it been?" he chides, cutting, his scissors flying. Sharp, quick, he cuts and pulls out the stiffened tendrils. I am horrified. "That jasmine bush is the best thing about this house. *Don't* cut it down *so much!*" He eyes me through the branching limbs.

"Nothing's going to happen to it, this is going to sprout in spring." He goes over to the bougainvillea and shakes his head. "If this could speak it would be yelling. If you let this go any longer without pruning, it would eventually have died, it's already drying up." No buds. Marko cuts, pulls stiff lengths scraping through the trellis. He blinks, nonplussed when I warn of thorns. "This is my job," he grins. "You have to love what you do." I listen the way I have learned to listen to Stella, to Theologos, to Stavros, to almost everyone I've met on the island. He is telling me a story about advice an apparent expert was giving one of the rich home owners in Hora. "He wanted to cut down his trees in August." Even I groaned, "*August?*" The pile of dead bougainvillea and jasmine vines covered the ground. "If these branches could talk," Marko says again, interrupting himself, "they would be cursing you." He tells me he told the rich home owner that he refused to prune anything in August; it would kill the growth, so the home owner allowed the so called expert to do the pruning for a good sum. The leaves on the lemon tree were the first to darken. The home owner called Marko to check the sap that wouldn't stop seeping from the cut limbs.

"If I cut my arm at the elbow right now won't I bleed to death?" he asks.

I left Greece in August, in full summer. I didn't bleed to death, but my dreams were full of sap, the smell of sea, the smell of my lover's skin. Now it's late February, a safe time to cut away the dead branches.

I slip my sweater over the two long-sleeved T-shirts I slept in. I think of making coffee in Stella's house but it's too cold. Maria upstairs has central heating. Her house is cluttered with comfort, from the always filled refrigerator to the fruit bowl that never has less than three kinds of fruit in it. Today it's full of bananas, apples and kiwi. She had a party the night before and proudly shows me the pineapple she decorated with toothpicks of broccoli, olives and cauliflower. I give her two boys the Disney underwear I brought them and some Mission Master Batman dolls. I sent Maria a Disney sweatshirt from the States which she says she loves but wishes I had brought her the Disney cookie jar. I tell her it was too heavy to carry. She is smiling. She understands but wishes she had it anyway. "We'll see," I tell her, explaining that maybe I could coax my mother to send it. She wonders why Disney took Greece off its list of countries they mail to. When I first met Maria she collected Disney catalogues but had no idea she could actually order anything from Patmos. When I suggested she get a VISA card to do it, she immediately placed three large orders in six months to be sent to Patmos. By the eighth month Greece

194

was removed from the Disney list of 'Countries We Ship To' which included Bulgaria, Turkey, Romania and others. I feel badly that I didn't manage to get Maria her cookie jar. I think there is little she lacks in her warm house. Stella has made it her purpose to provide her daughter with all she never had, including marrying her to a devoted man. She tells me she can only give to her children and grandchildren now, after having lost her son, after her husband's brutality and infidelities; she gives them nurture to defy her lack. But Maria describes her obsession with Disney products as *lissa*, something she can never have enough of.

I have lunch with Kyria Fotini, Stella's sister, who tells me of her son Gerasimos's wedding this past fall, how she spent days making Patmian sweets to pass out to everyone in the village. Then I see Stavros in his carpentry shop, we chat. Today he tells me, "Life is like an onion, the more you peel it open the more it makes you cry."

The ironsmith takes a look at the picture from a magazine I brought from the States to see how I want to replace the rusting pipes holding up the bougainvillea in the garden. "I'll paint it dark green," I say. "Or would you paint it?"

He shakes his head, "Next year. You have to let the iron sit exposed so it absorbs the salt through a full summer and winter. Otherwise the paint will peel off in a few months."

Weather determines so much of life on the island, whether the boats and ships will travel or not, whether helicopters can transport emergency cases, whether the grapes will manage a good wine crop. "We have all four seasons," the man at the travel office tells me, "but no hospital," so accidents happen and people die who might not have in the city. Then again people die in the city without realizing they have. "Suffering has kneaded my soul," Stella says, "so I am full." Another weathering.

There are special seasons for cutting so the suffering is worthy, if we can say trees suffer, or wood, the Patmians call them *kalofengo* (good moon) and *kakofengo* (bad moon) times. "A *kalofengo* season is just after the full moon, as it begins to empty." Marko says. He believes the doors and window frames of the monastery on Patmos have survived these 600 years because the old wood was cut during *kalofengo* seasons, but the newer windows and doors don't last, the times of cutting were not respected.

Not only how one cuts but how you have been cut will determine the outcome and worth of what you build. "Logs used to travel down rivers in the Amazon after they were cut," Aleko explains, "before they were shipped and used for building. The wood had enough time to die; it was exposed to all kinds of weather. Logs sat in water, traveled over rocks in different currents. Now the big companies have their huge machines for cutting the trees. They peel, slice, section up and ship them off, in a matter of hours." The cut wood is still hurting, sap still flows in the finer sinews of bark as it is being nailed.

Stella tells me she went to America to visit her first love to give herself time to let her feelings for her husband die completely. "I took my sewing, my needle. They almost took my needle from me on the plane. They said it could hurt someone, but I begged the airline hostess, 'My dear I won't be able to travel without my needle.'" She tells me she sewed the whole way across the Atlantic. Up in the clouds she thought she would see her dead son's face. It would have been the most natural thing to have seen his face. When she got to the United States she had no idea 'Kennedy' was New York. She kept hearing 'Kennedy' being announced as the plane landed. Someone at the airport helped her make her call from a pay phone to the man who was waiting for her in Orlando, Florida. He told her how to get the next plane, where to pick up her ticket. She says it was easy after that. He was waiting for her.

"I flew to America to shame myself into shock; I had to do *something*!" she says. She tells me her teeth are all new because her husband smashed them one night.

She doesn't know why she stayed all these years with her husband, what power he had to make her stay. Her first love is now in his seventies and married but the marriage was never good, arranged years ago by the archbishop in the village because of the family's money. Stella's first love made the mistake of leaving her only to regret it for the rest of his life. Now an old man, he wants to make up for what happened at the beginning and won't accept that some things can't be made up. The hurt was a *kakofengo* cut. "It's too late," Stella tells him. She says her soul is empty though she can feel for his passion which is why she let him approach her again. "There was only one person I loved passionately in my life and it was my son. Now I have my grandsons, my daughter and son-in-law." She tells her first love, "We can't simply do what we want to."

I will leave the new iron trellis unpainted, leave the lighter clothes I brought with me packed. I am still wearing the two undershirts I slept in. I haven't even changed my underwear. Listening to Stella I'm learning what it is to want and not have, allow the dying wood its death. The sea urchins are full of eggs during the full moon. People wait for the moon to fill to fish the urchins from their rock ledges and deep sea lagoons. Cutting open a fertile urchin is tricky; their black needles still move. They can break deep in your flesh, lodging stubbornly in palms and fingertips. The slicing has to be done with a sharp knife, carefully.

Stella describes to me how her first love won't give up. He calls her every other day, wakes her at four in the morning to hear her voice. I tell her he must be suffering. "Now he sees who I am and what his wife is and he can't believe he lost me." He describes his wife as a woman who is never satisfied, who never has enough; her *lissa* is without bounds. Stella is anxious when he visits Patmos because he insists on meeting wherever they can manage it, usually in the cemetery where Stella goes twice a day to see her son. "I tell him this is a small place, but he's like a child. I ask him what he wants or expects from me: to say, 'I love you,' to have sex?" I ask her if she has sex with him and she says yes; despite his age he is a good lover and satisfies her. But she doesn't want the things he insists on giving her: a leather jacket, bathrobes, dresses with their price tags still on them.

"I never had anything and now he wants to give me everything. But it's too late." He even brings things for Maria's sons and expensive fishing bait for Aleko, Maria's husband. Stella goes into her bedroom to show me the ring he gave her. Two linked diamond hearts. "It doesn't fit over my callouses," she laughs.

The clothes stay in their closet. The teas and American vitamins are given away. "I ask him why he keeps buying these things. Where am I going to wear these clothes? When I'm cleaning houses and washing steps?" He can't accept the fact that Stella won't take his gifts and continues to call her and send packages, bringing suitcases of American products every time he visits. "I've been oppressed all my life," she goes on, "and I take pills to help me sleep; when he calls me I always ask him if he's eaten anything. He tells me he can't enjoy his meals without me."

Satisfaction is mysterious. The Lenten *Sarakosti* gives us specific days to eat specific foods so we slowly wean ourselves of appetite through Holy Week, *Megali Evdhomadha* in Greek, when we eat the barest foods. Maria wants me to satisfy her *lissa* for the Disney cookie jar, and a Disney desk set for her younger son (her older son got a Disney desk set years ago). She believes if she lived in the States she wouldn't be satisfied until she did her entire house in Disney products. Sometimes it satisfies me just to be a part of my lover's satisfaction; sometimes my body is too tired or too hungry, I go into a trance, my body becomes a sea.

When Marko finishes with the pruning I want to pay him. He tells me to give him whatever I want to give. I insist he name a price. "*Please*. I'm not a gardener," I say. "I don't know what people get for this work."

He repeats, "Whatever you want to give." I am stubborn. He looks unhappy, troubled, his eyes cast down on the ground.

"Please?" I repeat.

After a minute, he says quietly, "Is 50 euros too much?" And explains he will fertilize, gather and throw away the dead branches.

Can we know what we want before the cutting? After I had been cut, I realized I was full of sap.

"Don't worry, don't worry yourself," Theologos said to me as I worried about his payment for the work he was doing on the house. I watched him plough through the century old stone wall with a small bulldozer. I was building a new bathroom. Everything was covered in yellow dust. "If you don't break things up you can't build anything," he smiled. Payment would come, later, now he wanted me to understand the mess was nothing to be upset about. Markos kept cutting without any intention of stopping until he had freed the bougainvillea of its dead limbs. He was embarrassed to speak of costs. The visit to the States cost me a lover who cut in a *kakofengo* season impatient with hurt. My loneliness is a skin I cannot part from; the paint will not peel off.

Badly cut, the Greeks still speak of a history that bled into seas. The sounds are hard to part from, and keep us awake.

References Consulted

Beedham, Brian. "A Country on the Edge," in *The Economist*, May 22, 1993.

Carson Anne. *Economy of the Unlost*, Princeton UP, Princeton 1999.

Dunn, Stephen. *Different Hours*, W.W. Norton, NY 2000.

Gilson, George. "'New Ethos' hits old sleaze,'" in the *Athens News* (English language newspaper), January 30, 2004.

Gounelas-Parkin, Ruth. "Introduction" *The Other Within* Vol. 1, Athanasios A. Altintzis, Thessaloniki, 2001.

Homer. *The Odyssey* (trans. Robert Fagles), Penguin, NY 1996.

Holst, Gail. *Road to Rembetika, music of a Greek sub-culture, songs of love, sorrow & hashish*, Denise Harvey & Co., Athens 1975, 1977.

Hooks, Bell. *Yearning: race, gender and cultural politics*, South End Press, Boston 1990.

Kalliri, Fotini. "Corruption and Nepotism are Tumors on the Body Politic" in *Kathimerini* (Athens newspaper), February 12, 2003.

Kristeva, Julia. *Strangers to Ourselves* (trans. Leon S. Roudiez) Columbia UP, NY 1991.

Mason, David. "Reading Greece" in the *Hudson Review*, New York, Autumn, 2002.

Montaigne, Michael de. *Essays* (trans. J.M. Cohen), the Penguin Classics, Penguin Books, London 1961.

Naipul, V.S.. *The Middle Passage, a Caribbean Journey*, Picador, London 2001.

Paley, Grace. "A Conversation with my Father" in *Enormous Changes at the Last Minute*. Virago, London 1986.

Psaropoulos, John. "State Education: A great oxymoron?" Editorial in the *Athens News*, September 5, 2002.

Ritsos, Yannis. *Ritsos in Parentheses* (trans. Edmund Keeley), Princeton UP, Princeton 1979.

Sarbanes, Janet Matina. "'Ach, m'efages preza': The Junkie's Pain in Rebetiko Music and Culture: Toward an Aesthetic Model of the Self" presented at "The Flesh Made Text": Bodies, Theories, Cultures in the Post-Millennial Era. Aristotle University, Thessaloniki, May 14-18 2003.

Seferis, George. *George Seferis, Collected Poems*, (trans. Edmund Keeley and Philip Sherrard), Princeton UP, Princeton 1981.

Spires, Elizabeth. *I Am Arachne, Fifteen Greek and Roman Myths*, Farrar, Straus and Giroux, New York, NY 2001.

Stallings, A.E.. *Hapax*, Triquarterly Books/Northwestern, Evanston, Illinois 2006.

Yiannopoulos, Dimitris. "The Many Faces of a Land Scandal" in the *Athens News*, January 30, 2004.

Glossary of Greek Names

To name is to give identity, and in Greek lore, destiny.

By Way of Preface

Greki: from the Latin *Graeci* and *Graecia*, derivative of *Graii* the local name of a tribe in west Thessaly. Later used pejoratively by the Ottoman Turks to refer to the colonized Greeks as 'servants' or 'slaves'.

Costas Mitsotakis: former Prime Minister of Greece (1990-93) from the party of the right, *Nea Democratia*.

The Sound

Aimilios: male name; in Greek Asia Minor (Constantinople), middle-class Greek families often picked foreign names of famous people (i.e. Emile Zola), to name their children.

Adrianna: from *Andriani*, and the Greek ανδρας (man); modern Greek female name.

EAM Hellas: the name of the group of Greek *andartes*, or Resistance fighters, that formed in 1941 to fight the German Nazi Occupation of Greece. EAM: the initials for *Ethniko Apelefterotiko Metopo*, the National Freedom Front.

Evangelos Averoff: an extreme right-wing Greek politician, who was an author of historical books.

Corinna: an ancient Greek lyric poetess from Tanagra in Boeotia; thought to be an older contemporary of Pindar.

Ismini: Oedipus and Jocasta's daughter, and Antigone's sister who refused to share in her actions (the forbidden burial of their brother Polyneices), but later chooses to share in her guilt and punishment.

Kalfopoulos (Kyrios): in Greek, the son of Kalfas; *kalfa*, Turkish for builder.

Kalliope: the first born of the nine Muses who were the daughters of Zeus. Kalliope was the Muse of heroic poetry; her son was Orpheus.

Karaghiozis: A puppet from the Greek Shadow Theater whose origins came from Turkey or the East, and later spread through the Balkans and Mediterranean. From *Karaghioz*, "black-eyed" in Turkish, this popular, subversive figure is best known for his cunning and charisma as he makes savvy use of his underprivileged status to get the better of those with authority, traditionally the Ottoman Pasha.

Kosta: nickname of Constantinos, common modern Greek male name.

Louizos: common male name on the island of Naxos, possibly with Italian roots.

Maniati (Kyrios): one from *Mani*, a coastal area of the Peloponnese.

Manolis Glezos: a national hero who made his name during the German Occupation of Athens in 1941; a young boy, he climbed the flag pole of the Acropolis and tore down the Nazi flag with the help of Lakis Santas.

Pantazi (Kyria): The Greek πάντα, means 'many' or 'plenty'.

Antonis Skillitsizis: former Mayor of the port town of Piraeus in Athens during the Greek Junta (1967-1974).

Tiporini: a name of village women in Naxos, possibly with Italian roots.

Traffic Politics

Rebetes (or rembetis): "The *rembetis* is the suffering, wronged, hunted man – the *rembetika* [music] was written for him." Tasos Skorelis and Mikis Oikonomides in *A Rembetis: Yirogos Rovertakis*.

Academic Phallicisms

(The mythological names are taken from '*Pronouncing Glossary*' in Homer's *The Odyssey*, translated by Robert Fagles, and also from Elizabeth Spires' *I Am Arachne*)

Agios Isidoros: the Saint of many gifts; from δώρο, meaning gift.

Anastasia: from *Anastasi* (Ανάσταση) meaning resurrection: popular modern Greek name for women.

Athena: goddess, daughter of Zeus, defender of the Achaeans; and the patroness of human ingenuity and resourcefulness.

Arachne: a mortal who challenged Athena in a weaving contest and lost. Athena changed her into a spider.

Arete: queen of Phaeacia, wife of Alcinous, mother of Nausicaa. Also a common female name in contemporary Greece; from αρετη, Greek for virtue.

Circe: goddess and enchantress of Aeaea, who changes men to swine.

Costas Simitis: former Prime Minister of Greece; 1998-2003.

Ctimene: younger sister of Odysseus.

Echo: a nymph condemned by Hera never to speak first because she was so talkative; she could only repeat what others said to her. She had an unrequited, obsessive love for Narcissus.

Eurytion: a drunken Centaur.

George Papandreou: current opposition party leader of *PASOK*. The son of former Greek Prime Minister, Andreas Papandreou, and grandson of the Prime Minister, George Papandreou who was the founder of *Enosi Kentrou* (a Centerist party). Also named after Saint George, the dragon slayer.

George Seferis: the Greek poet and Nobel Laureate (1963); 1900-1971.

Kapodistria (Capo d'Istria), Ioannis: Governor of the first Greek Republic and former foreign minister to the Czar in Russia. Under his leadership (1828-1831) in the then-capital of Nafplion, Kapodistria came under attack by Greek feudal landowners who felt he did not represent their interests, but those of foreign powers. He was shot to death.

Kolokotronis, Theodoros: from Peloponnesus; he wrote a letter to the Russian Czar asking that foreign power be removed. In 1834 he was jailed in Nafplion for his resistance to the Bavarian rule in Greece at the time.

Cronus: the youngest and most important of the Titans, the older gods that preceded the Olympian gods. On the advice of his mother Gaia, Cronus castrated his father. He then married Rhea, his sister, and they parented many of the important Greek gods; because he knew he would be supplanted by one of them, he swallowed them all at birth. When Zeus was born Rhea handed Cronus a stone instead and hid the baby in Crete.

Lambri, (Kyria): from λαμπρα (bright).

Fates: ancient goddesses of destiny who decided how long a mortal would live. **Clotho**: the spinner; **Lachesis**: the disposer of lots in life; **Atropos**, "the inflexible one, carried shears and severed life's thread at the moment of death" (Spires 91).

General Makriyannis: famous in the Greek Revolution (1821), he later taught himself to write, and penned the now classic, *Memories of General Makriyanni*. He eventually turned against the royalist leadership of the Bavarian King Othon (Otto), and was instrumental in the formation of the first Greek *Syntagma* (Constitution) in 1844.

Mavromihalis: from *mavro*, Greek for black, and *Mihali*, Greek for Michael. Greek feudal landowner from Peloponnesus (*Mani*), shot Kapodistria to death in 1831.

Narcissus: a beautiful youth who fell in love with his own reflection in water and loved no one but himself.

Nikiforos Diamandouros: the Greek Ombudsman who later was elected by the European Parliament to be the Ombudsman for the European Union.

Oedipus: oidipous, (swollen-foot): the son of Laius, King of Thebes, who unknowingly killed his father and married Jocasta, his mother which, according to Sophocles' tragedy *Oedipus Tyrannus* precipitated a plague and famine that the Delphic Oracle proclaimed would only be averted when Laius' killer was found and expelled from the city. Upon discovering his role in his father's death, Jocasta hangs herself and Oedipus blinds and exiles himself.

Othon (Otto): "imported" Bavarian King to Greece who ruled 1832-1860.

Pallas, (Kyria): also known as Athena, or Pallas Athena, the goddess.

Pandora: from παν (all) δωρα (gifts), meant to be the perfect woman, given beauty, charm, and other talents by the gods then sent down to earth with a box Zeus forbids her to open. When Pandora disobeys and opens the box, a myriad of sorrows and evil spirits are let loose on the world.

Pericles: (c. 495- 429); Athenian statesman. In his politics he supported the democracy and came into prominence as one of the state prosecutors of Cimon in 463.

Petros: brother of the apostle Paul, also derived from πετρα Greek for stone or rock.

Scylla: a man-eating monster that lives in a cliff side cavern opposite the whirlpool of Charybidis in *The Odyssey*.

Vitali: a name with Italian roots; from *Vitae* (life).

Yannis Michail: responsible for the Citizens' Advocate Committee.

The Story of the Wall

Agia Anna: Saint Anne, the mother of Mary.

Alexandros: Alexander; a popular male name after Alexander the Great.

Calypso: goddess-nymph, daughter of Atlas whose home is on the island of Ogygia.

Eleni: Helen, in English; also from Helen of Troy.

Fotini: from φωs (light).

Hieron: (478-67 B.C.) Tyrant of Syracuse; also founded the city of Aetna.

Hora: the name given to the main town on islands usually located at the tallest pinnacle of an island to sight pirating ships.

Lucas: Greek version of Luke; one of the apostles who wrote the New Testament.

Panagia: the Virgin Mary or Madonna; from παν (total) and αγια (saint).

Sideris (Kyrios): from σιδηρος (iron)

Simonides of Keos: poet of ancient Greece; 5th century B.C.

Stella: from αστερισμος (star).

Maria: Greek for Mary.

Niko: nickname of Nicholas, after Saint Nicholas.

Stavros: from the Greek σταυρος (cross).

Theologos: from θεος (God) and λογος (word).

Mourlos (Kyrios): from μουρλαθηκεs (crazy or to have gone crazy).

Chrisanthi: from χρυση (golden) and ανθη (flowers).

Yanni: Greek for John; a common Greek male name after John the Baptist or John the Divine.

Zoodohospigi: from ζωη (life) and πιγι (source).

Saints and Anarchists

Agios Antonios: Saint Anthony; first ascetic monk. Left his wealth to the poor and went to live in a cave in the Egyptian desert near Memphis. 250 A.D.

Agios Dimtrios: Saint Dimitri; the patron saint of Thessaloniki where he was born in 304 A.D.

Eleftherios Venizelos: the Greek leader from Crete of the *Fifeletheron* (Liberal) Party. Prime Minster of Greece (1910-20) and (1928-32). His father fought in the 1821 Greek Revolution. The new Athens airport is named after him.

Orestes: son of Agamemnon and Clytemnestra, and brother of Iphigenia and Electra. His killing of Clytemnestra and her lover Aegisthus brings on chaos that is only brought to order by Apollo's intervention who insists on Orestes being tried in Athens. He is freed, marries Hermione and becomes the ruler of Argos.

Theofani: from θεος (God) and φαινομαι (to appear).

Yiorgos, (Kyrios): Greek for George after St. George the dragon slayer.

Lenten Epilogue

Zoi: Greek for life; a popular modern Greek female name.

Markos: Greek for Mark; one of the four apostles who wrote, with Mathew, Luke and John, the *New Testament*.

About the Author

Adrianne Kalfopoulou is the author of a poetry collection, *Wild Greens*; a critical study, *The Untidy House, a discussion of the ideology of the American dream in the culture's female discourses*; and a poetry chapbook winner, *Fig*, also translated into Polish. She teaches literature and creative writing in Athens, and in the Scottish Universities' Summer Schools program at the University of Edinburgh.

Printed in the United States
71575LV00001B/23-46